I0800209

IMAGES
*of America*

# WILTON MANORS

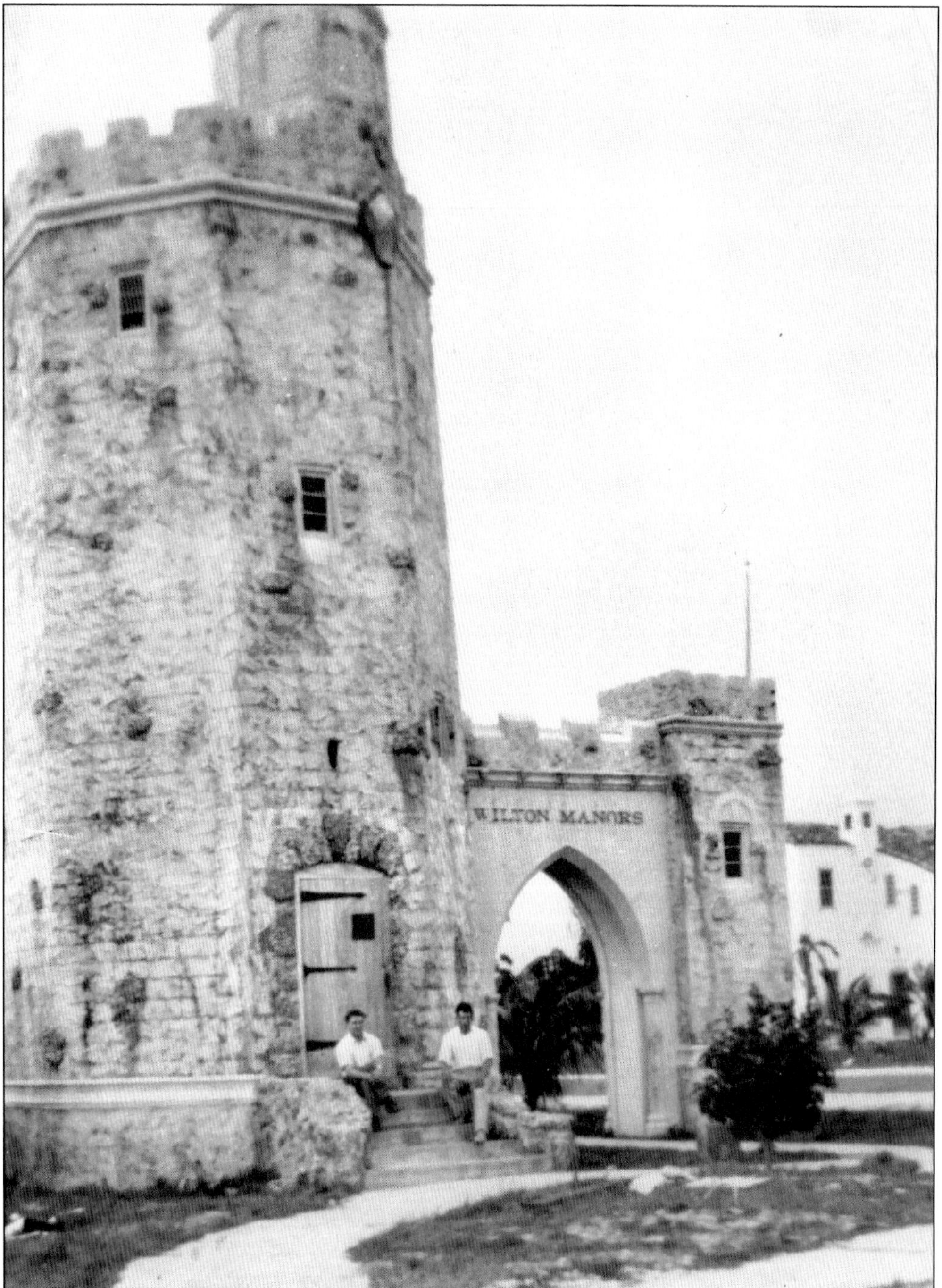


The Abreu entryway set the theme for the booming 1920s community of Wilton Manors. (Wilton Manors Historical Society.)

IMAGES
*of America*

# WILTON MANORS

Cynthia Thuma

ARCADIA
PUBLISHING

ISBN 978-0-7385-1741-4

Published by Arcadia Publishing
Charleston, South Carolina

Printed in the United States of America

Library of Congress Catalog Card Number: 2004116049

For all general information contact Arcadia Publishing at:
Telephone 843-853-2070
Fax 843-853-0044
E-mail sales@arcadiapublishing.com
For customer service and orders:
Toll-Free 1-888-313-2665

Visit us on the Internet at www.arcadiapublishing.com

## *Dedication*

*Love, care, and instilling a passion for education and learning are among the best gifts parents bestow on their young. So are roots and wings. My brother Joe's and my roots and wings came from our parents, Anthony and Madgeline Thuma, who were among Wilton Manors's early residents and were active in the community's formative years. My father served on the volunteer fire department and the auxiliary police and once ran for city council. My mother was active in church and school activities, leading a Brownie troop, among other things. Our values came from a tight-knit immediate family and repeated exposure to the extended family of the people on Northeast Twenty-fifth Street and beyond: the Williams, Potteiger, Caro, Brace, Cole, Rees, Reed, and Moyer families, and others. No matter how far away I wander, my wings always bring me back to Wilton Manors. It was a wonderful place to grow up back then and is still a wonderful place to live.*

*The past few years have been an exciting time in Wilton Manors, and the work of several recent mayors and city commissioners has been particularly important and meaningful to the community's growth. The hard work of Jack Seiler, John Fiore, Jim Stork, Scott Newton, Gary Resnick, Craig Sherritt, Ted Galatis, and Joe Angelo has been integral in awakening the city and revitalizing it. The city's administrative staff, headed by city manager Joseph Gallegos, and its work force are uncommonly devoted to service and preservation, and they deserve public recognition for their efforts. Also, the members of the Wilton Manors Historical Society are working hard to preserve the community's past.*

*I dedicate this book to my parents, my brother, my husband Jim, my son Nicholas, and to all the good people—past and present, dreamers and doers alike—who call or have called Wilton Manors home.*

# Contents

# ACKNOWLEDGMENTS

Compiling a visual history of Wilton Manors has been an exciting undertaking; it would not have been possible without the assistance of a small army of kind, generous folks who want to make sure this vibrant, diverse city never forgets its past. Starting with the inspirational and hard-working president of the Wilton Manors Historical Society, Diane Cline, the group has embraced this project, and its members and officers, past and present, have been crucial in finding photographs and archival materials for this book and for the city's archives. I thank them all.

Chris Eck, administrator of the Broward County Historical Commission, along with Denyse Cunningham, its curator, and Helen Landers, its historian, and the commission's staff were outstanding in their assistance, going above and beyond the call. Merrilyn Rathbun, director of research services, and Todd Bothel, curator at the Fort Lauderdale Historical Society, also were immensely kind and helpful. Thanks also go to the Middle Georgia Archives at the Macon-Bibb County Public Libraries for information about Ned Willingham.

Thanks go to the good people who looked through their personal scrapbooks, provided pictures and other memorabilia, and shared their memories or expertise: Paul M. Bradley Jr., Brenda Clanton, Bruce Connolly, Sharon Davis, Michael Dougherty, Cindy Exterkamp, Rob and Kathleen "Poco" French, the Haberstitch family, Hope and Joe Gallegos, Susan Gillis, Steve Kelley, Sharon Kerwick, Paul Kuta, Rick Leffel, Ann Lunsford, Jim McGivern, Marilyn Menchini, Karen Miga, John and Ruth Miller, Ruby Peak, Jillian Printz, Ward Robbins and Russotto Realty, Marlene and Wayne Schotanus, George and Shirley Schneider, Bud and Marilyn Scott, Nancy Stafford, Becky Thacker, Dianne Thompson, Joe Thuma, and Dawn Walker. Thanks also go to the office staff at Wilton Manors Elementary School and St. Clement Catholic Church, Linda at Wilton Manors Baptist Church, Juanita at First Christian Church of Wilton Manors, and Sudie Shipman and Jana Carnes of Religious Science of Fort Lauderdale. I tip my hat to you.

And finally, thanks go to my mother, Madgeline Thuma, with appreciation for her great memory and for giving me *carte blanche* in the family photo albums.

To all the good people whose names are listed here and to any others I may have inadvertently neglected, I offer my heartfelt thanks.

# INTRODUCTION

By the numbers, Wilton Manors, Florida, is home to little more than 12,000 people, and is only a smidgen more than 2.6 square miles in size.

But Wilton Manors is so much more than a dry recitation of statistics. Originally conceived as an all-white development, Wilton Manors is today a proudly diverse community. Once back on its heels and struggling, Wilton Manors is now vibrant and prosperous.

A 2004 study by Robert Carr and Victor Longo of the Archeological and Historical Conservancy revealed that the land on which the city's Richardson estate was constructed had in fact been home to indigenous settlers as long ago as 1000 to 1400 A.D.

The contemporary history of Wilton Manors harkens back to the early 1890s, when William C. Collier, an affable farmer, moved from Alabama to Florida and established a homestead on the south bank of the north fork of the Middle River. There, he grew oranges and became friendly with the Native Americans who stopped by to trade with him.

At about the same time, Duncan Upshaw Fletcher, one of several transplanted Georgians to make a mark in Wilton Manors's history, bought 1,310 acres on the north and south sides of the Middle River. There, he established the Florida Fiber Company for the purpose of growing sisal hemp to use for rope, cordage, and other coarse fabrics. The land was poorly suited for the task, and the company lost money. In 1891, the company petitioned Dade County for tax relief. Florida Fiber Company later shut down its operations and plotted its land to be sold as Progresso. Fletcher's career fared better than Florida Fiber—he went on to serve five terms in the United States Senate.

Frank Stranahan, whose cousin owned a stage line that stretched from Lantana to Lemon City (Miami), came south from Ohio to operate a ferry that crossed the New River in Fort Lauderdale. Stranahan opened a trading post at the ferry.

The arrival of Henry Flagler's railroad in 1896 put Stranahan's ferry out of business, but his trading post and other ventures prospered. Stranahan, generally regarded as the father of Fort Lauderdale, opened a bank and made some land purchases, including a parcel that later became the Coral Point subdivision in eastern Wilton Manors.

Development in the northeastern tip of Dade County was prospering by 1910, and land speculators were gobbling up huge parcels for future development. In 1915, the communities from Deerfield Beach to Hallandale decided it was time to form a county of their own. In 1915, Broward County was established. That same year, Dixie Highway was completed, linking Broward County to the rest of the world for automobile travel.

Winborn Joseph Willingham, an eloquent auctioneer from Macon, Georgia, was hired by Fort Lauderdale pioneer Tom Bryan to help auction land about 1911. Willingham returned home to the Peach State with tales of beautiful beaches, pine forests, beautiful rivers, Seminole Indians, and incredible opportunity. Willingham, who earned the nickname "Windy Joe" for his speaking ability, persuaded one of his cousins, Edward John Willingham, to join him on his return to southeastern Florida.

Edward John Willingham, better known as Ned, was born August 18, 1861, in Allendale, South Carolina. He was one of 18 children born to Benjamin Lawton Willingham and Elizabeth Martha Willingham (née Baynard). Both were South Carolina natives, college graduates, and deeply principled people. Thirteen of their children reached adulthood, and all were college educated. Ned Willingham was both a good son and a good businessman. He and brother Ernest Pringle Willingham established a furniture manufacturing plant in Macon, and Ned Willingham was a founder of the Bibb National Bank and owned peach orchards and pecan groves. When his cousin dazzled him with tales of opportunity in South Florida, Ned Willingham had the capital to become a player.

Upon arriving in South Florida in 1923, Ned Willingham worked with a few other land speculators and developers, such as Melvin I. Anglin, developer of Lauderdale-by-the-Sea, and Lake Park developer Harry Kelsey. Ned then went out on his own. In 1924, he bought a dairy farm owned by Billy Johnson, located just north of Middle River and west of Dixie Highway. He purchased as many nearby parcels as he could, such as a 30-acre plot from Merle C. Slagle, a retired Kansas educator. After the Slagle purchase, Willingham had acquired 345 acres, a sufficient amount of land for his development: Wilton Manors.

Civil engineer J.S. Rhine completed the first plat for Wilton Manors in October 1925. With the exception of Prospect Road (now Northeast Twenty-sixth Street) and Wilton Boulevard (now Wilton Drive), all the roadways in the city were called avenues, and most had Native-American names: Algonquin, Altamaha, Apachee, Canooga, Cherokee, Chippewa, Choctaw, Hiawasee, Iroquois, Mohawk, Nakomis, Navajo, Okolona, Seneca, Sioux, and Wabash. Two, Ocmulgee and Oconee, were named after rivers near Macon, and other avenues were named Suwanee and Ludowici.

Willingham created a sales brochure and advertisements to tout his development. He hired the top architect in the county to design the gates to the city and his sales and administration building. Everything seemed to be in place. The lovely little community of Wilton Manors was a paper reality. All Willingham had to do was sell the lots.

History rarely is neat and clean and often varies from the paths others set out for it. Natural disasters and man-made calamities intervened, and the course of Wilton Manors did not follow the path Ned Willingham had planned. The following pages present the story of Wilton Manors in pictures and words.

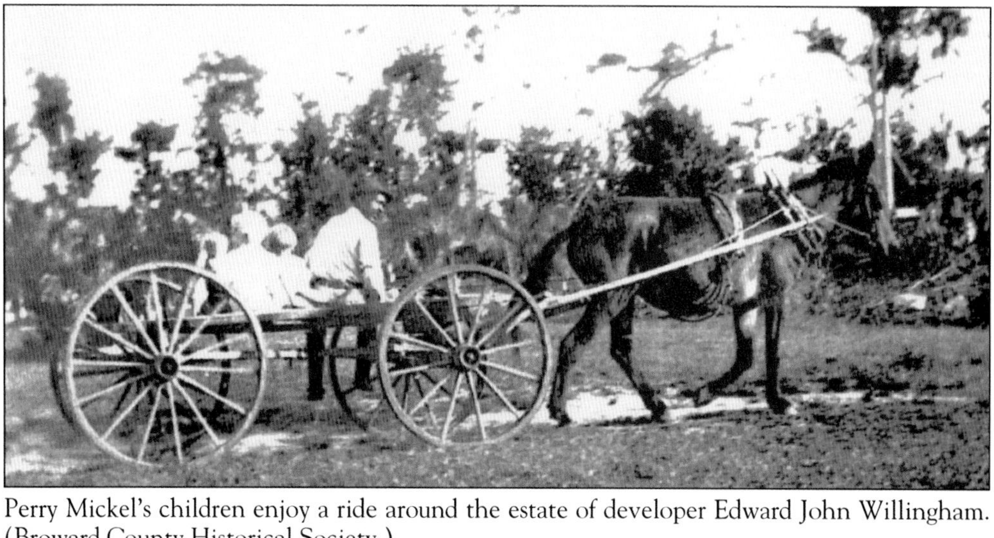

Perry Mickel's children enjoy a ride around the estate of developer Edward John Willingham. (Broward County Historical Society.)

# *One*

# A Strong Start (1910–1929)

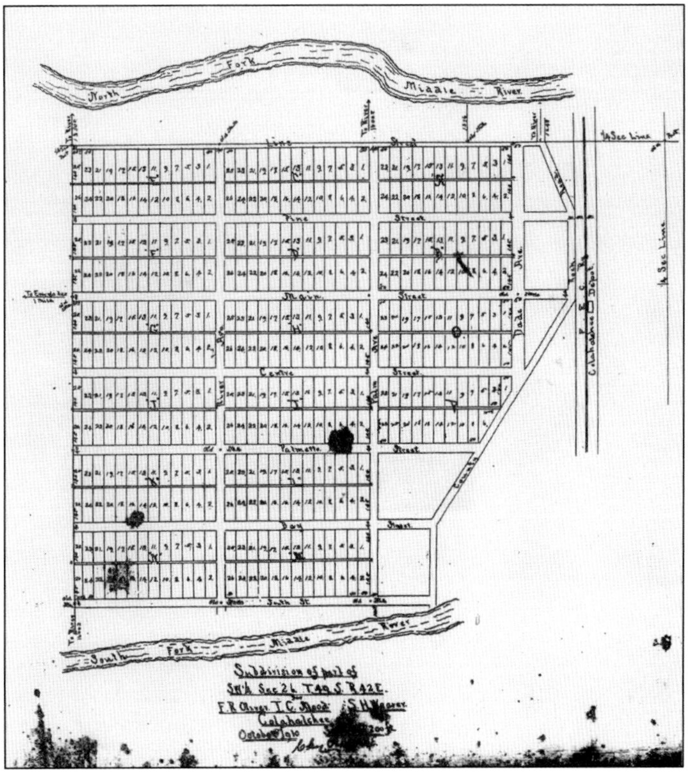


This is the plat for the town of Colohatchee, laid out by Frank Oliver, T.C. Moody, and S.H. Weaver in 1910, on property that later would become part of Wilton Manors. Colohatchee's streets, which ran east to west, were named Bay, Centre, Lime, Main, Palmetto, and Pine. Avenues, which ran north to south, included Dade and Palm. Colohatchee was part of Dade County. Broward County was formed in 1915 of pieces of Dade and Palm Beach Counties. It was named to honor Gov. Napoleon Bonaparte Broward of Jacksonville. (Broward County Historical Commission.)

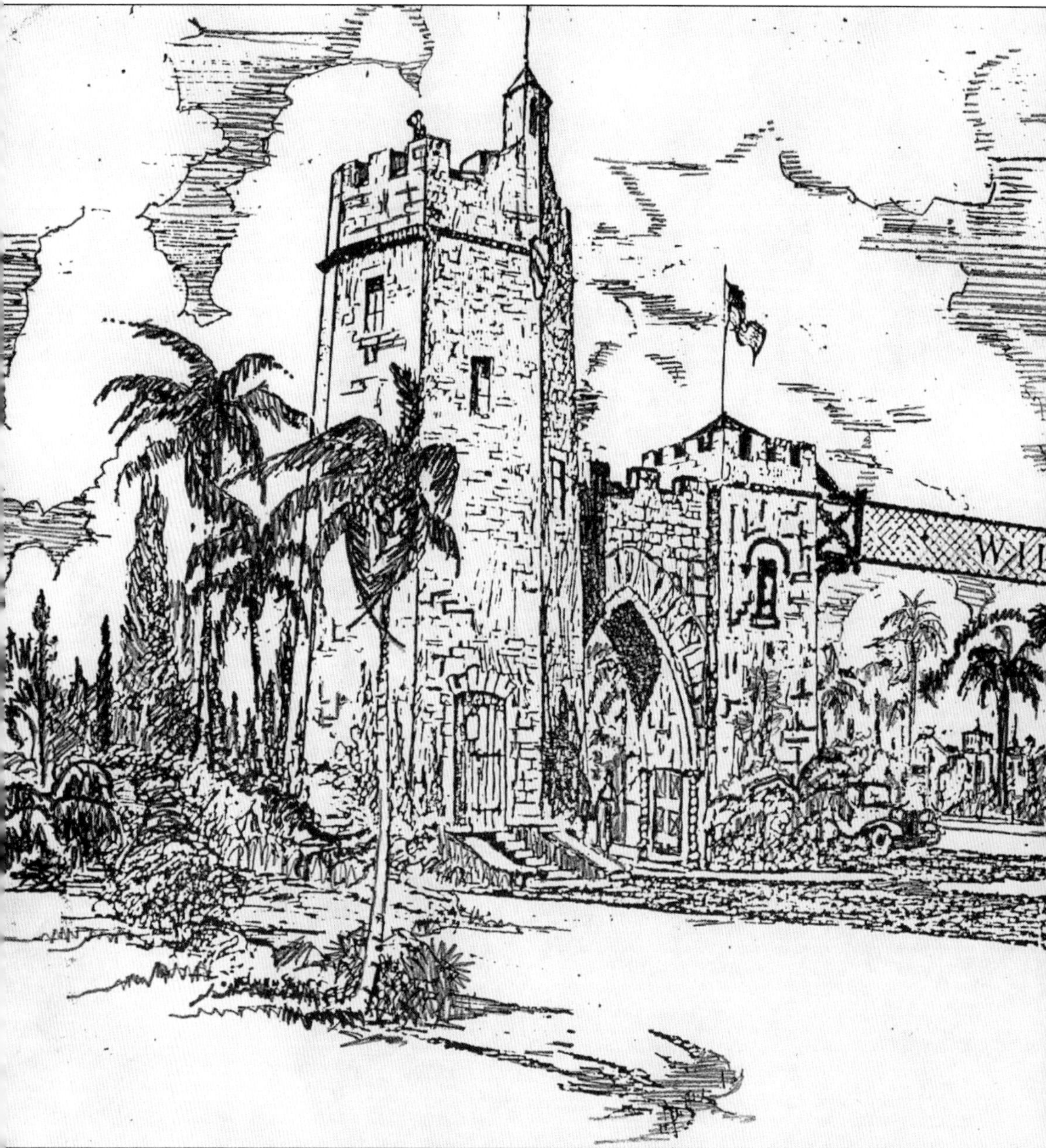


Francis Luis Abreu, whose romantic designs gave Fort Lauderdale its architectural cachet, designed the Italian Gothic–style field office, entrance gates, and observation towers for Willingham's Wilton Manors project. The son of a Cuban sugar plantation owner, Abreu spent his youth in Cuba and New York. He attended Cornell University and, after college, served in the United States Navy during World War I. After the war, he came to South Florida, where his family had relocated, and got his early commissions for homes from family and friends. The Jova House was the first home built on Fort Lauderdale's beach. It now serves as Casablanca Café. Among his other Florida designs are Himmarshee Court, one of Fort Lauderdale's first apartment buildings; Fort Lauderdale Country Club (1927); St. Anthony's School (1926); Dania Beach Hotel; Riverside Hotel; the Himmarshee branch of the United States Post Office (1926–1927),

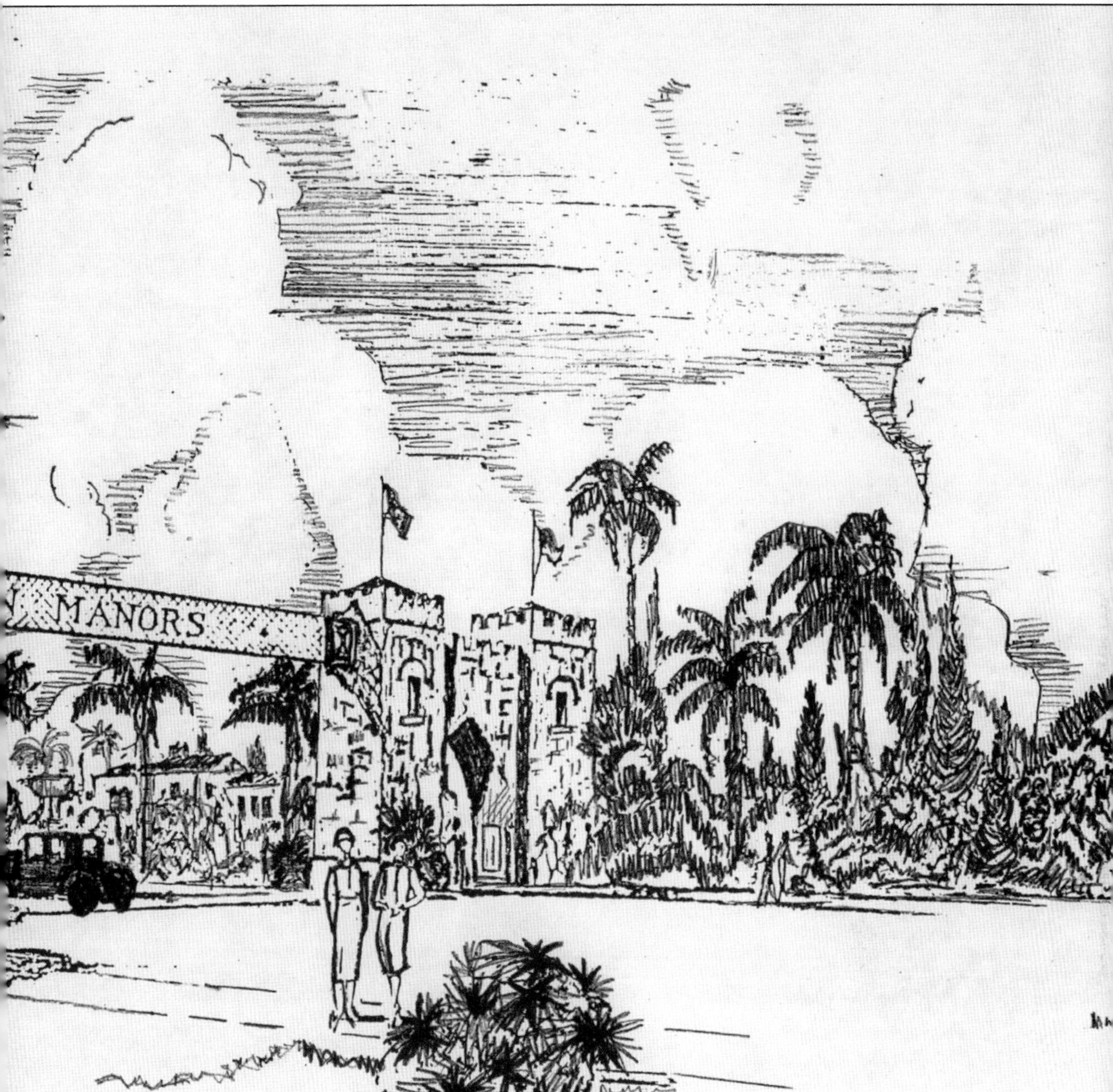


Fire Station No. 2 (1927), the Bryan House on the New River at Tarpon Bend (1925); and another New River home, Manga Reva (1933). In 1928, his firm was hired to design portions of the Cloister Hotel on Sea Island, Georgia. Abreu began splitting his time between South Florida and Georgia, then moved to Georgia permanently, where he created notable designs as well. Abreu's design fee for the Wilton Manors project was $50,000. He used the Casa de Salinas in Salamanca, Spain, as his inspiration for the project, and although the rendering makes the gates and towers look vast and expansive, they were actually rather modest in size. The contractors, Prescott and Boyd, charged $12,000 to construct the buildings, bringing the total cost of the project $62,000. Willingham's 345-acre development opened for business in February 1926. (Wilton Manors Historical Society.)

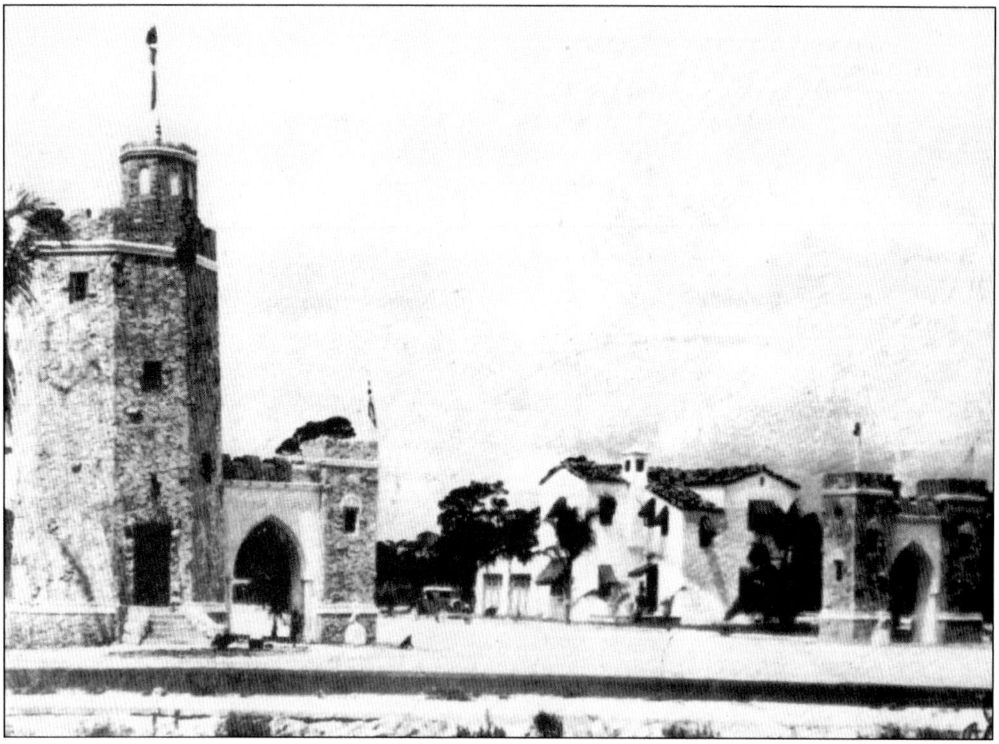

The plan had been for Willingham's sales force to take prospective investors and home buyers up into the tower to help them choose the property they planned to buy, then to go to the administration building to hammer out the details. Willingham's strategy was a good one, but events beyond his control changed the intended course. (Broward County Historical Commission.)

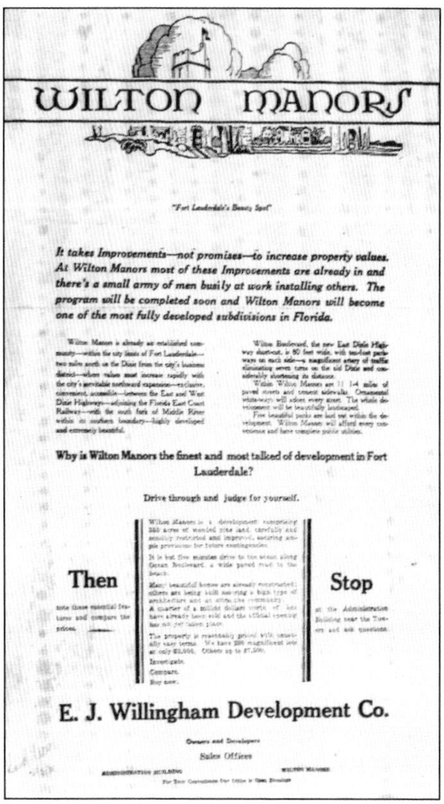


Willingham published full-page ads for Wilton Manors in the *Fort Lauderdale Herald*, *Fort Lauderdale Sentinel*, and *Fort Lauderdale Sun*. Though many of the land dealers of the era were not entirely scrupulous, Willingham's dealings were all above reproach. (Broward County Historical Commission.)

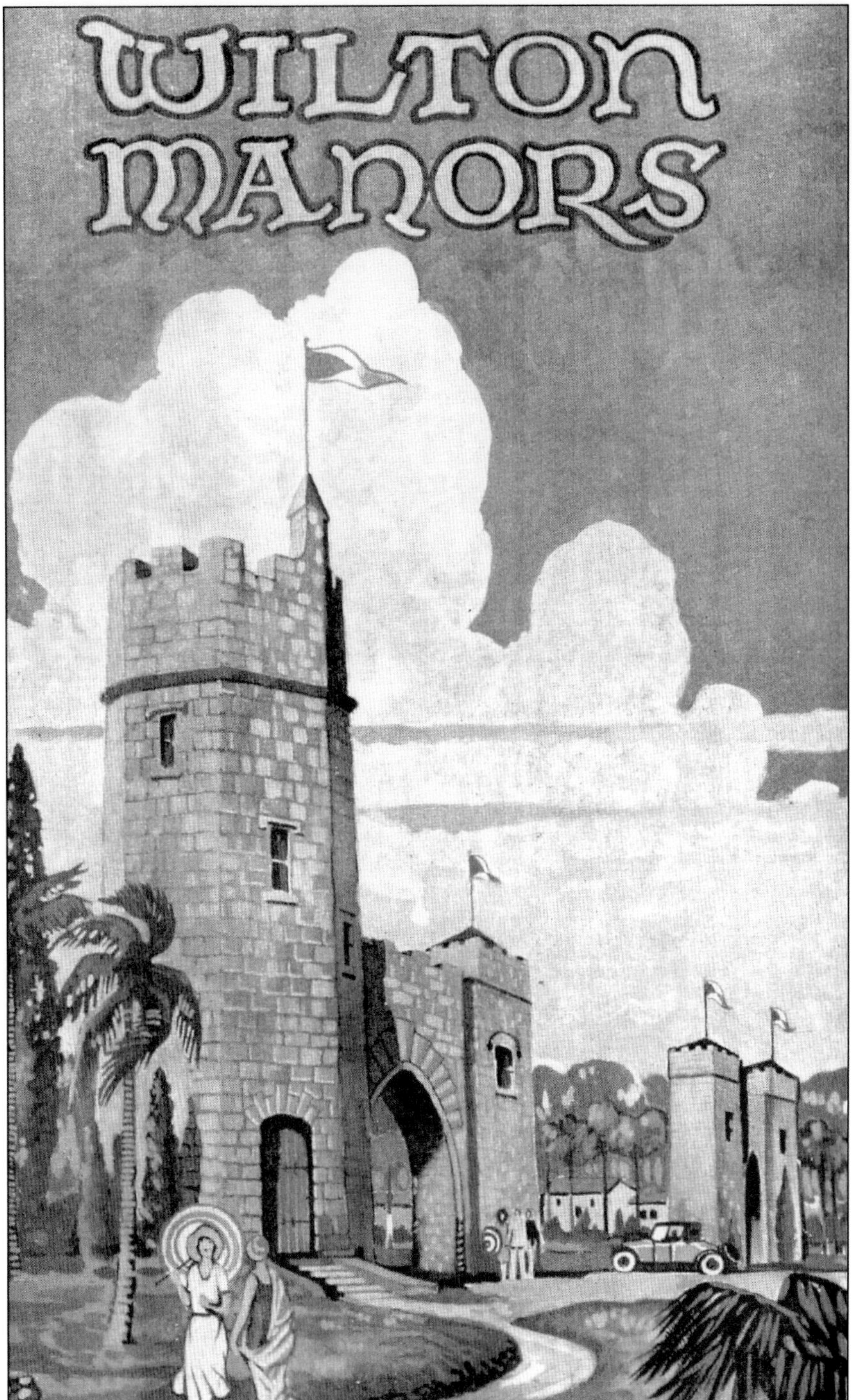


This is a cover of Willingham's colorful 1925 sales brochure. When Wilton Manors celebrated its 50th birthday in 1997, the city used this image for the cover of Stuart McIver's history of the city. The images on the following five pages come from this brochure. (Broward County Historical Commission.)

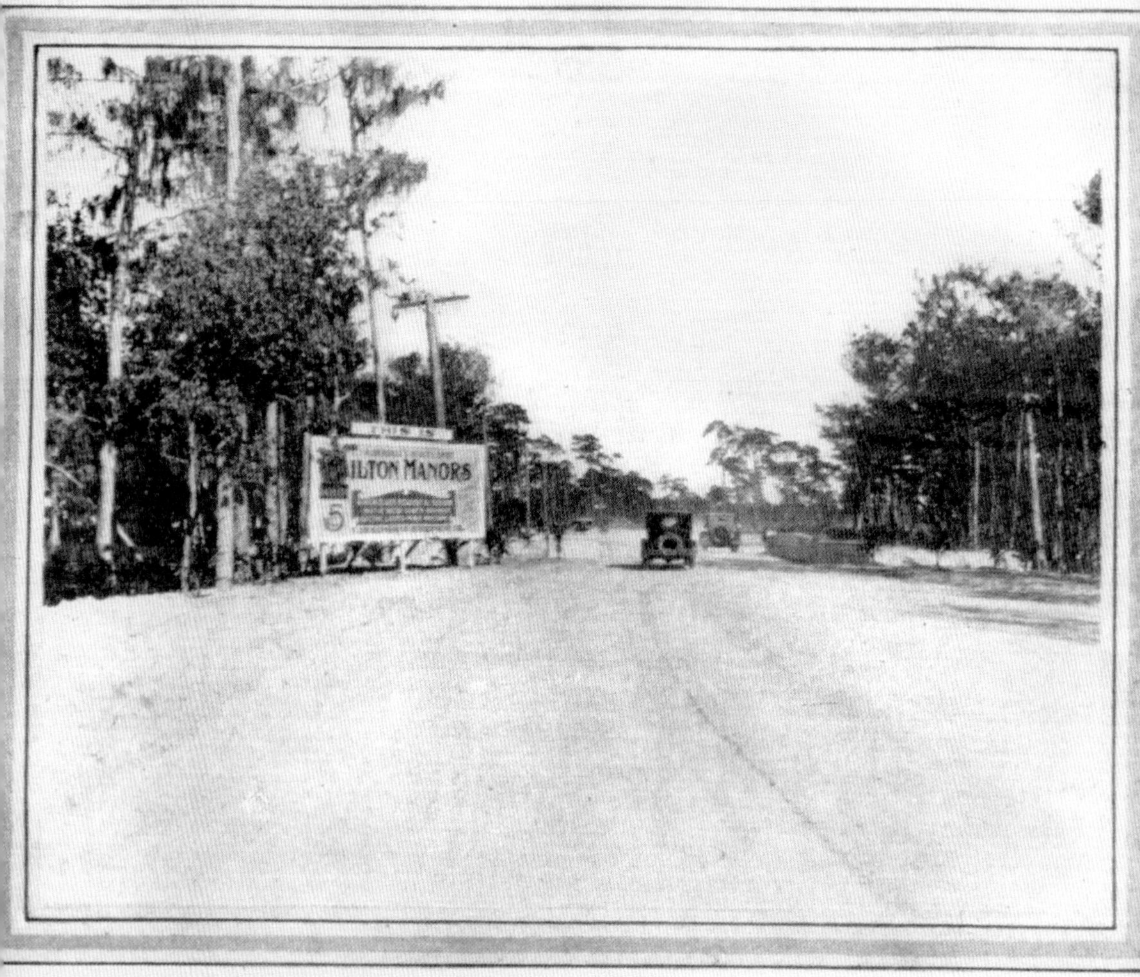

e southern approach to Wilton Manors over the South Fork (
beautiful Middle River.

Wilton Manors exists as an island in the middle of Broward County between the forks of the Middle River, but it did not become known as the Island City until the mid-1980s. In Willingham's other sales literature, he touts Wilton Manors as "enviably located within the city limits of Fort Lauderdale—two miles north on the Dixie from the center of the city's business district—between the East and West Dixie Highways." (Broward County Historical Commission.)

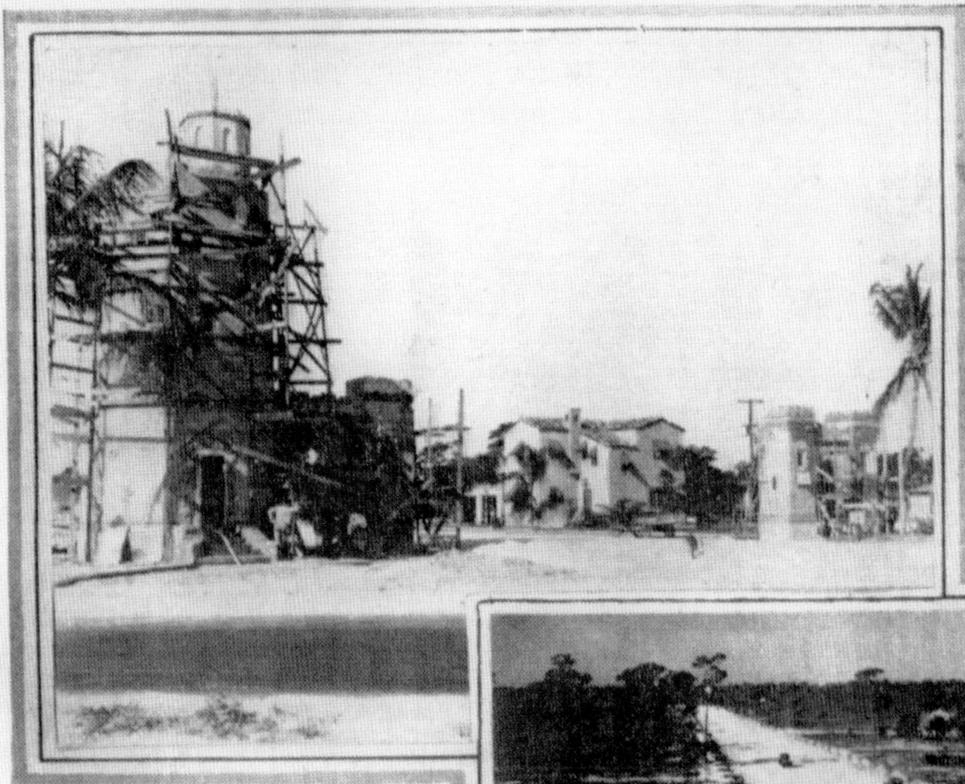

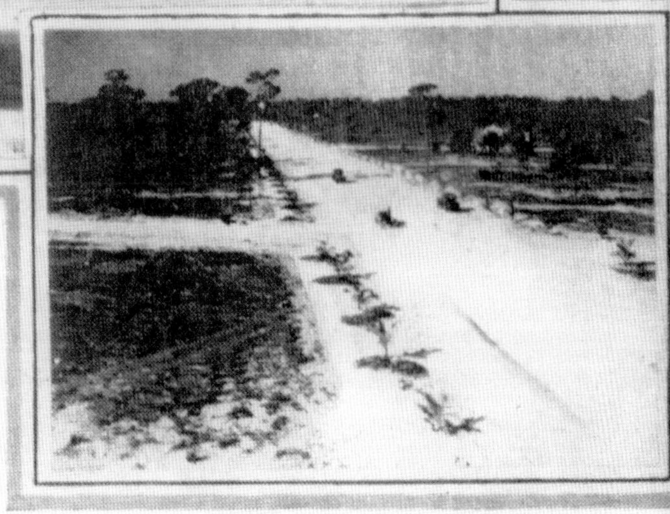

Top: "The Towers" comprising the magnificent entrance-way under construction.

Right: Looking along broad Wilton Boulevard.

The top photo shows the Abreu entryway under construction at what is now Five Points, where Wilton Drive, Dixie Highway, and Northeast Twenty-sixth Street meet. The administration building appears to have already been completed. (Broward County Historical Commission.)

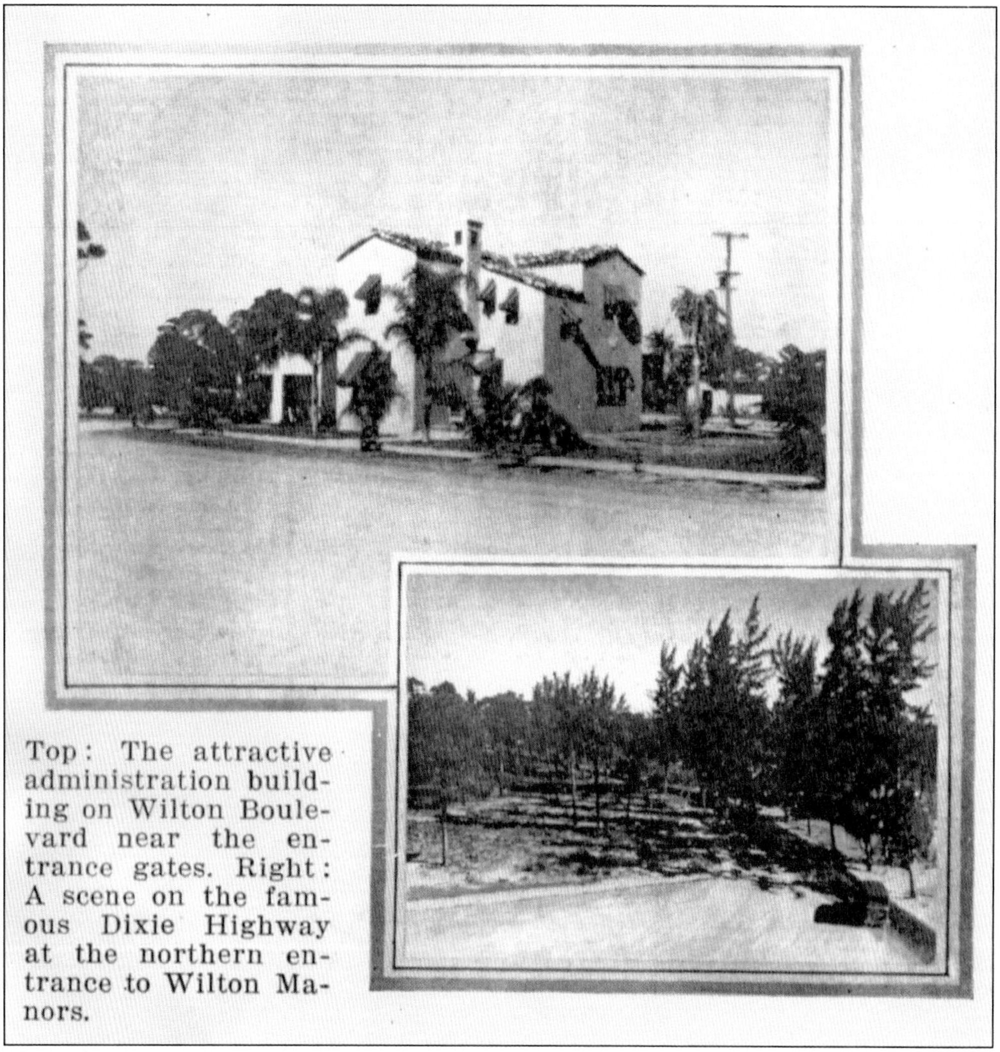
Top: The attractive administration building on Wilton Boulevard near the entrance gates. Right: A scene on the famous Dixie Highway at the northern entrance to Wilton Manors.

The administration building, with its barrel-tile roof, provided a Mediterranean feel to buildings. The tiles were used by many architects of the era, including Addison Mizner in Palm Beach County, who operated his own kiln to manufacture tiles in Boca Raton. Abreu used them extensively in the many South Florida homes he designed. (Broward County Historical Commission.)

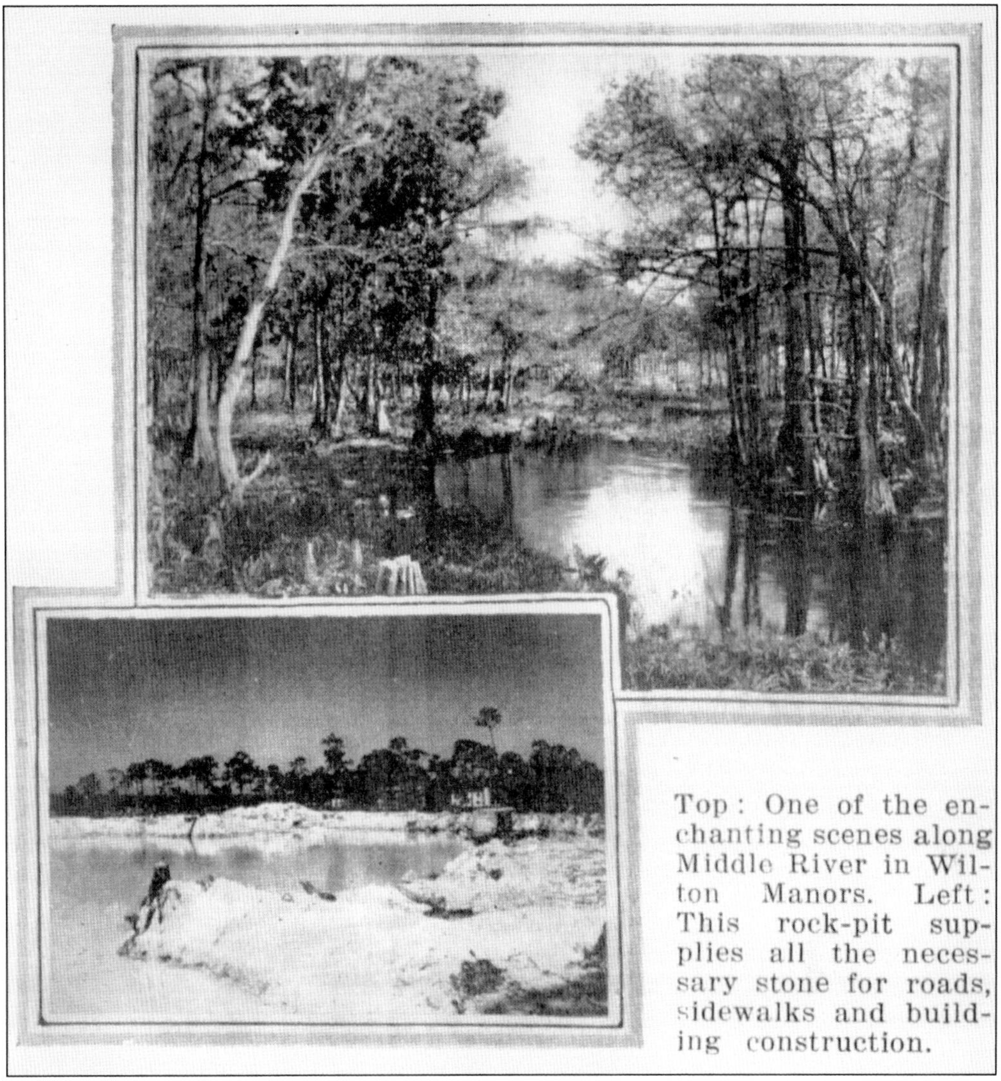
Top: One of the enchanting scenes along Middle River in Wilton Manors. Left: This rock-pit supplies all the necessary stone for roads, sidewalks and building construction.

The quarry in the picture was dug to supply raw building materials for Wilton Manors and became a town of its own, Lazy Lake, surrounded entirely by Wilton Manors. Willingham had originally intended to offer swimming, boating, and other aquatic activities at the lake, but contractor Hal Ratliff, accountant Charles Lindfors, and architect Clinton Gamble bought and developed the lake and the surrounding property in 1947, creating the village of Lazy Lake. In the 2000 census, Lazy Lake reported 38 residents living in 13 homes in the .02 square mile village. It has one street: Lazy Lane. (Broward County Historical Commission.)

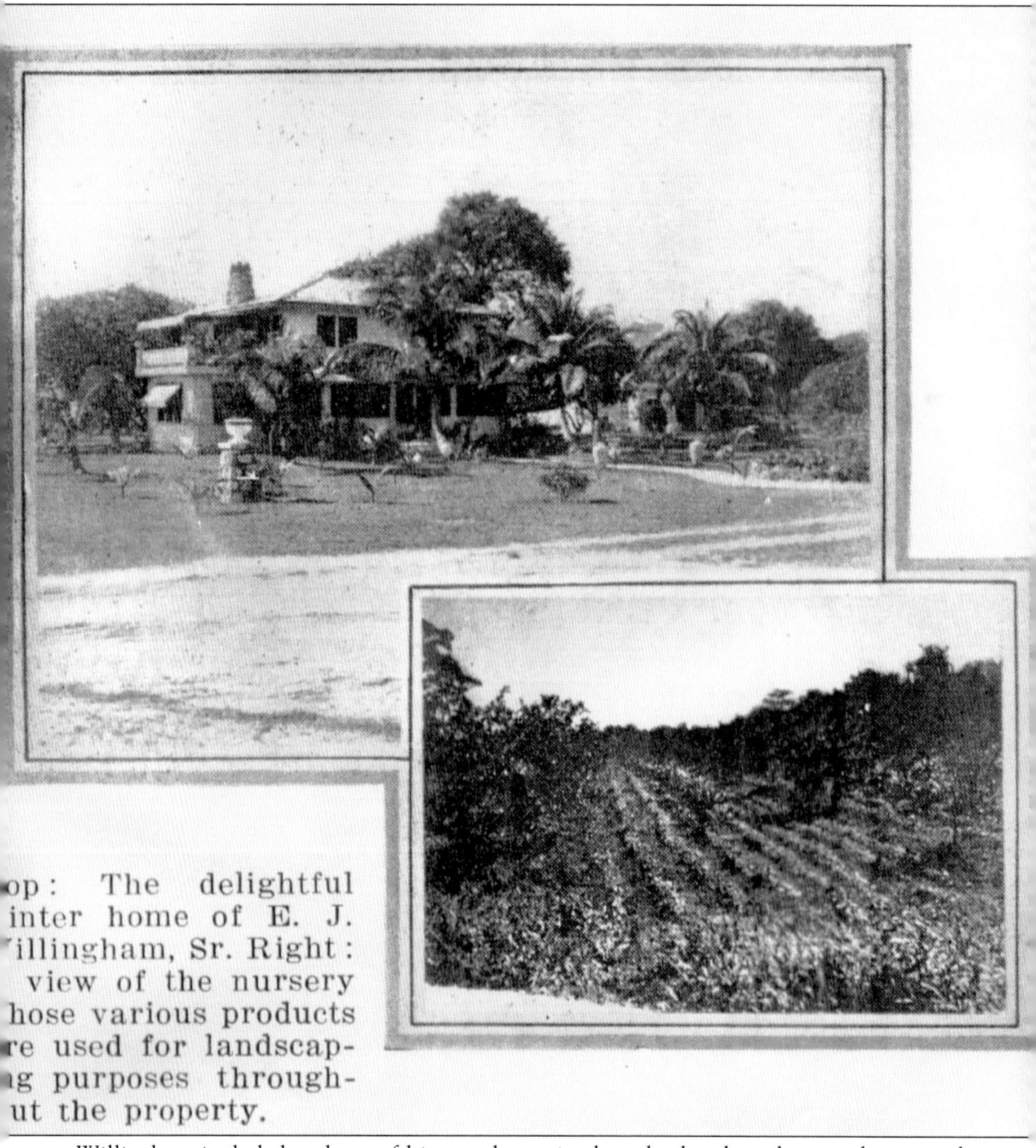


Willingham included a photo of his own home in the sales brochure because he wanted potential buyers to see he was a Wilton Manors homeowner, too. (Broward County Historical Commission.)

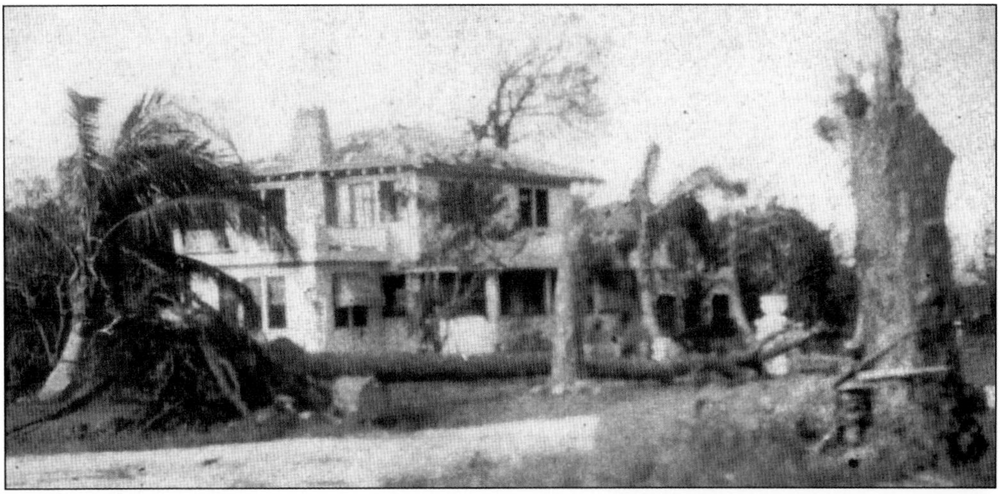

The swooning economy and the hurricane of 1926 doomed Willingham's project. Several plots of land were sold, and eight residences were erected. The Willinghams returned to Georgia. Eula Felton Willingham, Ned's wife, died in January 1927, and Ned Willingham died of a stroke on March 31, 1927, in Asheville, North Carolina. He was 66 years old. This picture shows hurricane damage to Willingham's house on Dixie Highway.

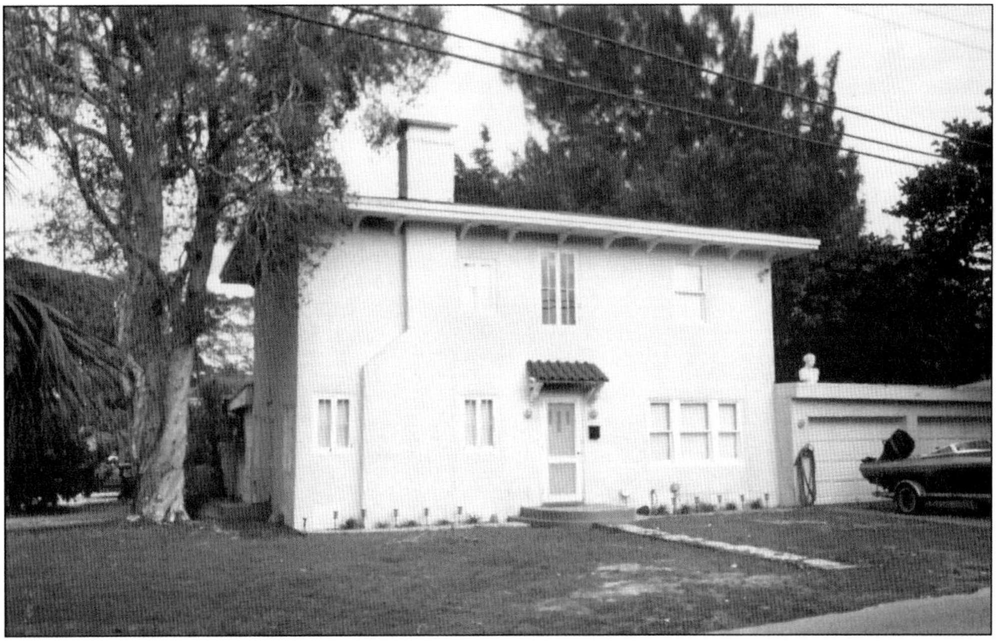

The Hiaasen house was the first home sold in Wilton Manors. The buyer was attorney Carl A. Hiaasen, partner in a locally prominent law firm, McCune, Casey, Hiaasen, and Fleming, which represented Willingham's company. The house was constructed on Northeast Twenty-first Court, across from where the Wilton Manors Women's Club now stands. A later Carl Hiaasen, a novelist and columnist for *The Miami Herald*, has made his family name famous.

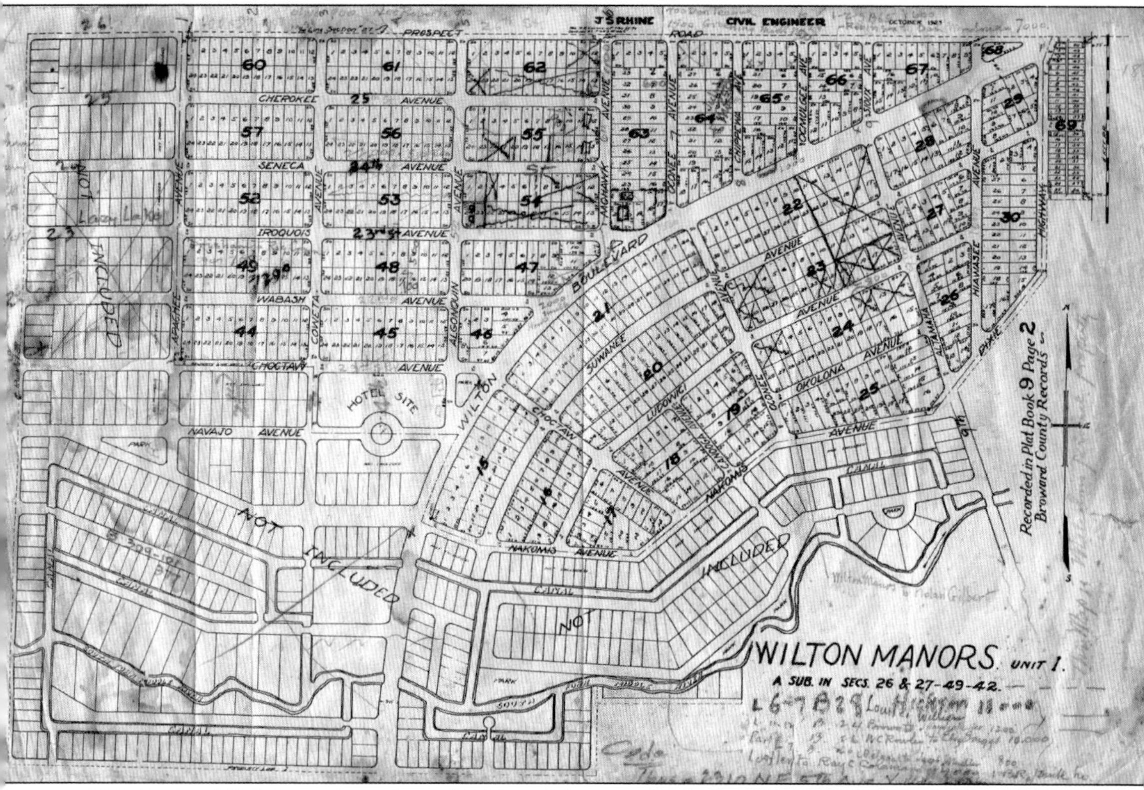


This is the J.S. Rhine first plat of Wilton Manors, filed in October 1925, featuring named streets. The northernmost thoroughfare, Prospect Road, became Northeast Twenty-sixth Street. Farther north in Fort Lauderdale is another Prospect Road, which still exists today. (Wilton Manors Historical Society.)

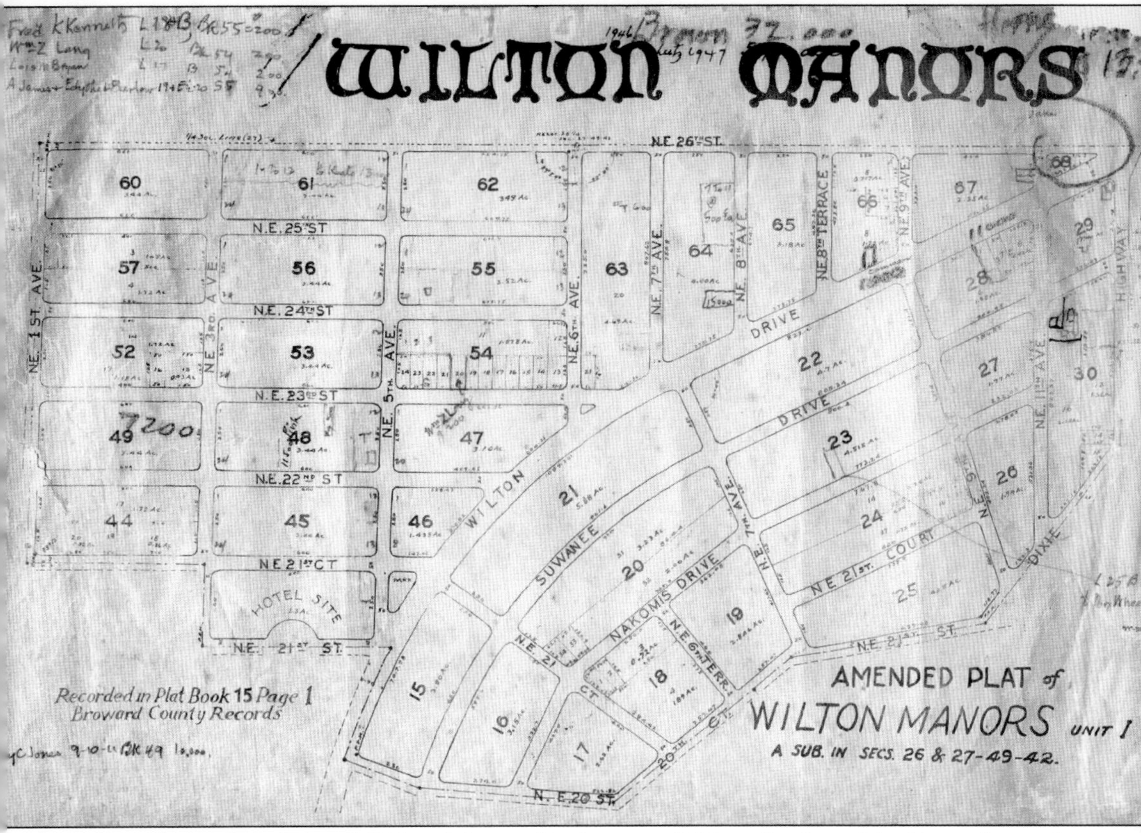


Here is the amended plat of Wilton Manors. By this time, Wilton Boulevard had been changed to Wilton Drive, and the only other named streets were Nakomis and Suwanee Drives. (Wilton Manors Historical Society.)

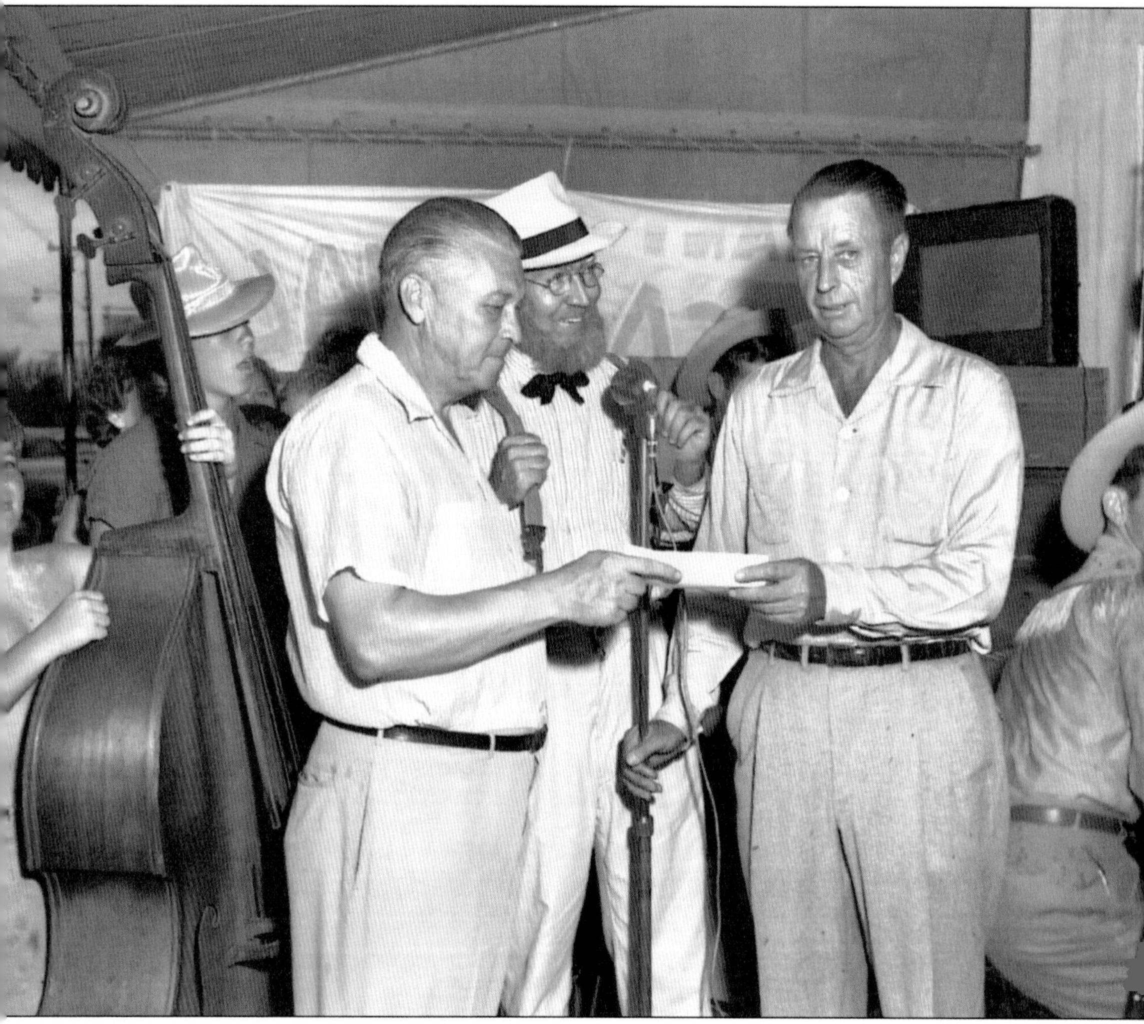

When Perry and Dorothea Mickel moved to South Florida, they lived in a garage apartment near the ocean, but found fate and the elements seemed to conspire against them. Mickel served as Willingham's sales manager and trusted associate, and after Willingham's departure, went on to sell lots in Wilton Manors. In 1952, he became its second mayor. He remained in office for three years and during that time, he started the police department. Much of his best work, though, was as a private citizen, such as leasing land for a baseball field to Wilton Manors Sports, Inc. for a dollar a year. Today's Mickel Field is named in his honor. He also was active in a variety of activities in the new community, including the civic association. In the picture above, he accepts a check for the city hall building fund. (Gene Hyde collection, Fort Lauderdale Historical Society, Inc.)

# *Two*

# Building a Community (1930–1949)

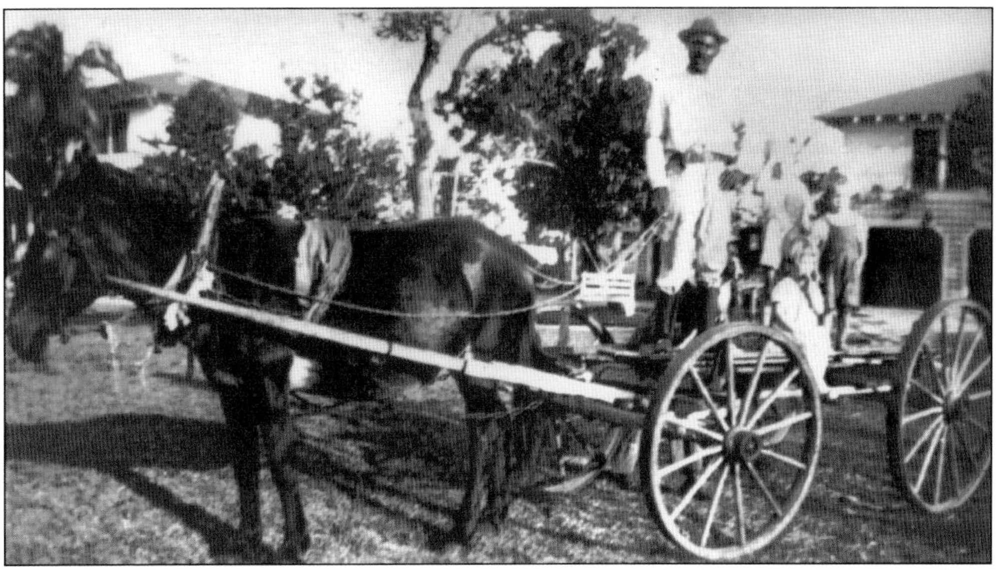

After Ned Willingham's departure, his son, E.J. Jr., remained behind to settle the family's affairs. Perry Mickel, who led Willingham's sales force, moved into the Willingham home with his wife Dorothea and their children to take care of the house. In this photograph, the Mickel children and driver get a buckboard ride around the property with Old Nelly. (Broward County Historical Commission.)

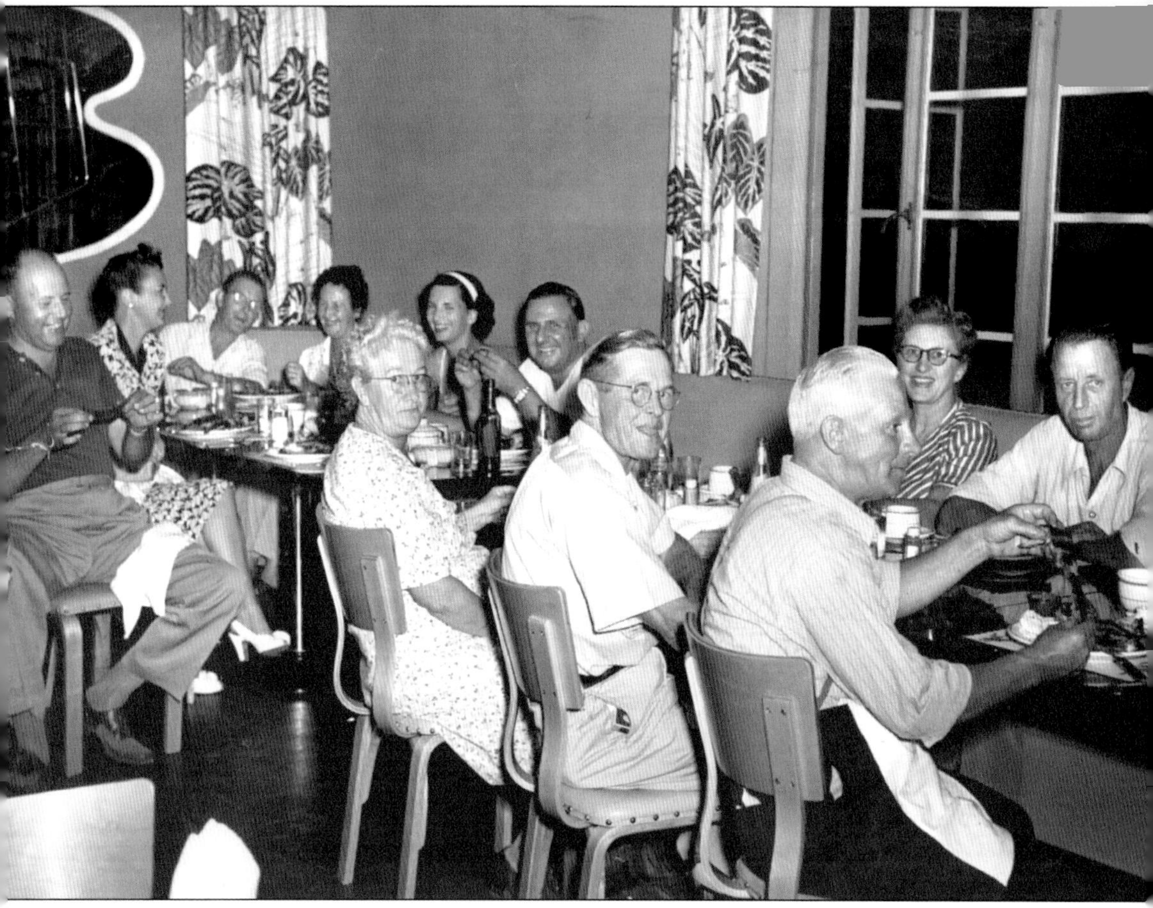

Without Willingham or his development, the community struggled to find cohesion, but over time, things took shape. George Richardson, who had constructed the golf course at the Fort Lauderdale Country Club, where Abreu designed the clubhouse, decided to retire in South Florida. He selected Wilton Manors as the location for his own golf course, and he purchased the property for a song. In Stuart McIver's book, *Island City: The Story of Wilton Manors*, Richardson's son, George Jr., told McIver, "The price we paid was so insignificant I'd be embarrassed to reveal it. It was out in the boonies, out beyond Progresso. In 1936, there were just three houses in town. One of them was owned by Carl Hiaasen." The nine-hole course was one of only three golf courses in the county (Orange Brook in Hollywood was the third). The 2,820-yard, par-68 course proved popular with tourists, undoubtedly enticing a few to remain longer. Dave Turner, son of Broward County's first sheriff, Aden Turner, returned home to South Florida after his military service to run a feed and fertilizer store. Among his many business pursuits, Turner acquired 283 lots from the Willingham estate for $12,500 and became a one-man sales force. As the community grew, its civic pride swelled. During the spring of 1946, members of the Wilton Manors Civic Association met for the first time over dinner at Alvar Hagen's bar. Alvar (far left) and Ginny Hagen, Ann and James Boyd (front row, center), and Perry and Dorothea Mickel (back row, far right) were among those who turned out to form the organization. Other members of the group included Katherine Johnston, Dave Turner, John Pedersen, A.F. Camman, James Farquhar, W.J. Robinson, and Harley Sanderson. The Village of Wilton Manors, population about 350, was incorporated on April 28, 1947. The state officially recognized the Village of Wilton Manors on May 13. Dave Turner became the village's first mayor and its municipal judge. (Wilton Manors Historical Society.)

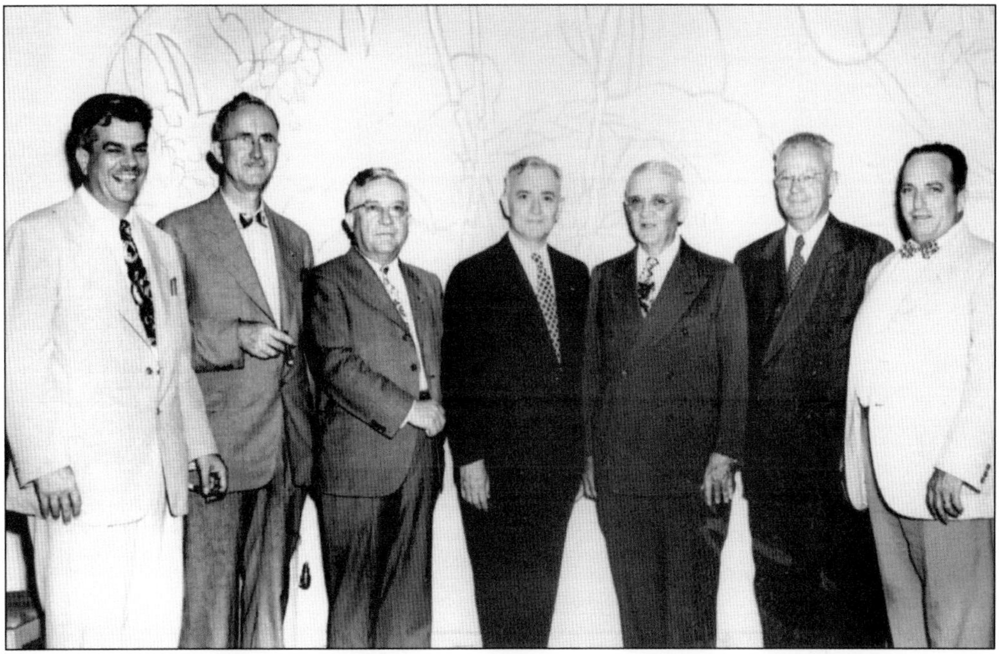

Turner, second from right, served as mayor from 1947 to 1952, when he stepped down. His career in public service had hardly ended. He helped several Broward communities through their growing pains. (Broward County Historical Commission.)

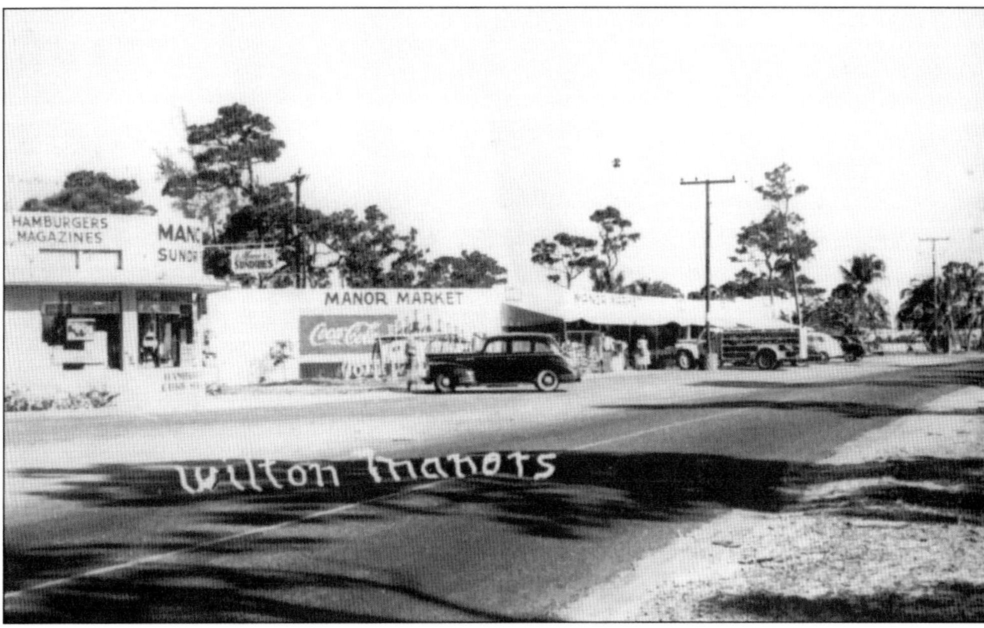


One hub of city life was Manor Market, which was opened in April 1946 by partners Lamar Braddy and J. Frank Starling. The original store had open sides and sawdust floors, and also was the site of the community's first public telephone. Braddy and Starling invested in other business ventures, including Cushionaire Mufflers at 2223 Wilton Drive, which they opened in 1956. Next door to Manor Market was Manor Sundries, owned by the Reed family. (Broward County Historical Commission.)

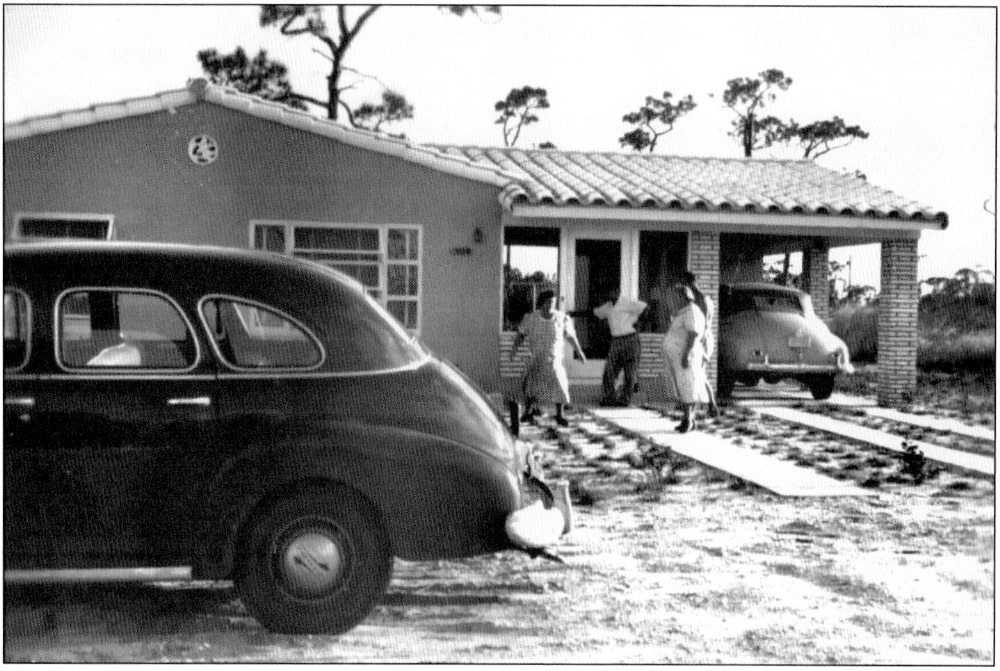

The Harold A. Keats development, just west of Wilton Drive, was the city's first subdivision. The postwar homes were perfect for returning servicemen and their spouses who were looking to start a family in the sunshine. Many northerners were amused at South Florida's interpretation of a garage—a covered, partially enclosed space called a carport.

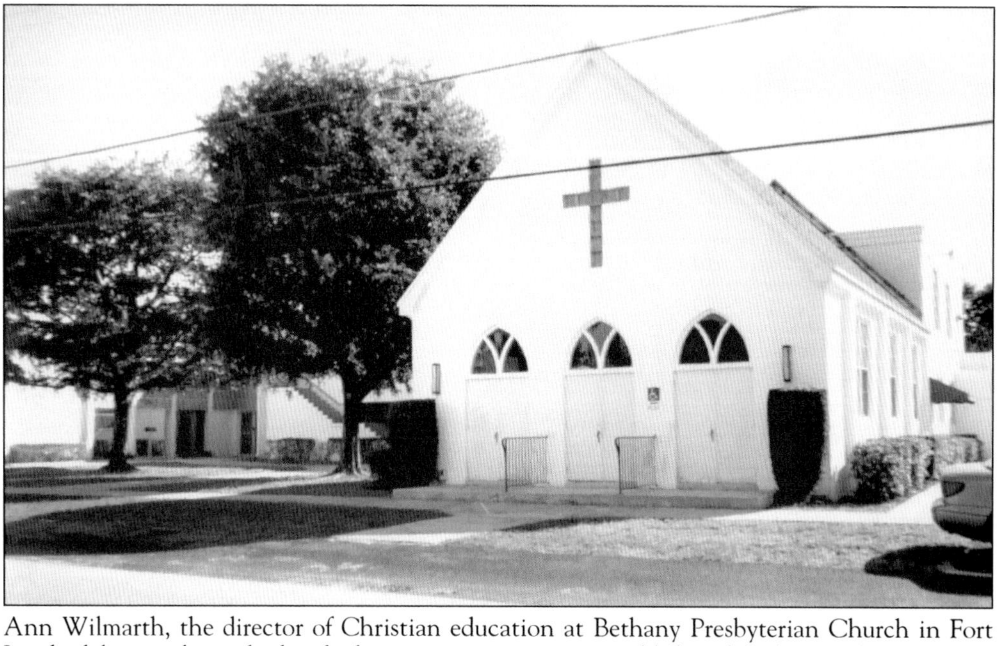

Ann Wilmarth, the director of Christian education at Bethany Presbyterian Church in Fort Lauderdale, was dispatched to find an appropriate site to establish a church in Wilton Manors. In January 1949, Covenant Presbyterian Church opened with Rev. Larry Love as its pastor. By October of that year, the church was incorporated. The first church, shown here, is now used for a variety of other purposes.

# *Three*

# The Next Step (1950–1959)

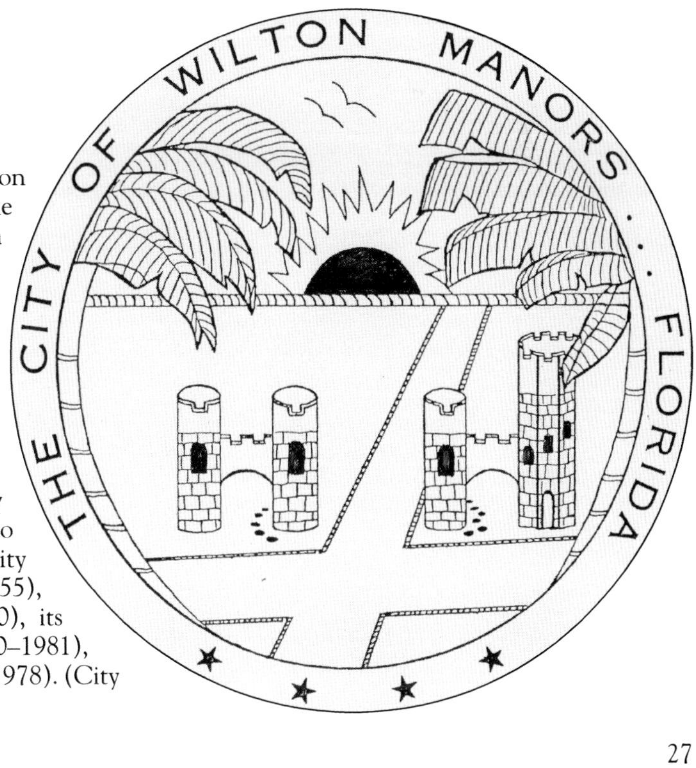


The citizens of Wilton Manors were ready to take the next step—becoming a city. James Dean, president of the village council, delivered the village's articles of incorporation to Tallahassee. On June 4, 1953, the village of Wilton Manors officially became a city. The city's first seal was designed by J. Frank Starling, who also served Wilton Manors as a city council member (1952–1955), its third mayor (1955–1960), its first city administrator (1960–1981), and as the city clerk (1960–1978). (City of Wilton Manors.)

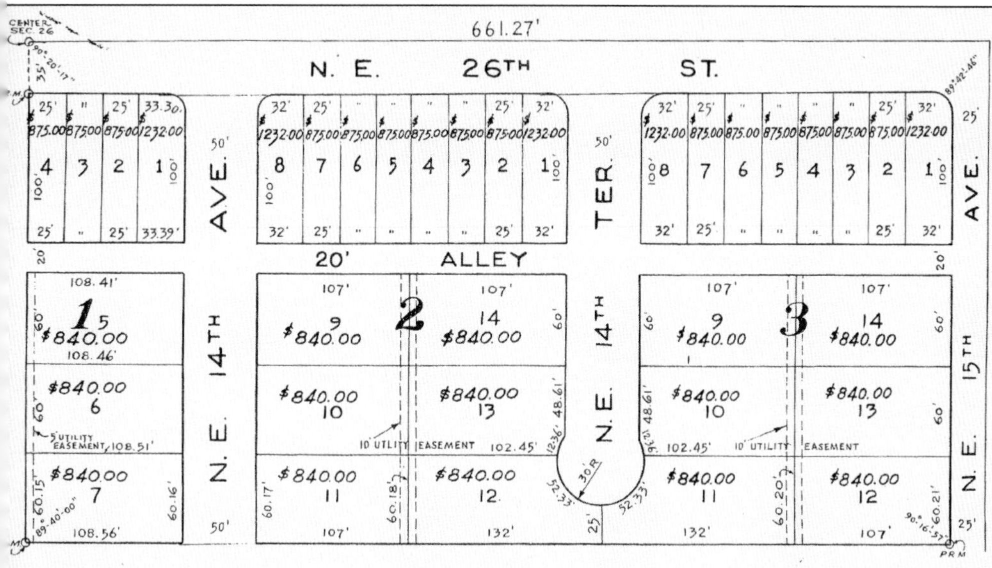


# /eber Heights

**Subdivision of Wilton Manor**
**Broward County, Florida**

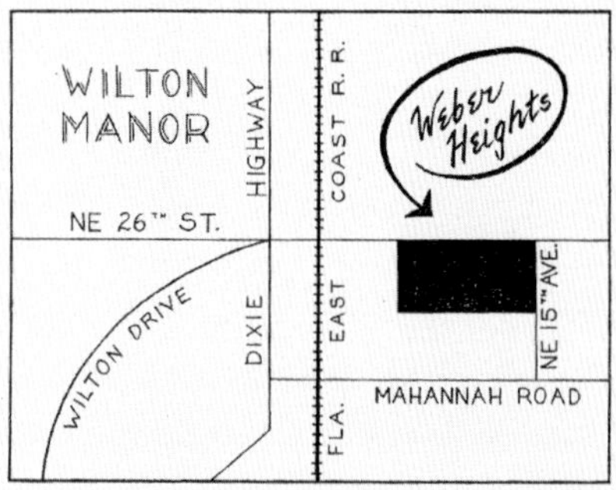


'e is choice residential and business property in the coming section of ton Manor, between the Florida East Coast R. R. and U. S. No. 1, fronting N. E. 26th Street, a 70-foot wide east-west artery.

de business lots are 25 feet wide and 100 feet deep, with a 20-foot alley he rear. Wilton Manor zoning requires a 20-foot setback on business tage, permitting construction of a 25 by 80-foot building on each lot. ner business lots are 32 feet wide. Business frontage is $35 per foot, with per cent premium for corner lots.

residential lots are 60 feet wide and are subject only to existing restrictions ecord. Residential frontage is $14 per foot.

street and alley easements as indicated on plat have been satisfied. Streets alleys are to be surfaced by subdivider.

**NOTE: All sales contracts are to carry the following stipulation: "Subject only to existing restrictions of record of the Village of Wilton Manor."**

*Every effort has been made to provide accurate information. However this offer is subject to errors, omissions, prior sale, or withdrawal without notice. The owner reserves the right to refuse any and all offers without explanation.*

As the Keats development took off, others joined the bandwagon. By the time Wilton Manors became a city, buyers had a wide selection of properties available to them, such as Coral Point, South Coral Point (1954), Middle River Estates (1952), Curva del Rio (1954), Hillbrook (1954), and Perry Mickel's developments. (Broward County Historical Commission.)

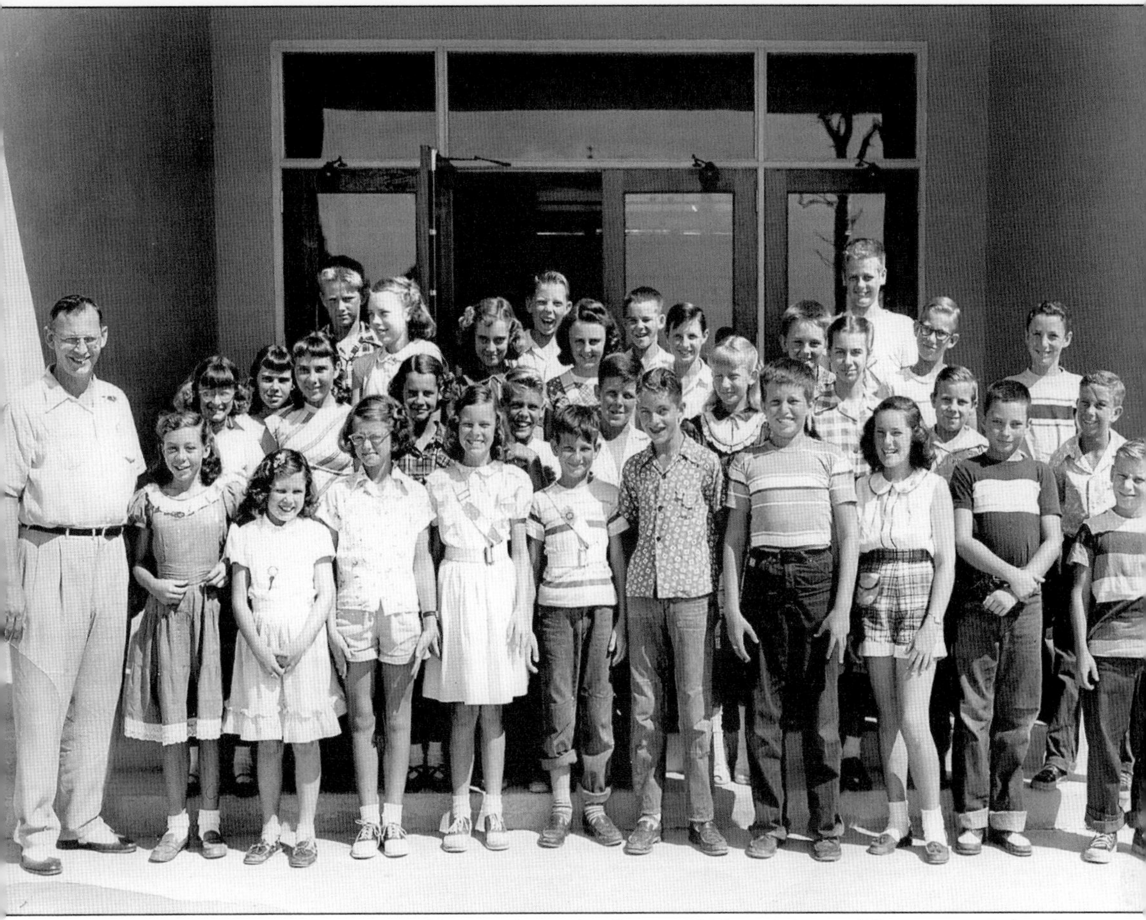

Teacher George Robinson III and his sixth grade class at Wilton Manors Elementary School pose at the school's main entrance near the end of the 1952 school year. Ground was broken for the school on April 2, 1951, on land earlier used as a chicken farm and across the street from a boarding house that saw double duty as a bordello. (It later became a home for the elderly.) The school opened before the end of the 1951–1952 year with 183 students, and within a year, it had grown to 302. (Wilton Manors Historical Society.)

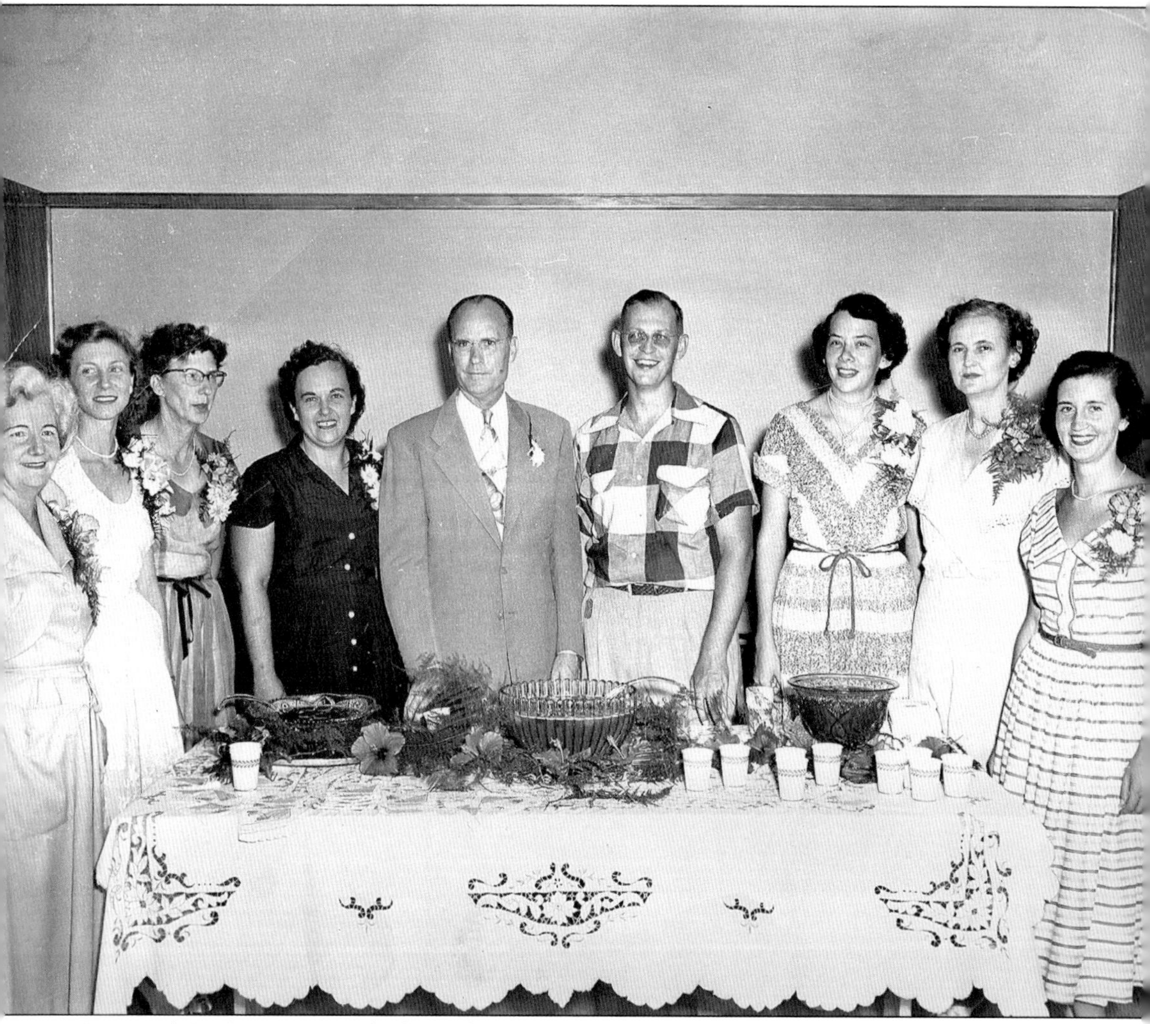

Principal W. Bryan Davis, looking dapper in his jacket and tie, and the founding faculty of Wilton Manors Elementary School are all smiles before they start ladling out the punch at a school event. The faculty for the school's second year included: Susie R. Meredith and Clare Welker, first grade; Jean E. Parker, second grade; Lilias Miller, third grade; Jacquelyn Robertson, fourth grade; Virginia Skeene, third and fourth grade; Billie K. Mattmuller and Edith Hammond, fifth grade; George Robinson III and Ina M. Tresca, sixth grade; and Ruth S. Van der Walt, music. (Wilton Manors Historical Society.)

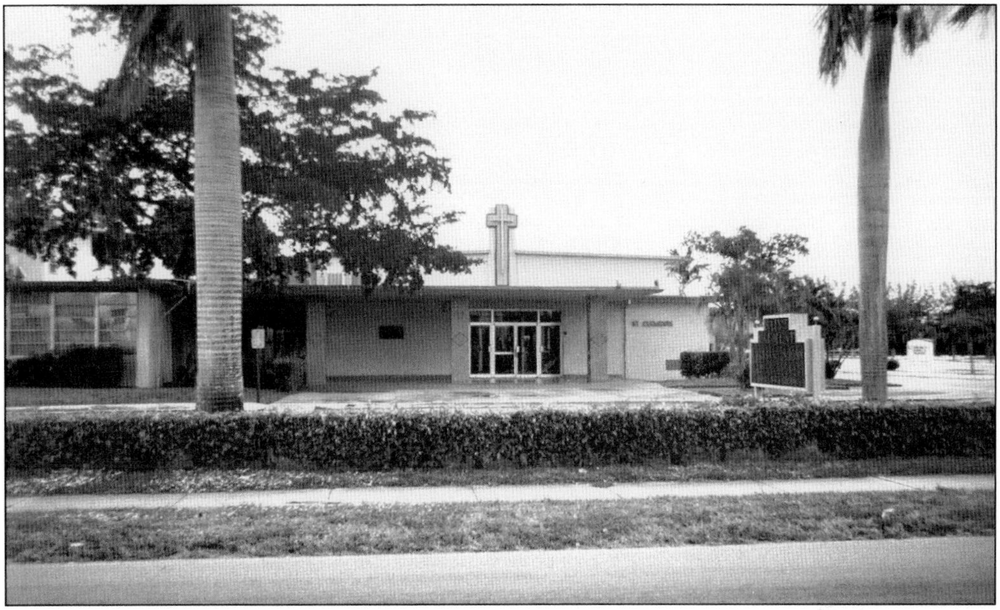

Archbishop Joseph Hurley of St. Augustine bought a 2.5-acre tract in Wilton Manors in 1952 to be developed to meet the needs of Catholics in north-central Broward County. Chosen as the founding pastor was Rev. James Keogh, from St. Margaret's parish in Clewiston. The congregation's first mass was celebrated in the church's temporary quarters at the Rivercrest Farms restaurant on Northeast Fourth Avenue in Fort Lauderdale. St. Clement parish was officially established on March 24, 1954. The parish moved into its permanent church on December 5, 1955.

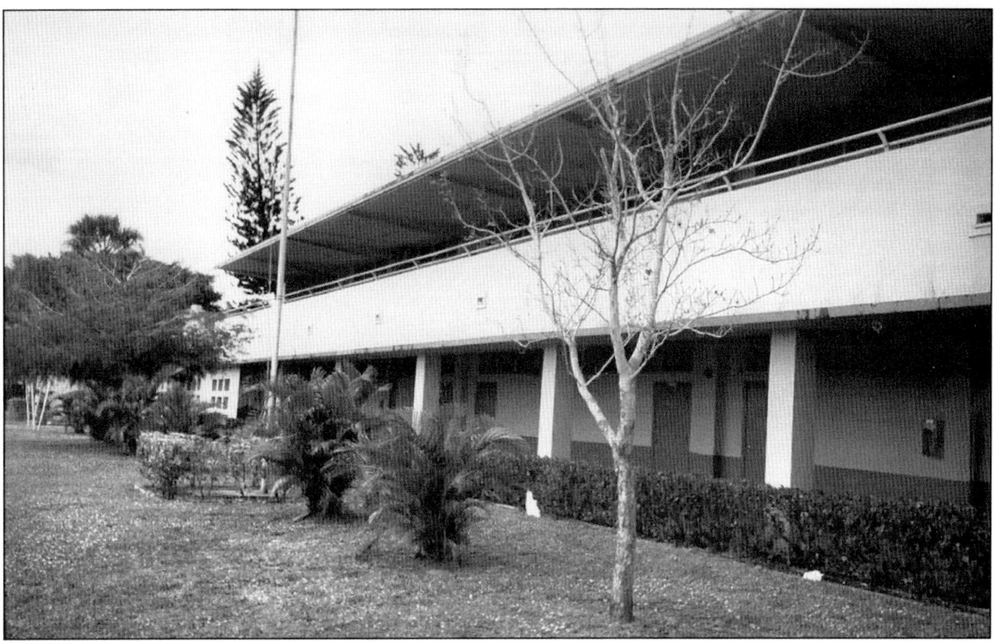

The parish received a building permit to add a two-story, eight-classroom school building in February 1956. Work was completed in time to open the school in September 1956. Sister Mary Theresine was the first principal.

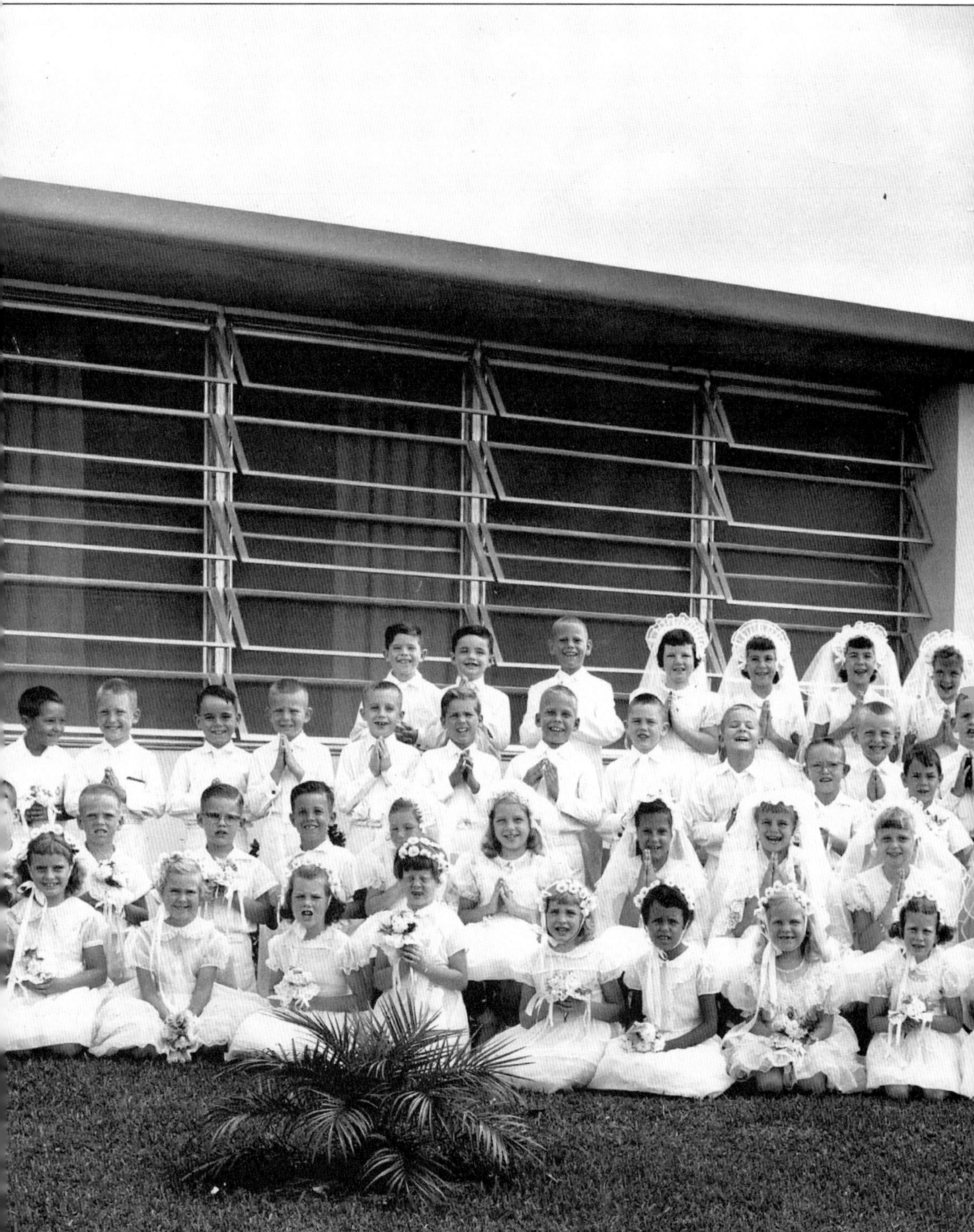

A St. Clement Church first communion class from the late 1950s flanks the parish's founding pastor, Rev. James Keogh. The parish celebrated the ordination of one of its own, Rev. James Kreitner, who had grown up in Wilton Manors and was approximately the age of

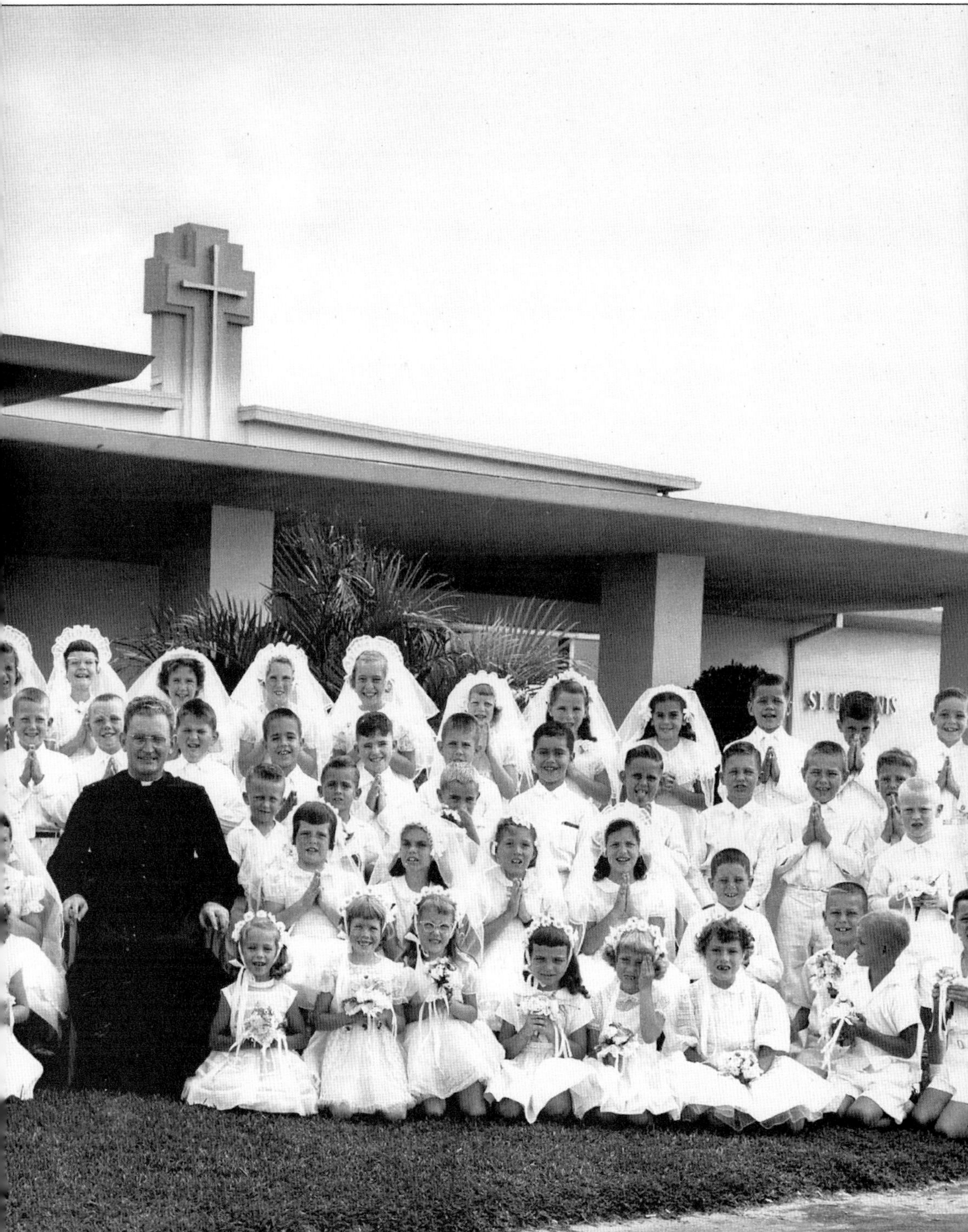

the communicants in the picture. Kreitner, who was affable, athletic, and well-liked by his peers, was ordained on May 17, 1975, but his service to the church did not last long. He died October 28, 1983.

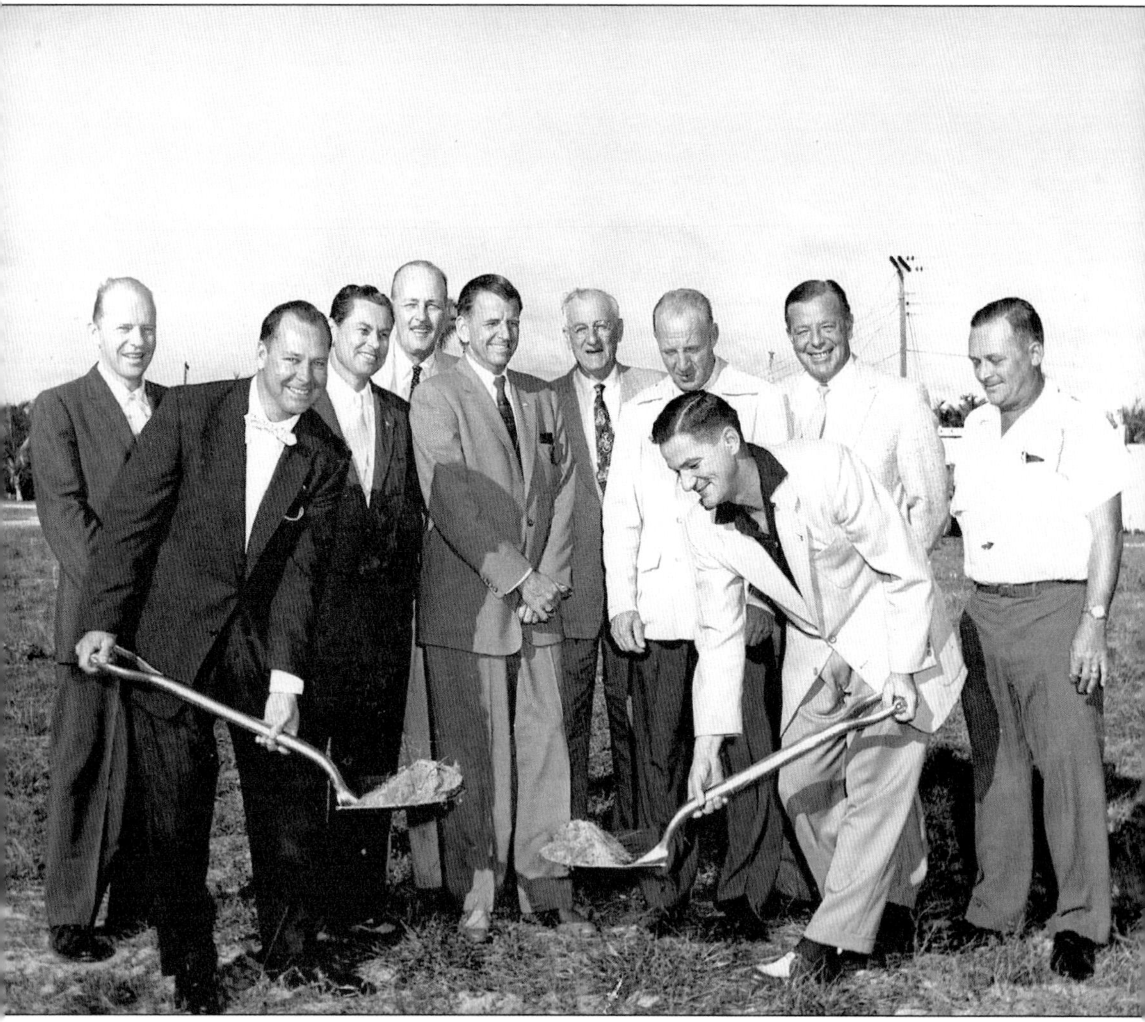

Wilton Manors became incorporated as a city on June 4, 1953, but most of the city records continued to be kept in city clerk Marcia Stafford's kitchen for a few years afterward. It wasn't until 1956 that work began on a city hall. Mayor J. Frank Starling, at left with shovel, and council member Fred J. Stevens, at right also with a shovel, handled the ceremonial duties at groundbreaking ceremonies for city hall. Joining in on the fun are (from left to right) George Richardson, the former city council president; Herman Quinn; council president Vernon Burnell; builder W.F. Seese; council member Earle Middleton; council member Harold T. Price; and business leader Bert Barry. The city moved into the present city hall, designed by William Bigoney, in 1957. The first city hall later became home to the library. (Wilton Manors Historical Society.)

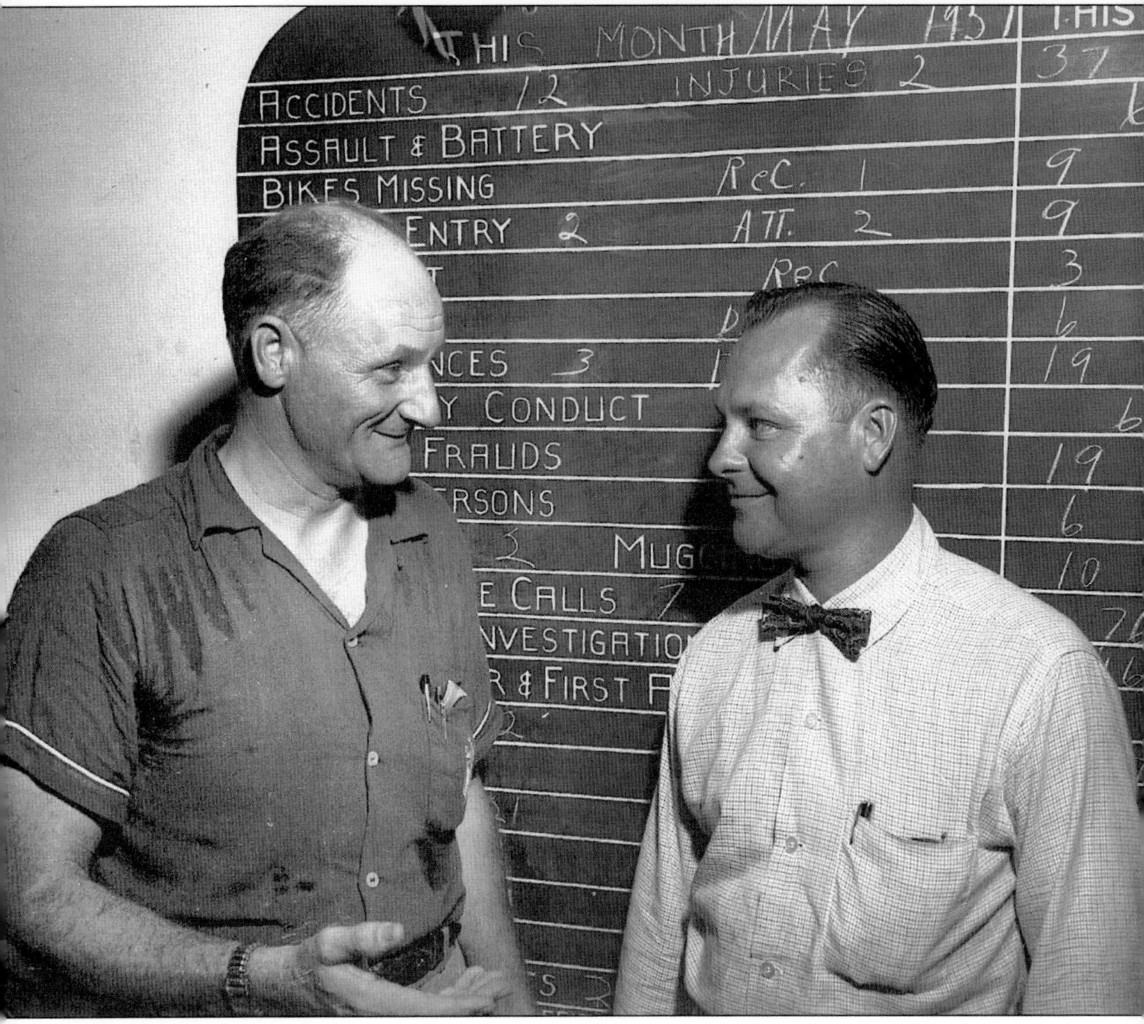


Richard Beaney, the city's first police chief, served from 1952 to 1957. He was removed from office largely for derogatory comments about the city he was alleged to have made. In the picture, he is shown with J. Frank Starling (right), discussing crime statistics. (Gene Hyde collection, Fort Lauderdale Historical Society, Inc.)

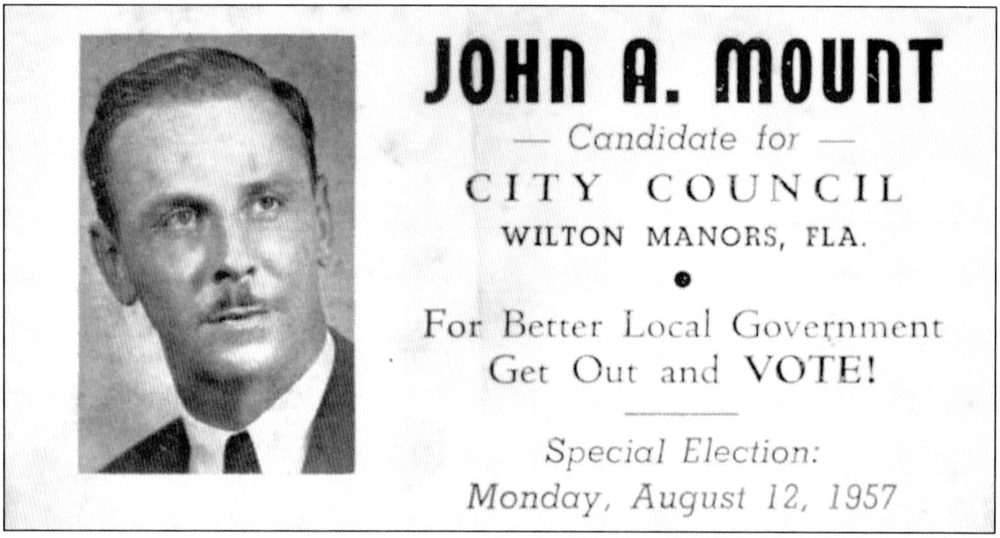


The council's dismissal of Beaney touched off a political maelstrom and an effort to recall the council members who voted for his dismissal: Vernon Burnell, Fred J. Stevens, and Harold Price. Beaney filed suit against the council members who voted to oust him and attempted to gain reinstatement. Many city employees signed a petition vowing to resign if Beaney got his job back. The recall's backers contended Beaney was improperly dismissed. First to file in the recall move was John Mount, a lawn supply business owner and political novice. (Marilyn Menchini.)

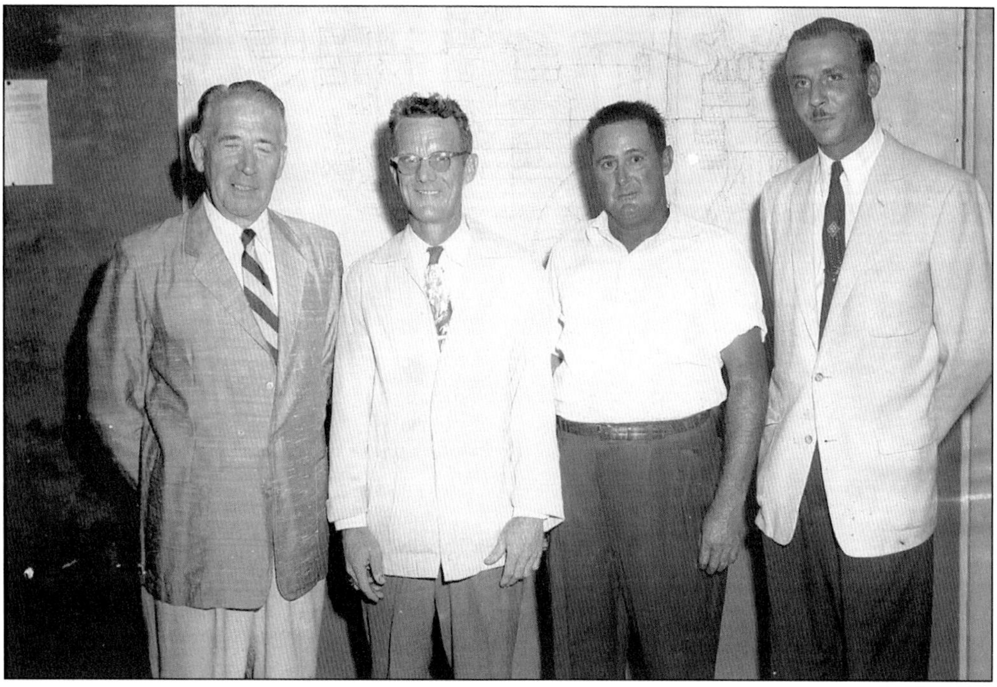

The recall movement attracted four candidates for the three seats: (from left): Lawrence C. Bailey, a plumbing contractor; John Broom, a Broward County employee; Guy Smith, a railway switch operator; and John Mount. Votes totalling 1,489 were cast against the recall, and 743 were cast in favor of it. (Marilyn Menchini.)

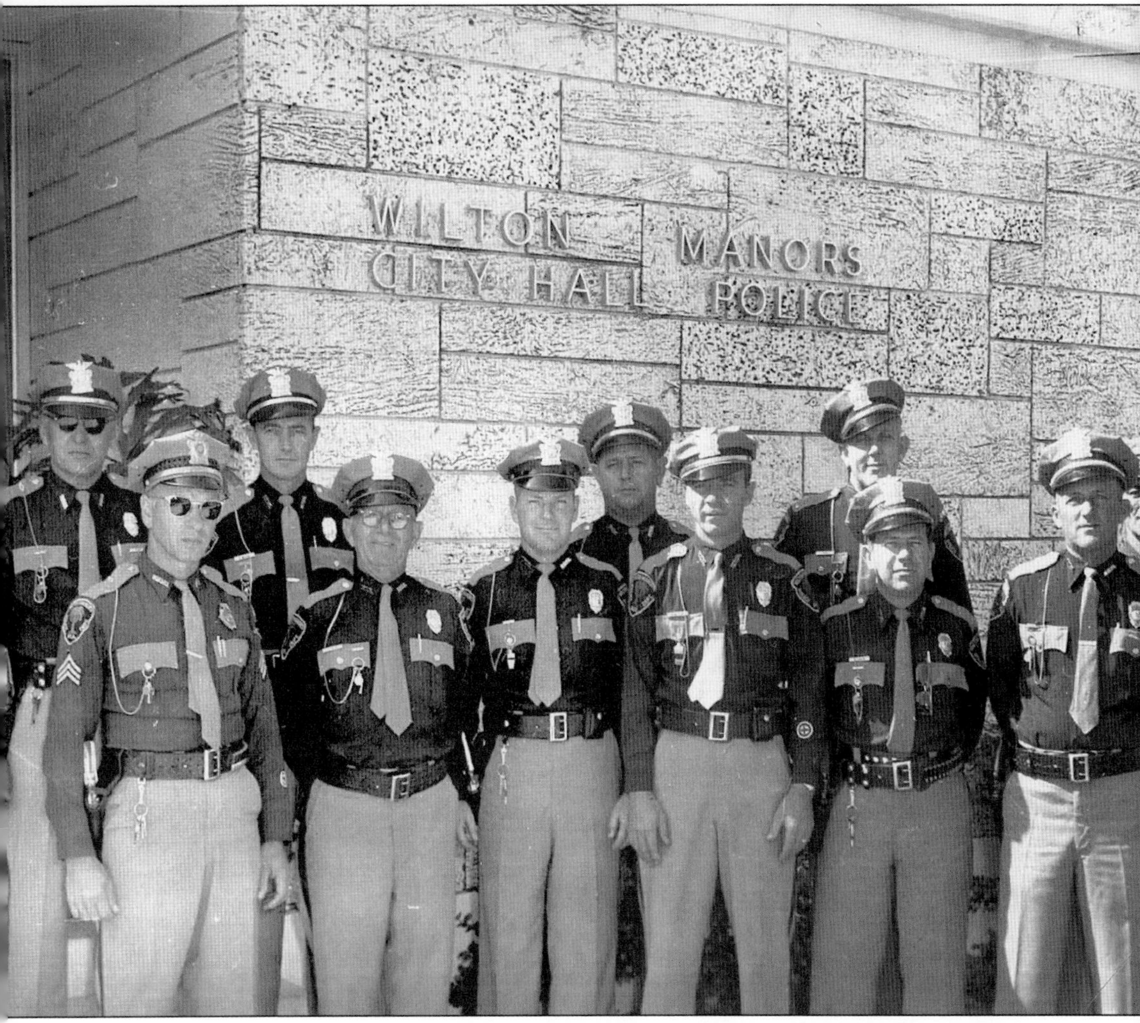


Tom Brace was appointed police chief after Beaney's dismissal. He set about forming an auxiliary police force to provide routine functions such as directing traffic, providing security details at public events, and accompanying sworn officers on routine patrol. Original members of the auxiliary include, from left to right, (front row) Police Sgt. Laddie Marolt, Bill Philbin, Don Ridenhour, Steve Gancarz, Steve Sharrow, and Bill McCabe; (back row) Ed Novy, Bob Merton, Capt. Tony Thuma, Dick Brandt, and Dave Salvino.

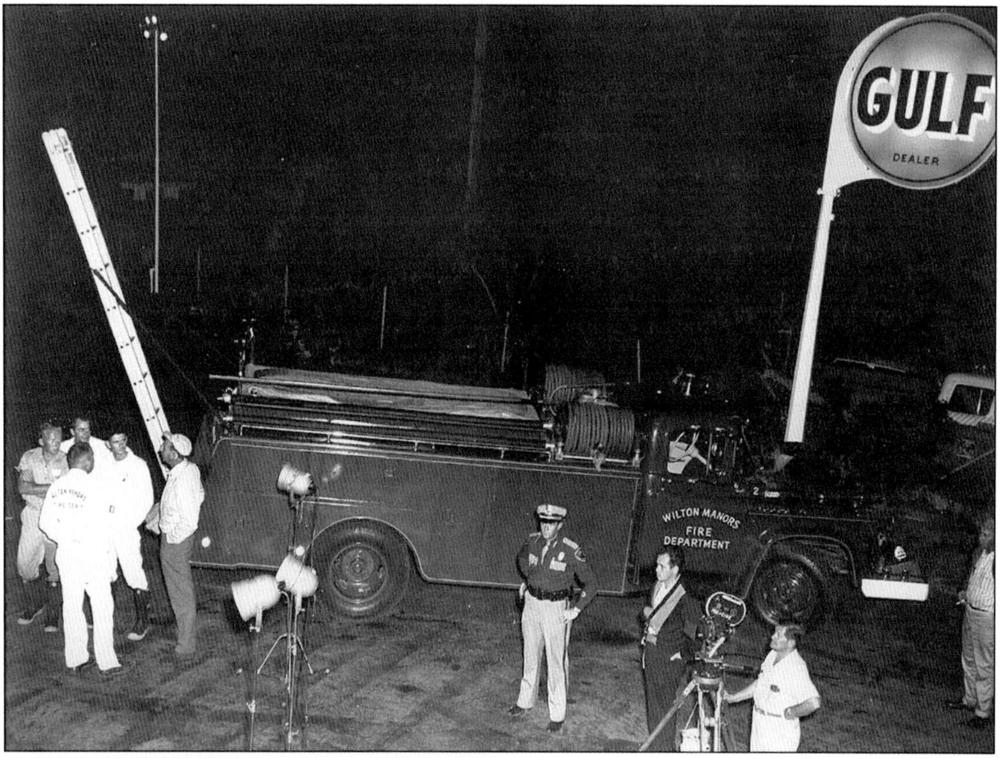


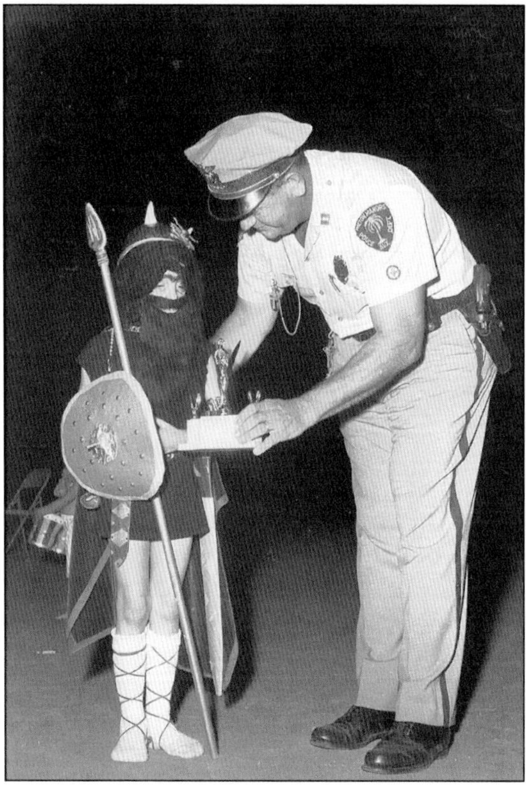

Firefighter John Miller (in cap in group at left) and Bob Merton, an auxiliary police officer (center), wait as film crews prepare to roll at the Wilton Drive Gulf station. Among the television episodes shot in Wilton Manors was one of *Candid Camera*, filmed at the car wash on Dixie Highway. Many years later, in 1995, several scenes for the movie *Striptease* were shot at the city's Middle River Trailer Park. (Wilton Manors Historical Society.)

By the 1950s, the recreation department had developed a well-rounded program for the city's residents. Among the events was the annual Halloween costume contest, a tradition that continues into the present.

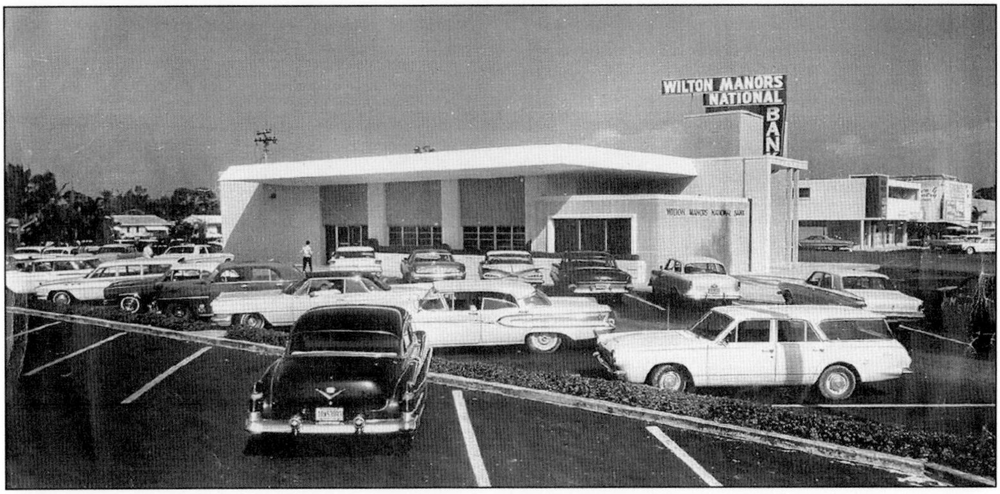

In December 1954, work began on the Wilton Manors National Bank, the anchor tenant for James Dean's Manor Gate Shopping Center. Dean originally had hoped to locate the bank in a 10-story office building topped by a restaurant. (Wilton Manors Historical Society.)

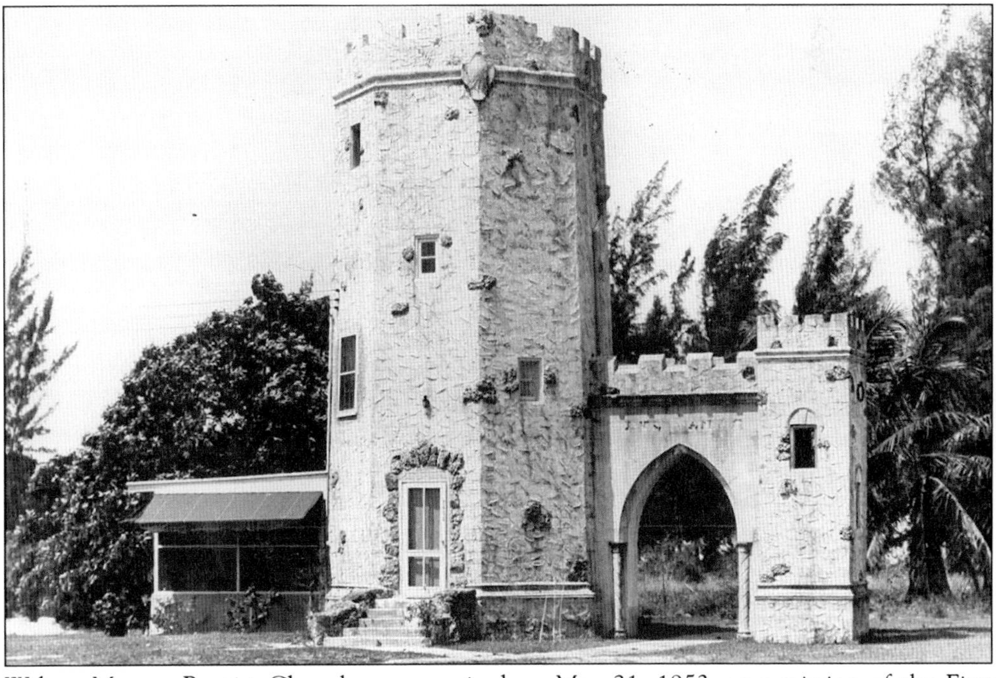
Wilton Manors Baptist Chapel was organized on May 21, 1953, as a mission of the First Baptist Church of Fort Lauderdale. Rev. A.D. Dawson was appointed its pastor on October 18 that year. Services were first held in the home of Robert and Grace Newton, then were moved to the tower building of the Abreu entryway. More than 100 worshippers squeezed into the tower and the adjoining enclosed area for Christmas services. A month later, ground was broken for the Wilton Manors Baptist Chapel at 116 Northeast Twenty-fourth Street, on land purchased from R.D. Cobb. The Abreu gates and tower that marked the city's formal entryway were torn down between 1958 and 1962, giving way to progress that came in the form of widening Wilton Drive and the construction of an A&W Root Beer drive-in restaurant. (Wilton Manors Historical Society.)

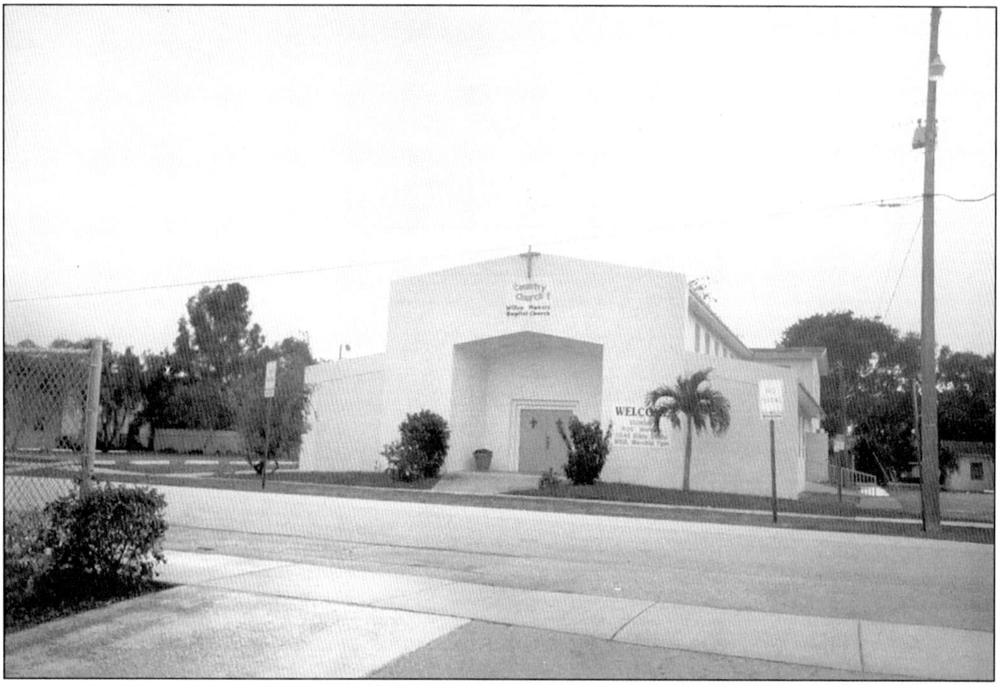

Rev. Kelly Blanton became pastor of the congregation and guided it through a period of intense growth, starting with the construction of its first permanent church in 1955. The mission became Wilton Manors Baptist Church on July 10, 1955, with 151 members. James Dean carried the city's incorporation papers to Tallahassee. He remains one of the church's deacons.

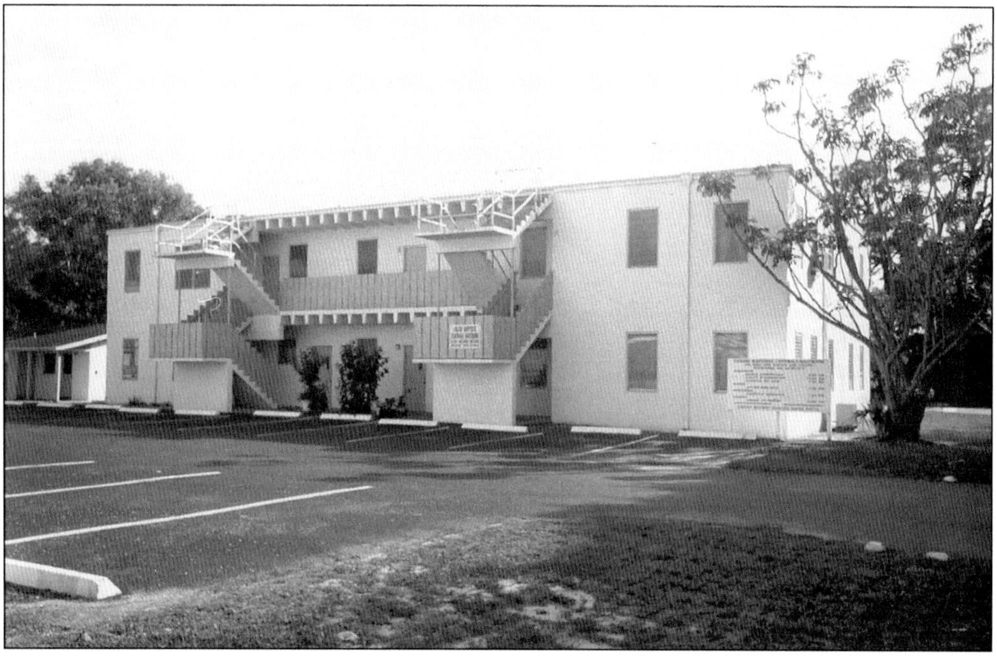

The church opened a kindergarten in September 1958 and completed its two-story educational building in October. The building is currently used by Eglise Baptiste Haitienne Centrale, a mission of the church, one of three sponsored since 1991.

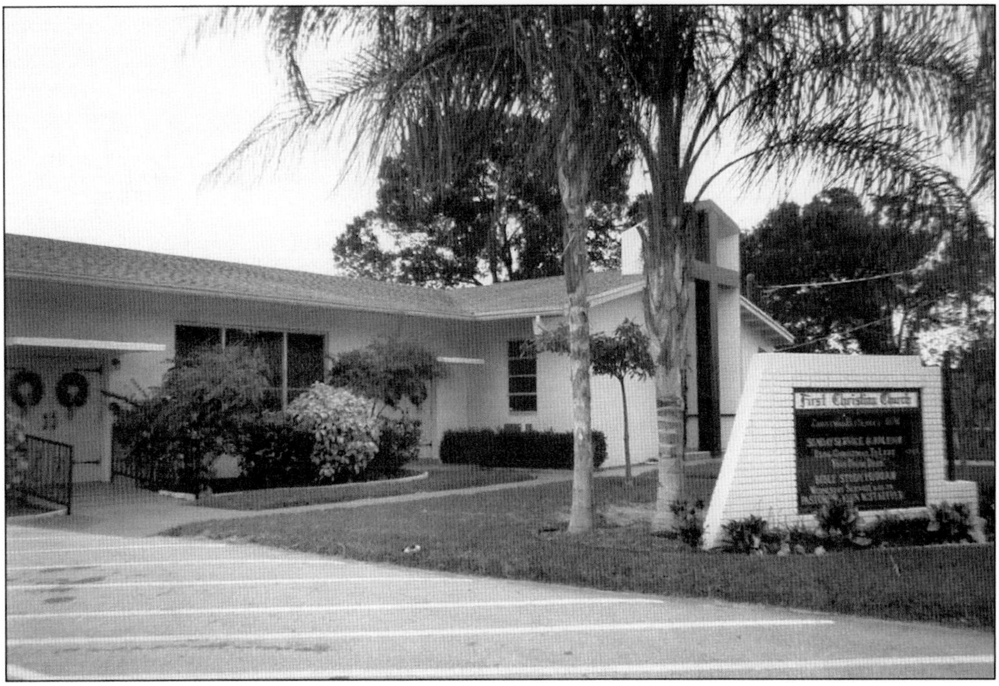

First Christian Church of Wilton Manors opened the doors to its sanctuary on April 10, 1955. The first worship service was held on Easter and was celebrated by the founding pastor, Rev. Clarence C. Stauffer. Often present at services was Rev. Stauffer's son, John, who decided at age 12 he wished to follow in his father's footsteps, which he did. Throughout the church's 50 years, a Stauffer has been the church's spiritual leader.

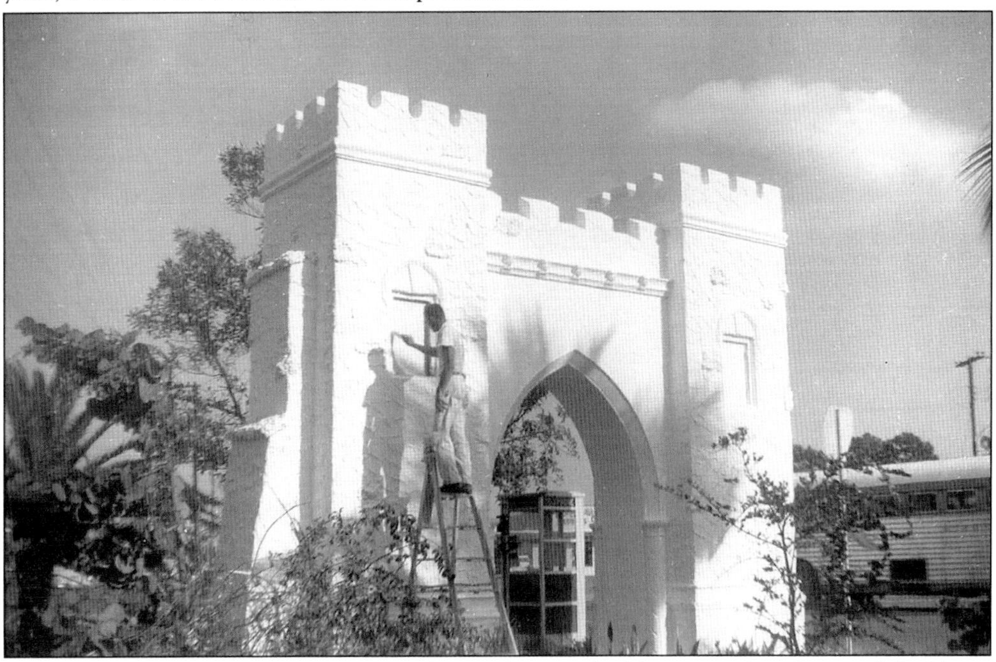

A workman paints over wood panels in the north tower building in 1955. The panels had been installed in place of glass windows, a target for vandals. (Wilton Manors Historical Society.)

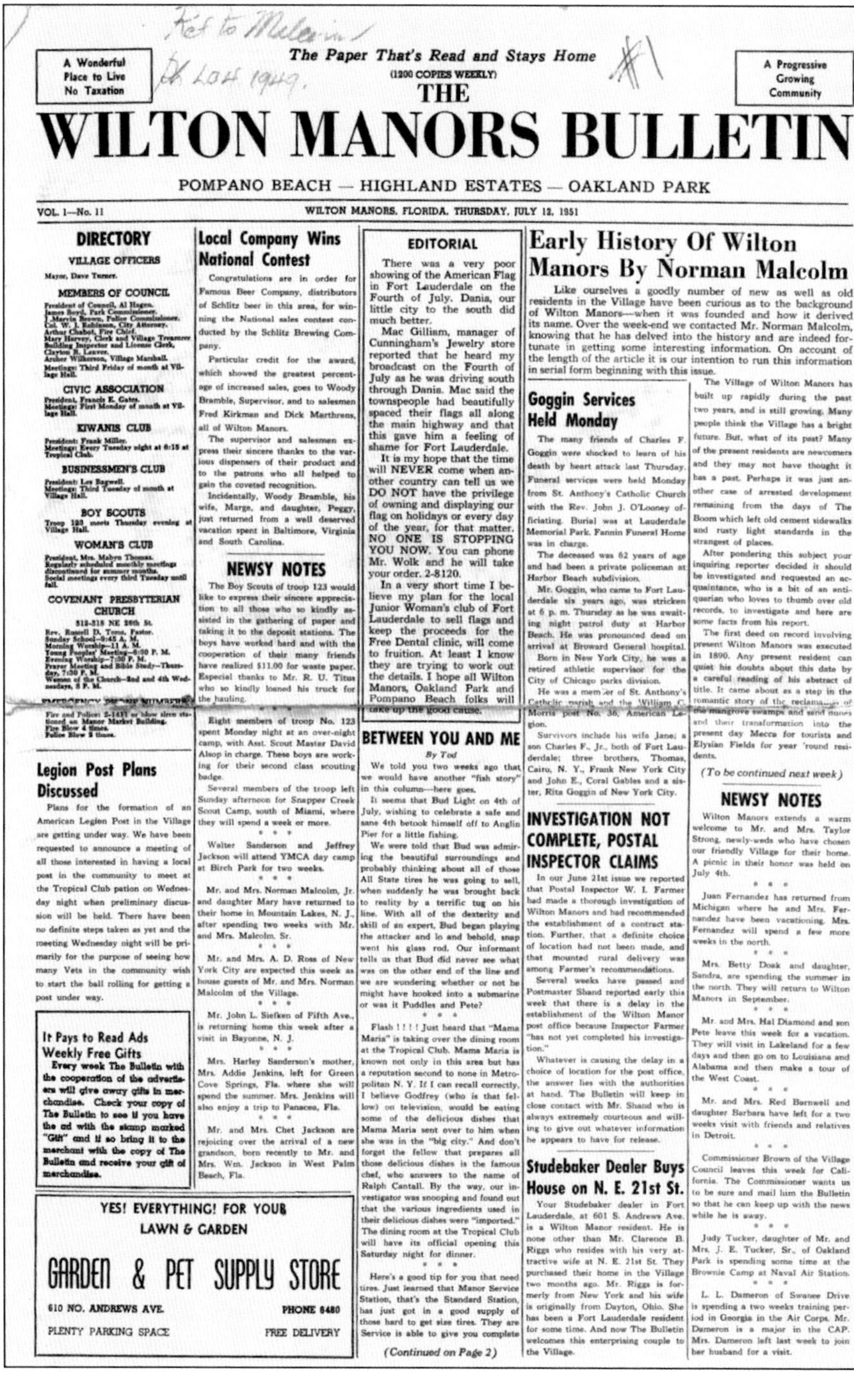

A Wonderful Place to Live No Taxation

*The Paper That's Read and Stays Home*

(1200 COPIES WEEKLY)

A Progressive Growing Community

# THE WILTON MANORS BULLETIN

POMPANO BEACH — HIGHLAND ESTATES — OAKLAND PARK

VOL. 1—No. 11 WILTON MANORS, FLORIDA, THURSDAY, JULY 12, 1951

## DIRECTORY

### VILLAGE OFFICERS

Mayor, Dave Turner.

### MEMBERS OF COUNCIL

President of Council, Al Hagen.
James Boyd, Park Commissioner.
J. Marvin Brown, Police Commissioner.
Col. W. J. Robinson, City Attorney.
Arthur Chabot, Fire Chief.
Mary Harvey, Clerk and Village Treasurer
Building Inspector and License Clerk, Clayton R. Leaver.
Archer Wilkerson, Village Marshall.
Meetings: Third Friday of month at Village Hall.

### CIVIC ASSOCIATION

President, Francis E. Gates.
Meetings: First Monday of month at Village Hall.

### KIWANIS CLUB

President: Frank Miller.
Meetings: Every Tuesday night at 6:15 at Tropical Club.

### BUSINESSMEN'S CLUB

President: Les Bagwell.
Meetings: Third Tuesday of month at Village Hall.

### BOY SCOUTS

Troop 123 meets Thursday evening at Village Hall.

### WOMAN'S CLUB

President, Mrs. Mabyn Thomas.
Regularly scheduled monthly meetings discontinued for summer months.
Social meetings every third Tuesday until fall.

### COVENANT PRESBYTERIAN CHURCH

512-518 NE 26th St.
Rev. Russell D. Toms, Pastor.
Sunday School—9:45 A. M.
Morning Worship—11 A. M.
Young Peoples' Meeting—6:30 P. M.
Evening Worship—7:30 P. M.
Prayer Meeting and Bible Study—Thursday, 7:30 P. M.
Women of the Church—2nd and 4th Wednesdays, 8 P. M.

### EMERGENCY [illegible] NUMBERS

Fire and Police: 2-1411 or blow siren stationed on Manor Market Building.
Fire Blow 4 times.
Police Blow 2 times.

## Legion Post Plans Discussed

Plans for the formation of an American Legion Post in the Village are getting under way. We have been requested to announce a meeting of all those interested in having a local post in the community to meet at the Tropical Club pation on Wednesday night when preliminary discussion will be held. There have been no definite steps taken as yet and the meeting Wednesday night will be primarily for the purpose of seeing how many Vets in the community wish to start the ball rolling for getting a post under way.

### It Pays to Read Ads Weekly Free Gifts

Every week The Bulletin with the cooperation of the advertisers will give away gifts in merchandise. Check your copy of The Bulletin to see if you have the ad with the stamp marked "Gift" and if so bring it to the merchant with the copy of The Bulletin and receive your gift of merchandise.

## Local Company Wins National Contest

Congratulations are in order for Famous Beer Company, distributors of Schlitz beer in this area, for winning the National sales contest conducted by the Schlitz Brewing Company.

Particular credit for the award, which showed the greatest percentage of increased sales, goes to Woody Bramble, Supervisor, and to salesmen Fred Kirkman and Dick Marthrens, all of Wilton Manors.

The supervisor and salesmen express their sincere thanks to the various dispensers of their product and to the patrons who all helped to gain the coveted recognition.

Incidentally, Woody Bramble, his wife, Marge, and daughter, Peggy, just returned from a well deserved vacation spent in Baltimore, Virginia and South Carolina.

## NEWSY NOTES

The Boy Scouts of troop 123 would like to express their sincere appreciation to all those who so kindly assisted in the gathering of paper and taking it to the deposit stations. The boys have worked hard and with the cooperation of their many friends have realized $11.00 for waste paper. Especial thanks to Mr. R. U. Titus who so kindly loaned his truck for the hauling.

* * *

Eight members of troop No. 123 spent Monday night at an over-night camp, with Asst. Scout Master David Alsop in charge. These boys are working for their second class scouting badge.

Several members of the troop left Sunday afternoon for Snapper Creek Scout Camp, south of Miami, where they will spend a week or more.

* * *

Walter Sanderson and Jeffrey Jackson will attend YMCA day camp at Birch Park for two weeks.

* * *

Mr. and Mrs. Norman Malcolm, Jr. and daughter Mary have returned to their home in Mountain Lakes, N. J., after spending two weeks with Mr. and Mrs. Malcolm, Sr.

* * *

Mr. and Mrs. A. D. Ross of New York City are expected this week as house guests of Mr. and Mrs. Norman Malcolm of the Village.

* * *

Mr. John L. Siefken of Fifth Ave., is returning home this week after a visit in Bayonne, N. J.

* * *

Mrs. Harley Sanderson's mother, Mrs. Addie Jenkins, left for Green Cove Springs, Fla. where she will spend the summer. Mrs. Jenkins will also enjoy a trip to Panacea, Fla.

* * *

Mr. and Mrs. Chet Jackson are rejoicing over the arrival of a new grandson, born recently to Mr. and Mrs. Wm. Jackson in West Palm Beach, Fla.

## EDITORIAL

There was a very poor showing of the American Flag in Fort Lauderdale on the Fourth of July. Dania, our little city to the south did much better.

Mac Gilliam, manager of Cunningham's Jewelry store reported that he heard my broadcast on the Fourth of July as he was driving south through Dania. Mac said the townspeople had beautifully spaced their flags all along the main highway and that this gave him a feeling of shame for Fort Lauderdale.

It is my hope that the time will NEVER come when another country can tell us we DO NOT have the privilege of owning and displaying our flag on holidays or every day of the year, for that matter. NO ONE IS STOPPING YOU NOW. You can phone Mr. Wolk and he will take your order. 2-8120.

In a very short time I believe my plan for the local Junior Woman's club of Fort Lauderdale to sell flags and keep the proceeds for the Free Dental clinic, will come to fruition. At least I know they are trying to work out the details. I hope all Wilton Manors, Oakland Park and Pompano Beach folks will take up the good cause.

## BETWEEN YOU AND ME

*By Tod*

We told you two weeks ago that we would have another "fish story" in this column—here goes.

It seems that Bud Light on 4th of July, wishing to celebrate a safe and sane 4th betook himself off to Anglin Pier for a little fishing.

We were told that Bud was admiring the beautiful surroundings and probably thinking about all of those All State tires he was going to sell, when suddenly he was brought back to reality by a terrific tug on his line. With all of the dexterity and skill of an expert, Bud began playing the attacker and lo and behold, snap went his glass rod. Our informant tells us that Bud did never see what was on the other end of the line and we are wondering whether or not he might have hooked into a submarine or was it Puddles and Pete?

* * *

Flash ! ! ! ! Just heard that "Mama Maria" is taking over the dining room at the Tropical Club. Mama Maria is known not only in this area but has a reputation second to none in Metropolitan N. Y. If I can recall correctly, I believe Godfrey (who is that fellow) on television, would be eating some of the delicious dishes that Mama Maria sent over to him when she was in the "big city." And don't forget the fellow that prepares all those delicious dishes is the famous chef, who answers to the name of Ralph Cantall. By the way, our investigator was snooping and found out that the various ingredients used in their delicious dishes were "imported." The dining room at the Tropical Club will have its official opening this Saturday night for dinner.

* * *

Here's a good tip for you that need tires. Just learned that Manor Service Station, that's the Standard Station, has just got in a good supply of those hard to get size tires. They are Service is able to give you complete

*(Continued on Page 2)*

## Early History Of Wilton Manors By Norman Malcolm

Like ourselves a goodly number of new as well as old residents in the Village have been curious as to the background of Wilton Manors—when it was founded and how it derived its name. Over the week-end we contacted Mr. Norman Malcolm, knowing that he has delved into the history and are indeed fortunate in getting some interesting information. On account of the length of the article it is our intention to run this information in serial form beginning with this issue.

The Village of Wilton Manors has built up rapidly during the past two years, and is still growing. Many people think the Village has a bright future. But, what of its past? Many of the present residents are newcomers and they may not have thought it has a past. Perhaps it was just another case of arrested development remaining from the days of The Boom which left old cement sidewalks and rusty light standards in the strangest of places.

After pondering this subject your inquiring reporter decided it should be investigated and requested an acquaintance, who is a bit of an antiquarian who loves to thumb over old records, to investigate and here are some facts from his report.

The first deed on record involving present Wilton Manors was executed in 1890. Any present resident can quiet his doubts about this date by a careful reading of his abstract of title. It came about as a step in the romantic story of the reclamation of the mangrove swamps and sand dunes and their transformation into the present day Mecca for tourists and Elysian Fields for year 'round residents.

*(To be continued next week)*

## Goggin Services Held Monday

The many friends of Charles F. Goggin were shocked to learn of his death by heart attack last Thursday. Funeral services were held Monday from St. Anthony's Catholic Church with the Rev. John J. O'Looney officiating. Burial was at Lauderdale Memorial Park. Fannin Funeral Home was in charge.

The deceased was 62 years of age and had been a private policeman at Harbor Beach subdivision.

Mr. Goggin, who came to Fort Lauderdale six years ago, was stricken at 6 p. m. Thursday as he was awaiting night patrol duty at Harbor Beach. He was pronounced dead on arrival at Broward General hospital.

Born in New York City, he was a retired athletic supervisor for the City of Chicago parks division.

He was a member of St. Anthony's Catholic parish and the William C. Morris post No. 36, American Legion.

Survivors include his wife Jane; a son Charles F., Jr., both of Fort Lauderdale; three brothers, Thomas, Cairo, N. Y., Frank New York City and John E., Coral Gables and a sister, Rita Goggin of New York City.

## INVESTIGATION NOT COMPLETE, POSTAL INSPECTOR CLAIMS

In our June 21st issue we reported that Postal Inspector W. I. Farmer had made a thorough investigation of Wilton Manors and had recommended the establishment of a contract station. Further, that a definite choice of location had not been made, and that mounted rural delivery was among Farmer's recommendations.

Several weeks have passed and Postmaster Shand reported early this week that there is a delay in the establishment of the Wilton Manor post office because Inspector Farmer "has not yet completed his investigation."

Whatever is causing the delay in a choice of location for the post office, the answer lies with the authorities at hand. The Bulletin will keep in close contact with Mr. Shand who is always extremely courteous and willing to give out whatever information he appears to have for release.

## Studebaker Dealer Buys House on N. E. 21st St.

Your Studebaker dealer in Fort Lauderdale, at 601 S. Andrews Ave. is a Wilton Manor resident. He is none other than Mr. Clarence B. Riggs who resides with his very attractive wife at N. E. 21st St. They purchased their home in the Village two months ago. Mr. Riggs is formerly from New York and his wife is originally from Dayton, Ohio. She has been a Fort Lauderdale resident for some time. And now The Bulletin welcomes this enterprising couple to the Village.

## NEWSY NOTES

Wilton Manors extends a warm welcome to Mr. and Mrs. Taylor Strong, newly-weds who have chosen our friendly Village for their home. A picnic in their honor was held on July 4th.

* * *

Juan Fernandez has returned from Michigan where he and Mrs. Fernandez have been vacationing. Mrs. Fernandez will spend a few more weeks in the north.

* * *

Mrs. Betty Doak and daughter, Sandra, are spending the summer in the north. They will return to Wilton Manors in September.

* * *

Mr. and Mrs. Hal Diamond and son Pete leave this week for a vacation. They will visit in Lakeland for a few days and then go on to Louisiana and Alabama and then make a tour of the West Coast.

* * *

Mr. and Mrs. Red Barnwell and daughter Barbara have left for a two weeks visit with friends and relatives in Detroit.

* * *

Commissioner Brown of the Village Council leaves this week for California. The Commissioner wants us to be sure and mail him the Bulletin so that he can keep up with the news while he is away.

* * *

Judy Tucker, daughter of Mr. and Mrs. J. E. Tucker, Sr., of Oakland Park is spending some time at the Brownie Camp at Naval Air Station.

* * *

L. L. Dameron of Swanee Drive is spending a two weeks training period in Georgia in the Air Corps. Mr. Dameron is a major in the CAP. Mrs. Dameron left last week to join her husband for a visit.



Wilton Manors could hardly be thought of as a media hub, but at times, particularly in the 1950s, it served as home to several newspapers. The first appears to have been the *Wilton Manors Bulletin*, which began publication in May 1951. Betty Dickens served as publisher and Tom E. Hinds served as editor. By July of that year, Hinds had become editor and publisher. One of the *Bulletin*'s early projects was a three-part history of the village, written by Norman Malcolm. (Wilton Manors Historical Society.)

MARCH 1, 1956

# Wilton Sunrise News

VOLUME 3 NO. 9 ......WILTON SUNRISE PUB. CO., 2183 WILTON DRIVE, WILTON MANORS FLA.

## Local Druggist Gives Away $5 Bills

KERBEL PHARMACY APPRECIATIVE UP TO 400 WILL BENEFIT

Ervin and Evelyn Kerbel, owners and operators of Kerbel's Pharmacy at 2155 Wilton Drive, are so enthusiastic over the results of their advertising in the Clipper ads run each week in the Wilton Sunrise News that they are giving a new five dollar bill to each and every one who has presented a Clipper Coupon to them during the last three weeks of the running of the Clipper Ads.

The coupons quoted the following specials:

February 9 - 25% off on Valentine Heart box candy; February 16 - A free soda, sundae, or milk shake while waiting for a prescription; February 23 - free coke or 100 bottle of saccharine with purchase of each bottle of insulin.

Quotes Doc Kerbel: "This is our way of thanking the people of Wilton Manors for welcoming us to their lovely city, and we want to show our appreciation even if it breaks us !"

### SAXERS HAVE HOUSE GUESTS

The Charles A. Saxers have as their house guests Mr. and Mrs. Alfred E. Mason of Newark, New Jersey. They will be with the Saxers until they buy a house and get located.

Mrs. Saxer is particularly happy and excited about her guests since Mrs. Mason is her twin and only sister.

The Masons got 'sand in their shoes' sometime back and resolved to settle here after Mr. Mason's retirement. So, he is now retired from the automobile business and their resolution has now become a reality. They will, no doubt, be quite busy for awhile, but not too much to enjoy the ideal weather we all are now enjoying.

### SPORTS, INC. WILL GIVE 1956 FORD AWAY

In the planning stage is a double header baseball game sponsored by Wilton Manors Sports, Inc., to be held March 17th, "St. Patrick's Day," at Mickel Field—27th Street and NW 7th Ave.

Past the planning stage, however, is the give-away of a brand spankin' new 1956 Ford station wagon. It is on hand now and is on display at various places of business in and around Wilton Manors. Tickets to the game will be sold also where the car is displayed.

### LITTLE LEAGUE & WILTON MANORS SPORTS TO MEET

Wilton Manors Sports will meet Monday, March 5th at 7:30 PM at Wilton Manors Elementary School. This meeting will be held at the same time as Little League.

### LAUDERDALE MANORS SCHOOL PTA

Lauderdale Manors PTA plans a discussion group for their meeting on Tuesday, February 28th, at 7:30 PM.

The topics to be discussed are an outgrowth of previous discussions that arose at the November meeting. This meeting is planned to give parents an opportunity to discuss their problems and to share their experiences.

All topics pertain to the guidance of children. Those scheduled are 1) homework. 2) whether or not children should be rewarded for what they do. 3) How parents should interpret report cards and of what value are grades. 4) Should a child be compared with other children in the family and with others in the neighborhood. 5) What should be done with children who have the feeling of rejection 6) What should be done about the children who have real ability but do not work up to their capacity. 7) How can TV be used so that it is a constructive rather than a destructive influence upon children.

All parents are cordially invited to attend this worthwhile meeting and to contribute to these discussions.

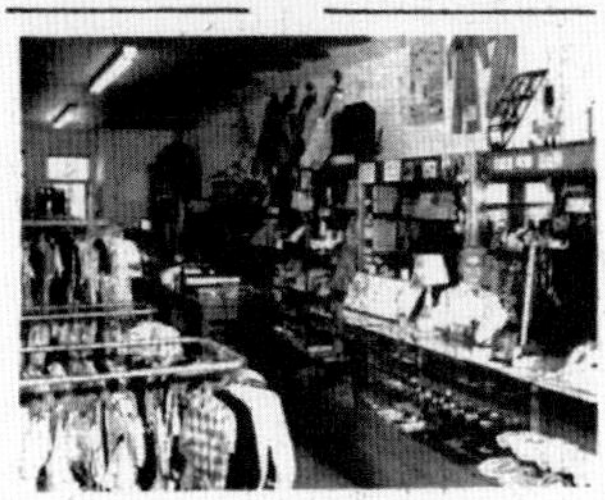

SHOP THRIFTY, 2039 WILTON DRIVE, A UNIQUE SHOP DEALING IN RARETIES OF ALL SORTS, IS PROOF THAT NOVEL IDEAS PAY OFF.

USE THE CLASSIFIED ADS

## 100 NEW STORES, WILTON MANORS

40 IN MIRACLE MILE

Federal, Times Square, Oakland Park Blvd. and Federal, this rapidly expanding area will soon take on a metropolitan appearance.

Trading zone of the Wilton Manors shopping area is populated with close to 30,000 persons, providing a tremendous market to draw from.

If construction of homes in this vicinity, reaching an all time high continues, the population figures could double in just a few short years.

Subdivisions recorded in the past few months, has made available in Wilton Manors about 500 additional home building sites.

Well into the final stage is the planning of 40 new store facilities to be erected on Wilton Drive in the 2200 block. With a depth of 400 feet, the center will have plenty of parking space.

On North Andrews Avenue construction in the near future is slated for 25 modern store rooms in Herald Square shopping center.

Breaking of ground on 26th Street, East of the FEC Railway for new business houses is scheduled, when plans come off the drawing board.

Along with other commercial construction in the immediat community at Crossroads, 26th and

### SMALL BUSINESS

Some members of Congress are concerned about the large number of failures among small business. There will be a move to lower taxes on small business when the Bill on Corporation Rates for another year comes up.

### BAR-B-Q AT OAKLAND PARK MARCH 17TH.

Members of Oakland Park Methodist Church plan a barbecue for March 17th, 5:30 PM to 8 PM at the Muncipal Youth Center, East of Railroad. The affair is to raise funds for Educational Building Fund.

### 'TIS SAID

Talk on the street is that land will be donated by a large chain company to the City of Wilton Manors for a City Hall site. Information pieced together indicates there will be plenty of room for complete municiaplity facilities, including plenty of parking space.

Although not officially announced at time of this writing, it appears the deal is approved by all parties concerned.

### BUILDING PERMIT ISSUED FOR ST CLEMENTS SCHOOL

The Wilton Manors Building department issued a permit last week for construction of an eight room, two-story school building.

This first step in establishing a Catholic school in the North part of this area will help relieve crowded school conditions to some extent.

### WILL IKE RUN?

Friends think he will. From his attitude they think he leans towards the affirmative.

He has indicated that people ought to be aware that he cannot put in the long hours the job calls for.

Nomination is a sure thing if he says yes, and if he does, Nixon will be his vice pres.

It's been said many times that Ike thinks no man is indispensable, but on the other side of his thinking, if he believes his presence in the job will be for the best interest of his country, then he will run. (as of Feb.29, 1956)

The *Wilton Sunrise News*, which started out as a mimeographed sheet with stenciled headlines, covered news in Wilton Manors and neighboring parts of Fort Lauderdale. It was founded by L.A. Bagwell in February 1954. Papers were distributed by mail (with a 2¢ stamp), and an annual subscription cost $2.50. (Wilton Manors Historical Society.)

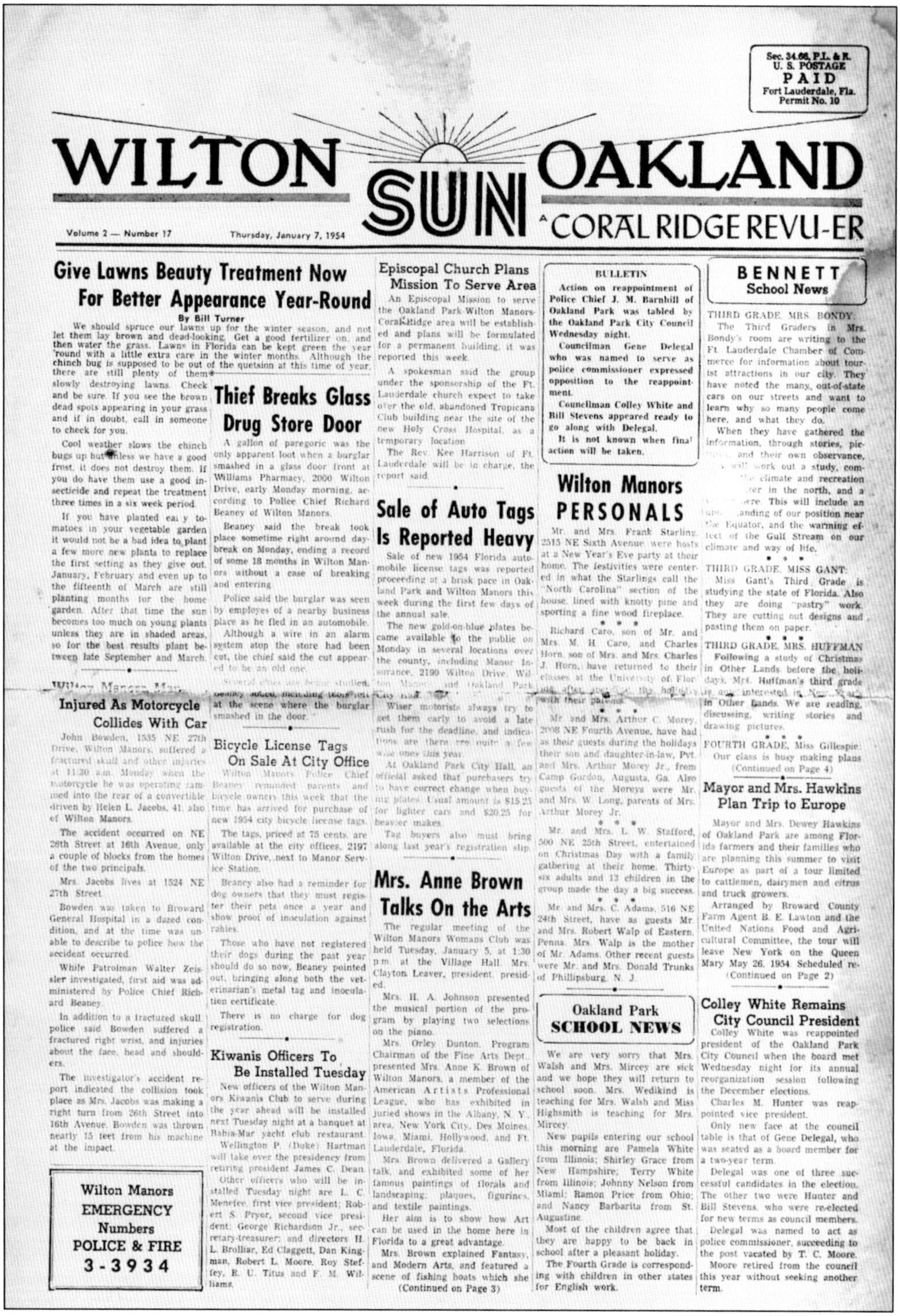

Sec. 34.66, P.L. & R.
U. S. POSTAGE
PAID
Fort Lauderdale, Fla.
Permit No. 10

# WILTON SUN OAKLAND

A CORAL RIDGE REVU-ER

Volume 2 — Number 17 Thursday, January 7, 1954

## Give Lawns Beauty Treatment Now For Better Appearance Year-Round

By Bill Turner

We should spruce our lawns up for the winter season, and not let them lay brown and dead-looking. Get a good fertilizer on, and then water the grass. Lawns in Florida can be kept green the year 'round with a little extra care in the winter months. Although the chinch bug is supposed to be out of the quetsion at this time of year, there are still plenty of them slowly destroying lawns. Check and be sure. If you see the brown dead spots appearing in your grass and if in doubt, call in someone to check for you.

Cool weather slows the chinch bugs up but unless we have a good frost, it does not destroy them. If you do have them use a good insecticide and repeat the treatment three times in a six week period.

If you have planted early tomatoes in your vegetable garden it would not be a bad idea to plant a few more new plants to replace the first setting as they give out. January, February and even up to the fifteenth of March are still planting months for the home garden. After that time the sun becomes too much on young plants unless they are in shaded areas, so for the best results plant between late September and March.

## Injured As Motorcycle Collides With Car

John Bowden, 1535 NE 27th Drive, Wilton Manors, suffered a fractured skull and other injuries at 11:30 a.m. Monday when the motorcycle he was operating rammed into the rear of a convertible driven by Helen L. Jacobs, 41, also of Wilton Manors.

The accident occurred on NE 28th Street at 16th Avenue, only a couple of blocks from the homes of the two principals.

Mrs. Jacobs lives at 1524 NE 27th Street.

Bowden was taken to Broward General Hospital in a dazed condition, and at the time was unable to describe to police how the accident occurred.

While Patrolman Walter Zeisler investigated, first aid was administered by Police Chief Richard Beaney.

In addition to a fractured skull, police said Bowden suffered a fractured right wrist, and injuries about the face, head and shoulders.

The investigator's accident report indicated the collision took place as Mrs. Jacobs was making a right turn from 26th Street into 16th Avenue. Bowden was thrown nearly 15 feet from his machine at the impact.

**Wilton Manors EMERGENCY Numbers POLICE & FIRE 3-3934**

## Episcopal Church Plans Mission To Serve Area

An Episcopal Mission to serve the Oakland Park-Wilton Manors-Coral Ridge area will be established and plans will be formulated for a permanent building, it was reported this week.

A spokesman said the group under the sponsorship of the Ft. Lauderdale church expect to take over the old, abandoned Tropicana Club building near the site of the new Holy Cross Hospital, as a temporary location.

The Rev. Kee Harrison of Ft. Lauderdale will be in charge, the report said.

## Thief Breaks Glass Drug Store Door

A gallon of paregoric was the only apparent loot when a burglar smashed in a glass door front at Williams Pharmacy, 2000 Wilton Drive, early Monday morning, according to Police Chief Richard Beaney of Wilton Manors.

Beaney said the break took place sometime right around daybreak on Monday, ending a record of some 18 months in Wilton Manors without a case of breaking and entering.

Police said the burglar was seen by employes of a nearby business place as he fled in an automobile.

Although a wire in an alarm system atop the store had been cut, the chief said the cut appeared to be an old one.

Several clues are being studied, Beaney noted, including ... at the scene where the burglar smashed in the door.

## Bicycle License Tags On Sale At City Office

Wilton Manors Police Chief Beaney reminded parents and bicycle owners this week that the time has arrived for purchase of new 1954 city bicycle license tags.

The tags, priced at 75 cents, are available at the city offices, 2197 Wilton Drive, next to Manor Service Station.

Beaney also had a reminder for dog owners that they must register their pets once a year and show proof of inoculation against rabies.

Those who have not registered their dogs during the past year should do so now, Beaney pointed out, bringing along both the veterinarian's metal tag and inoculation certificate.

There is no charge for dog registration.

## Kiwanis Officers To Be Installed Tuesday

New officers of the Wilton Manors Kiwanis Club to serve during the year ahead will be installed next Tuesday night at a banquet at Bahia-Mar yacht club restaurant.

Wellington P. (Duke) Hartman will take over the presidency from retiring president James C. Dean.

Other officers who will be installed Tuesday night are L. C. Menefee, first vice president; Robert S. Pryor, second vice president; George Richardson Jr., secretary-treasurer; and directors H. L. Brolliar, Ed Claggett, Dan Kingman, Robert L. Moore, Roy Steffey, R. U. Titus and F. M. Williams.

## Sale of Auto Tags Is Reported Heavy

Sale of new 1954 Florida automobile license tags was reported proceeding at a brisk pace in Oakland Park and Wilton Manors this week during the first few days of the annual sale.

The new gold-on-blue plates became available to the public on Monday in several locations over the county, including Manor Insurance, 2190 Wilton Drive, Wilton Manors, and Oakland Park City Hall.

Wiser motorists always try to get them early to avoid a late rush for the deadline, and indications are there are quite a few wise ones this year.

At Oakland Park City Hall, an official asked that purchasers try to have correct change when buying plates. Usual amount is $15.25 for lighter cars and $20.25 for heavier makes.

Tag buyers also must bring along last year's registration slip.

## Mrs. Anne Brown Talks On the Arts

The regular meeting of the Wilton Manors Womans Club was held Tuesday, January 5, at 1:30 p.m. at the Village Hall. Mrs. Clayton Leaver, president, presided.

Mrs. H. A. Johnson presented the musical portion of the program by playing two selections on the piano.

Mrs. Orley Dunton, Program Chairman of the Fine Arts Dept., presented Mrs. Anne K. Brown of Wilton Manors, a member of the American Artists Professional League, who has exhibited in juried shows in the Albany, N. Y., area, New York City, Des Moines, Iowa, Miami, Hollywood, and Ft. Lauderdale, Florida.

Mrs. Brown delivered a Gallery talk, and exhibited some of her famous paintings of florals and landscaping; plaques, figurines, and textile paintings.

Her aim is to show how Art can be used in the home here in Florida to a great advantage.

Mrs. Brown explained Fantasy, and Modern Arts, and featured a scene of fishing boats which she

(Continued on Page 3)

**BULLETIN**

**Action on reappointment of Police Chief J. M. Barnhill of Oakland Park was tabled by the Oakland Park City Council Wednesday night.**

**Councilman Gene Delegal who was named to serve as police commissioner expressed opposition to the reappointment.**

**Councilman Colley White and Bill Stevens appeared ready to go along with Delegal.**

**It is not known when final action will be taken.**

## Wilton Manors PERSONALS

Mr. and Mrs. Frank Starling, 2515 NE Sixth Avenue were hosts at a New Year's Eve party at their home. The festivities were centered in what the Starlings call the "North Carolina" section of the house, lined with knotty pine and sporting a fine wood fireplace.

Richard Caro, son of Mr. and Mrs. M. H. Caro, and Charles Horn, son of Mrs. and Mrs. Charles J. Horn, have returned to their classes at the University of Florida after ... the holidays with their parents.

Mr. and Mrs. Arthur C. Morey, 2008 NE Fourth Avenue, have had as their guests during the holidays their son and daughter-in-law, Pvt. and Mrs. Arthur Morey Jr., from Camp Gordon, Augusta, Ga. Also guests of the Moreys were Mr. and Mrs. W. Long, parents of Mrs. Arthur Morey Jr.

Mr. and Mrs. L. W. Stafford, 500 NE 25th Street, entertained on Christmas Day with a family gathering at their home. Thirty-six adults and 13 children in the group made the day a big success.

Mr. and Mrs. C. Adams, 516 NE 24th Street, have as guests Mr. and Mrs. Robert Walp of Eastern, Penna. Mrs. Walp is the mother of Mr. Adams. Other recent guests were Mr. and Mrs. Donald Trunks of Phillipsburg, N. J.

## Oakland Park SCHOOL NEWS

We are very sorry that Mrs. Walsh and Mrs. Mircey are sick and we hope they will return to school soon. Mrs. Wedikind is teaching for Mrs. Walsh and Miss Highsmith is teaching for Mrs. Mircey.

New pupils entering our school this morning are Pamela White from Illinois; Shirley Grace from New Hampshire; Terry White from Illinois; Johnny Nelson from Miami; Ramon Price from Ohio; and Nancy Barbarita from St. Augustine.

Most of the children agree that they are happy to be back in school after a pleasant holiday.

The Fourth Grade is corresponding with children in other states for English work.

## BENNETT School News

THIRD GRADE, MRS. BONDY:

The Third Graders in Mrs. Bondy's room are writing to the Ft. Lauderdale Chamber of Commerce for information about tourist attractions in our city. They have noted the many out-of-state cars on our streets and want to learn why so many people come here, and what they do.

When they have gathered the information, through stories, pictures, and their own observance, ... will work out a study, comparing ... climate and recreation ... in the north, and a ... here. This will include an ... understanding of our position near the Equator, and the warming effect of the Gulf Stream on our climate and way of life.

THIRD GRADE, MISS GANT:

Miss Gant's Third Grade is studying the state of Florida. Also they are doing "pastry" work. They are cutting out designs and pasting them on paper.

THIRD GRADE, MRS. HUFFMAN

Following a study of Christmas in Other Lands before the holidays, Mrs. Huffman's third grade is now interested in New Year's in Other Lands. We are reading, discussing, writing stories and drawing pictures.

FOURTH GRADE, Miss Gillespie:

Our class is busy making plans

(Continued on Page 4)

## Mayor and Mrs. Hawkins Plan Trip to Europe

Mayor and Mrs. Dewey Hawkins of Oakland Park are among Florida farmers and their families who are planning this summer to visit Europe as part of a tour limited to cattlemen, dairymen and citrus and truck growers.

Arranged by Broward County Farm Agent B. E. Lawton and the United Nations Food and Agricultural Committee, the tour will leave New York on the Queen Mary May 26, 1954. Scheduled re-

(Continued on Page 2)

## Colley White Remains City Council President

Colley White was reappointed president of the Oakland Park City Council when the board met Wednesday night for its annual reorganization session following the December elections.

Charles M. Hunter was reappointed vice president.

Only new face at the council table is that of Gene Delegal, who was seated as a board member for a two-year term.

Delegal was one of three successful candidates in the election. The other two were Hunter and Bill Stevens, who were re-elected for new terms as council members.

Delegal was named to act as police commissioner, succeeding to the post vacated by T. C. Moore. Moore retired from the council this year without seeking another term.

The *Wilton-Oakland Sun* was published weekly to cover the news of Wilton Manors and Oakland Park. Carter Holmes served as its editor and publisher. (Wilton Manors Historical Society.)

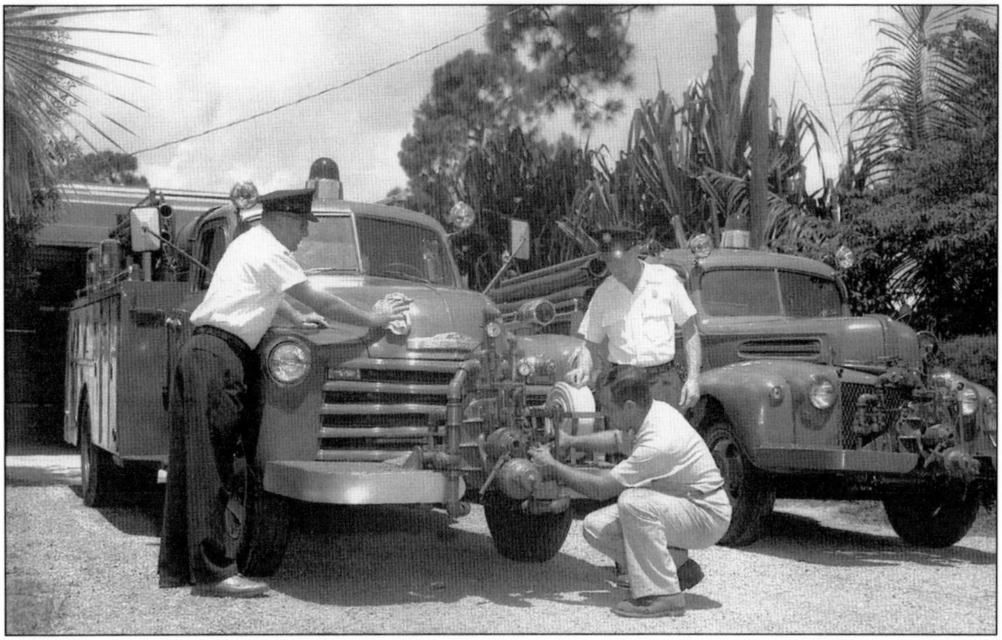

Members of the Wilton Manors Volunteer Fire Department buff one of the department's trucks. Founded in 1952, the fire department experienced difficulties in sustaining leadership at the start. Its first three chiefs lasted a year or less each. The fourth chief, Wally Wakely, held the post for six years, and Al Walker held it for two, until 1960. John Miller, known affectionately as "Coach," took on the post in 1960 and held it for 20 years. (Gene Hyde collection, Fort Lauderdale Historical Society, Inc.)

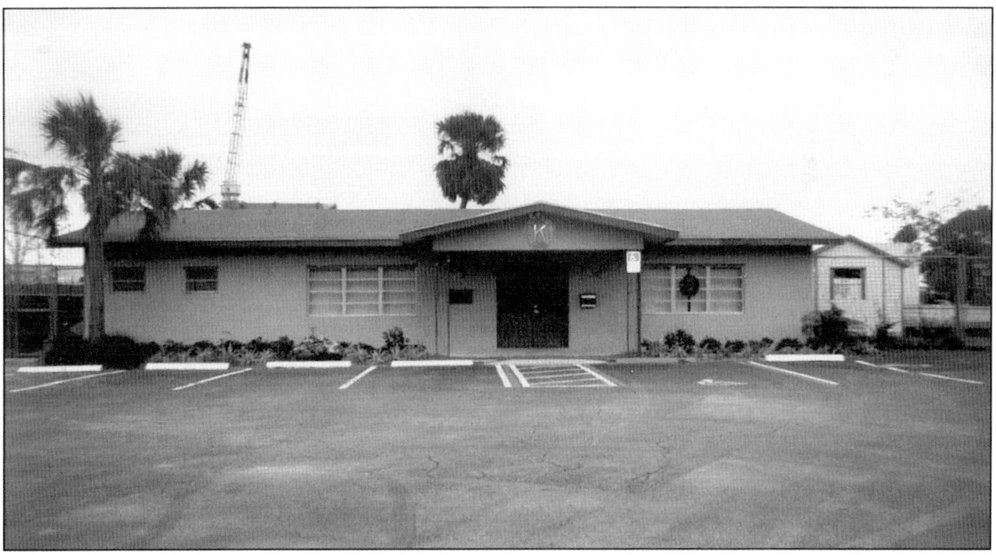

The 1950s were years of intense growth in the community's social infrastructure. One of the many organizations to get its start during that time was the Wilton Manors Kiwanis, who have devoted a half-century of hard work to serving the community and its youth. The Kiwanis motto is "We Build," and the Wilton Manors club has proven so for decades. The clubhouse, dedicated on November 25, 1958, is at 2749 Northeast Fourteenth Avenue, built on property donated by James Dean.

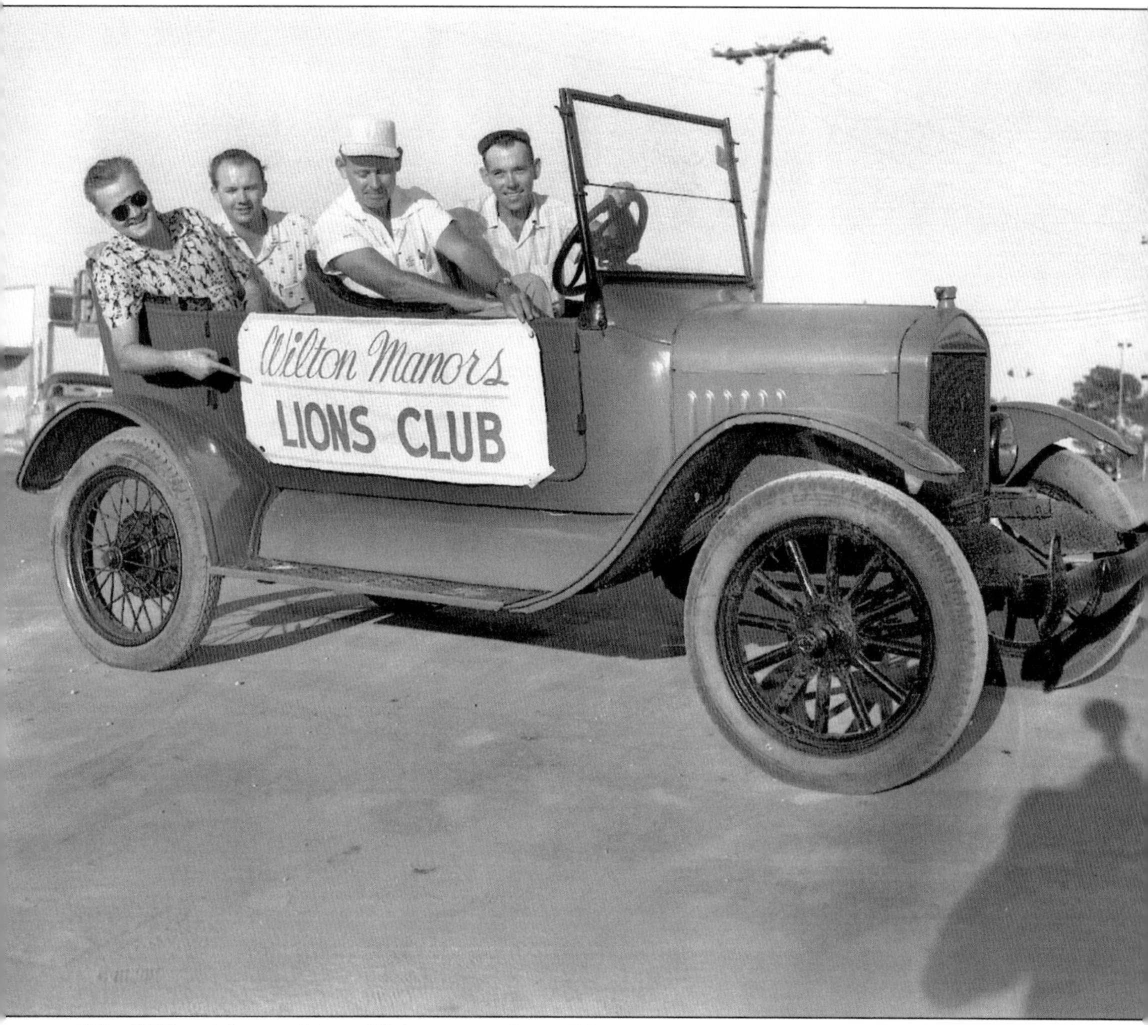


The Wilton Manors Lions Club was another of the community service organizations organized during the 1950s. In this picture, members ride in a parade along Wilton Drive. (Gene Hyde collection, Fort Lauderdale Historical Society, Inc.)

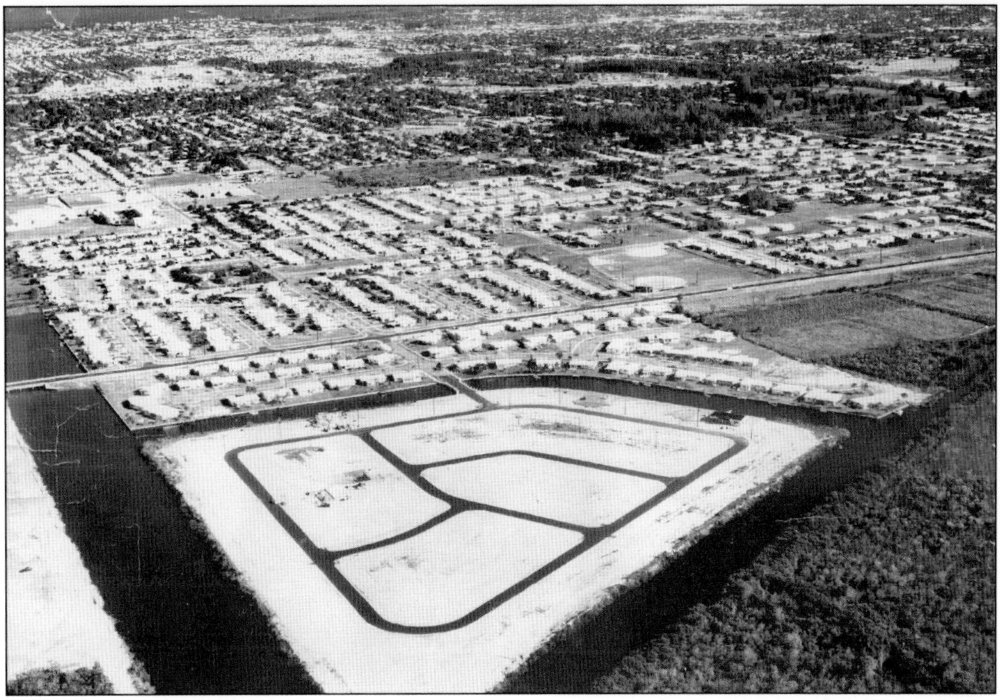

The Jenada Villas development moved the city's boundaries westward; builder Jens Rask pushed them farther west with the start of the community's first high-end, gated development, Jenada Isle, in 1959. (Wilton Manors Historical Society.)

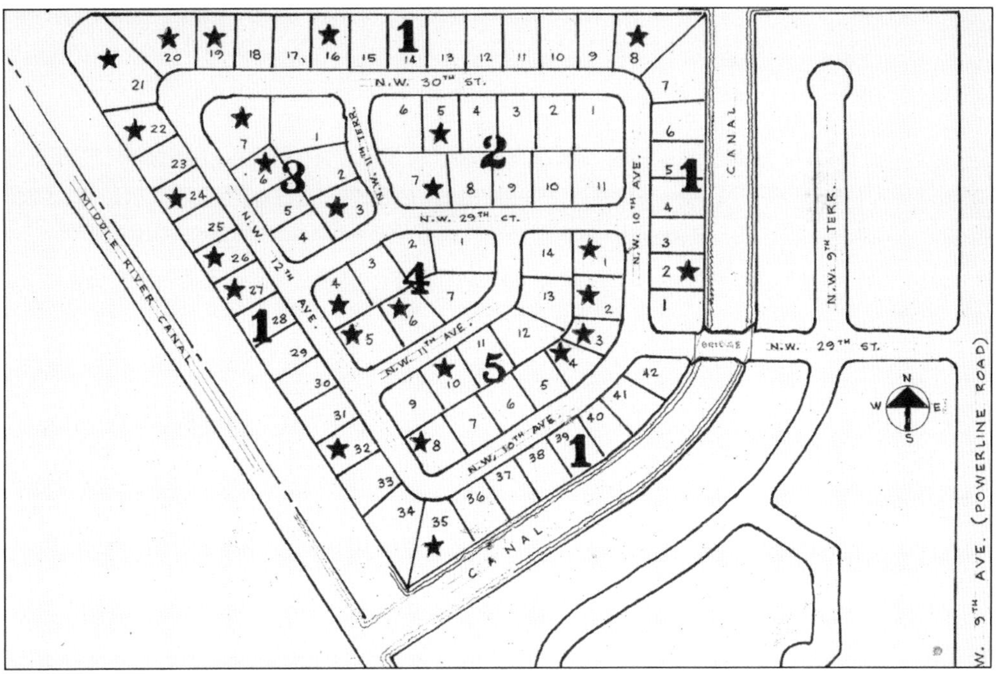


Arrowhead-shaped Jenada Isle was designed with an outer ring of 42 properties and 4 interior islands with a total of 39 properties. The stars denote properties for which architect Paul M. Bradley Jr. had designed homes. (Paul M. Bradley Jr.)

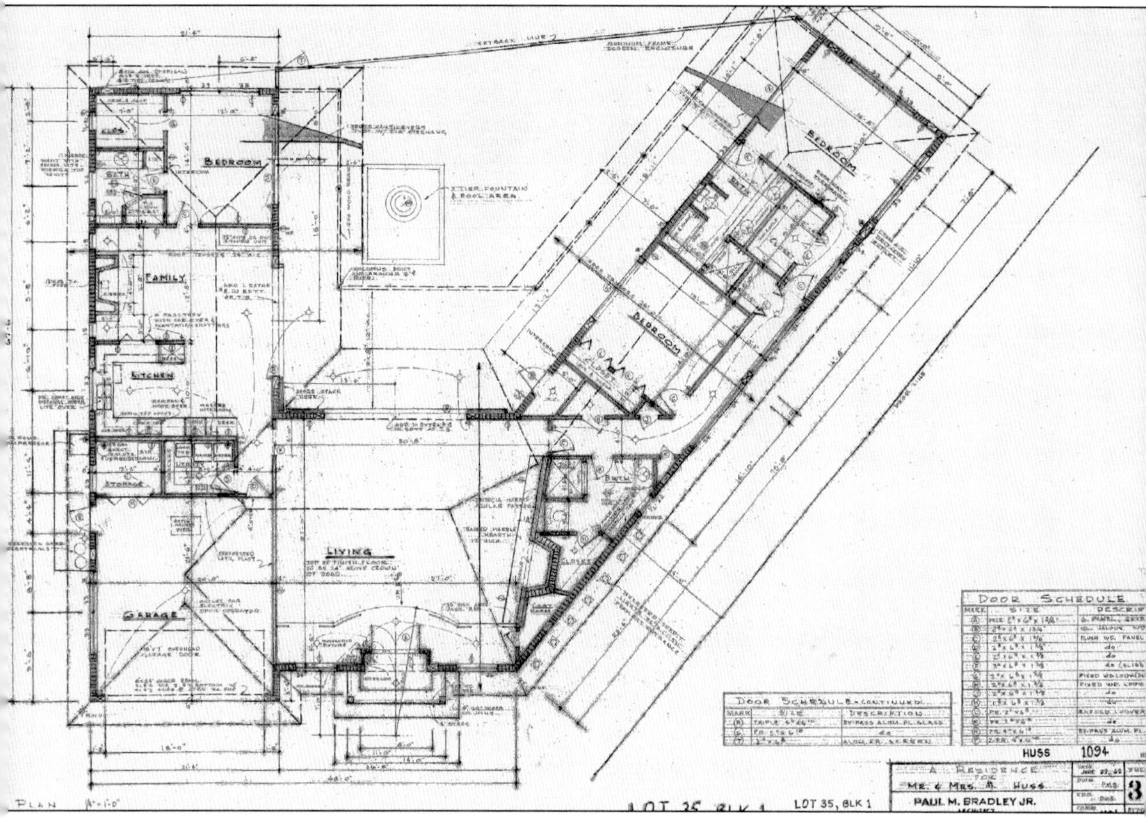


On lot 35, block 1 is a home originally designed for a Mr. and Mrs. Huss. Architect Bradley designed a dramatic, three-bedroom home for the asymmetrical, wedge-shaped corner lot. (Paul M. Bradley Jr.)

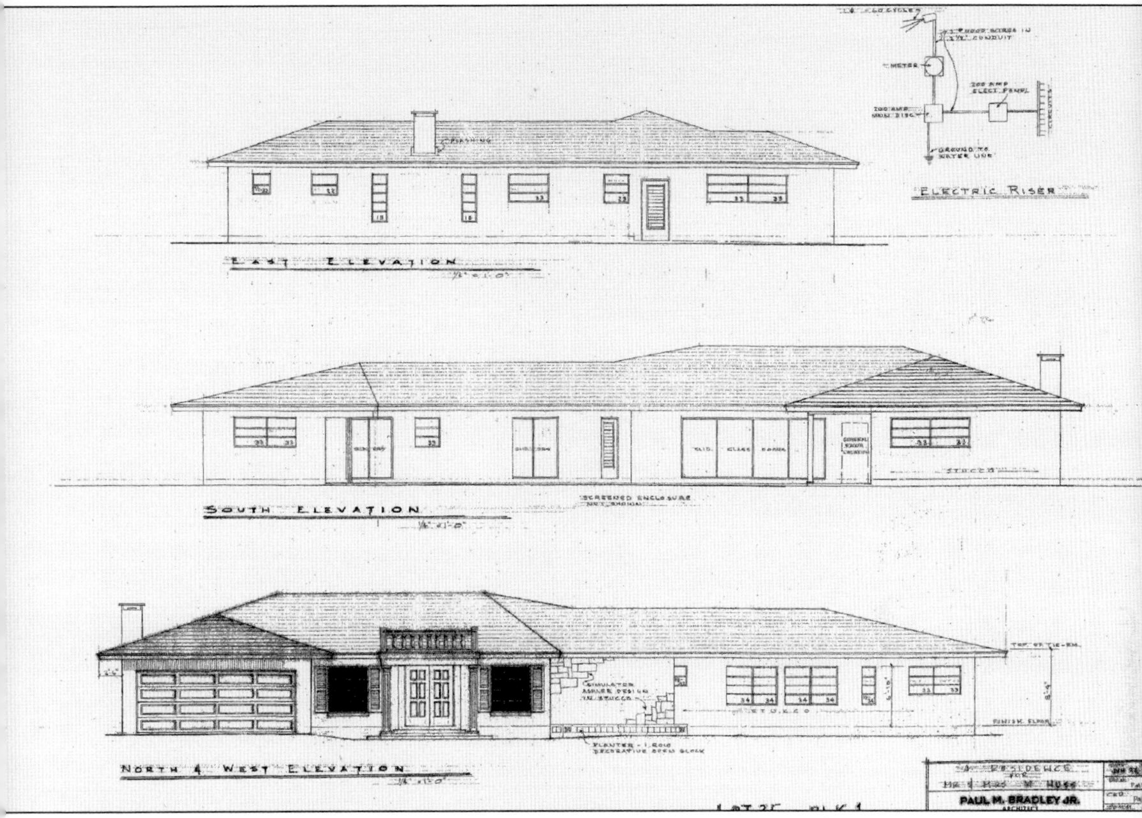


The home was later purchased by Donn and Susan Eisele, who moved to Wilton Manors in 1980. Colonel Eisele, an Apollo 7 astronaut, left the United States Air Force in 1972, worked for the Peace Corps in Thailand, and then came back to the States. During his years in Wilton Manors, he worked as an account manager for Oppenheimer & Company. He participated in Wilton Manors city politics by serving a year on the city council. Colonel Eisele moved to the Harbor Beach section of Fort Lauderdale in June 1987. He died of a heart attack while in Tokyo on business on December 2, 1987. (Paul M. Bradley Jr.)

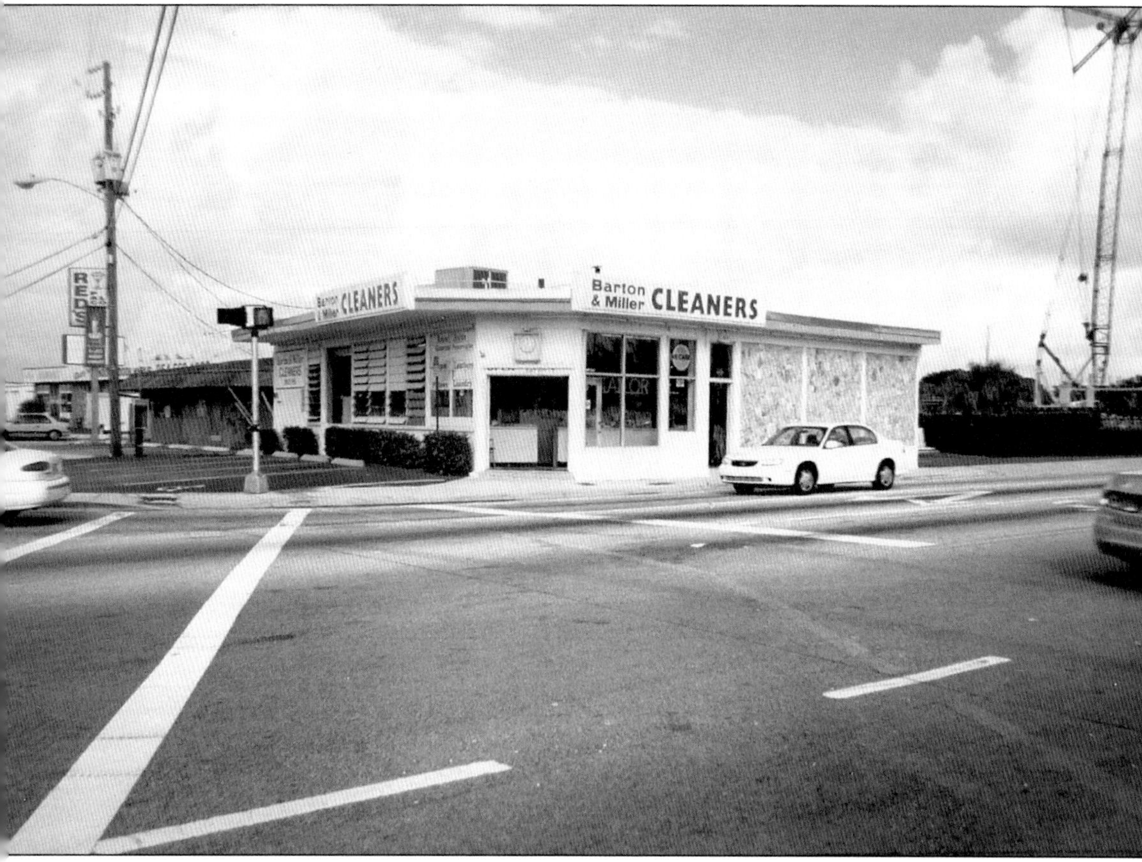


Buster Barton and Ed Miller constructed a building for a dry-cleaning establishment at Five Points in 1955 and opened Barton & Miller in 1956. The firm is one of the longest continuously operating business establishments in Wilton Manors.

*Four*

# Sports of All Sorts (1960–1969)

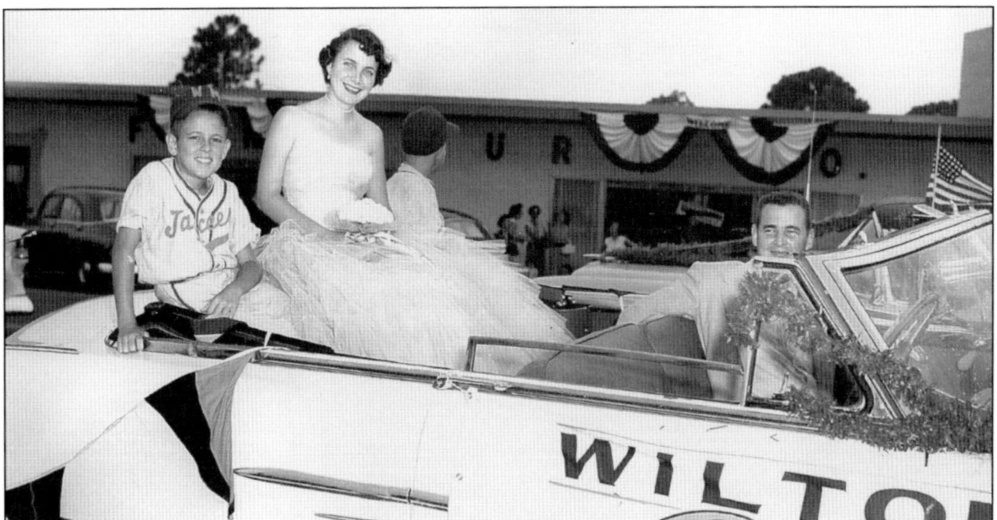


Baseball has been a popular sport in Wilton Manors since it was first offered in 1952. In that year, the Kiwanis team won the Optimist League championship, topping Coral Ridge 8-1 in the playoff game. Four of the team's players—shortstop George Sapp, catcher Ed Clagett, pitcher Tim Shelby, and third baseman Vic Langford—were named to the league's all-star team. Sapp also was named the league's most valuable player. But youth sports in Wilton Manors were more than just baseball. City youth also competed with honor in other sports, especially basketball and track and field under the direction of the city's recreation director, James McGivern. In addition to the city's facilities, Wilton Manors Elementary School was used for youth sports. The baseball diamonds at the school were dedicated May 25, 1952, when the Kiwanis team played Pompano Beach. In this picture, two ballplayers and a beauty queen cruise Wilton Drive in a parade. (Wilton Manors Historical Society.)

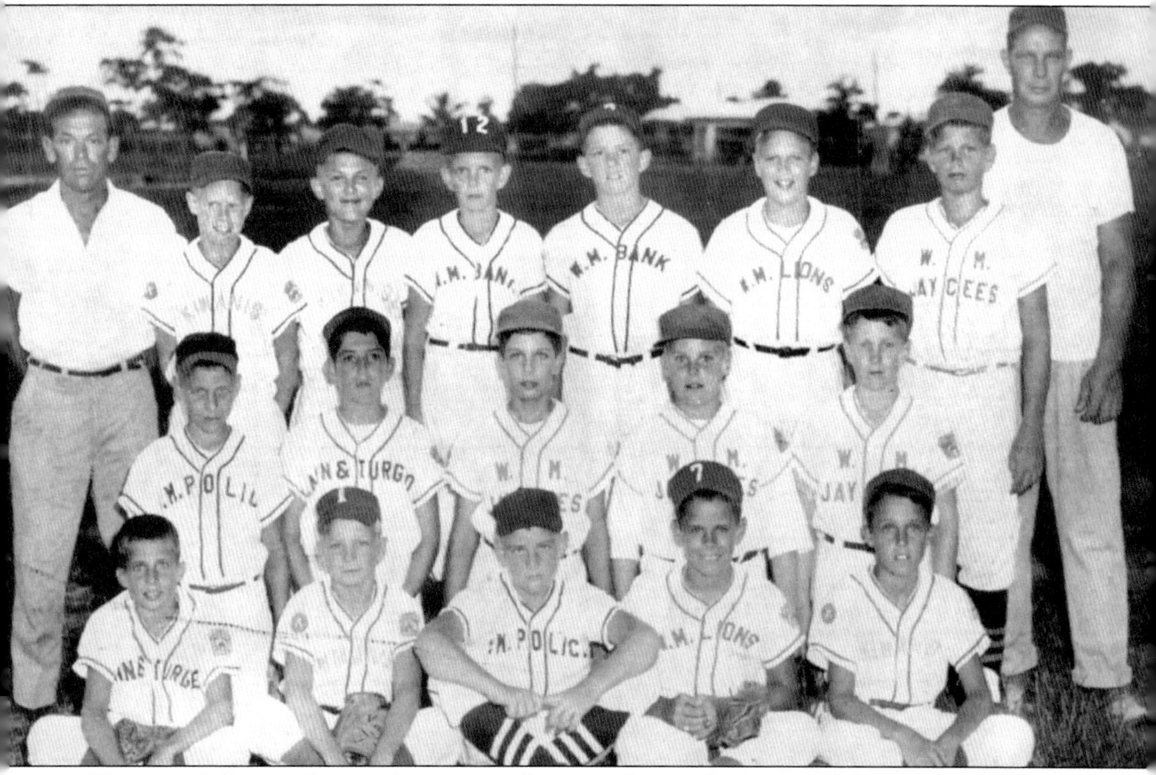


The year 1961 turned out to be a tremendous year for youth sports in the city. The recreation department team won the Broward County Recreation Association's Junior Relays in Hollywood, edging runner-up Fort Lauderdale 115 points to 111. Pompano Beach finished third. Sandy Moesta was named Relay Queen for her performance. The summer of 1961 was a particularly magical time for the young men of the Wilton Manors Little League, who, as District 7 representatives, qualified to travel to Blue Angel Park on the grounds of the Jacksonville Naval Air Station to compete for the state title. The players went by bus, accompanied by McGivern, Mayor Harold Price, Police Chief Tom Brace, and coaching staff. Parents followed in a caravan behind the team bus. Team members, from left to right, are (front row) Louis Cass, Scotty Maurer, Billy Ladd, Sid Millam, and Bobby Baird; (middle row) Pat Mealy, Bruce Connolly, Bobby Sagline, Bobby Jones, and Richard Verduin; (back row) manager Danny Beare, Pete Johnson, Bobby Beare, Steve Possinger, Kenny Hughes, Tony Schuber, Danny Ebersold, and coach Charlie Mitzel. Mickey Rodenbaugh is not shown. (James B. McGivern.)

The United States Navy housed the players from all the teams in officers' quarters and provided meals for the players and their parents throughout the tournament, but there were still expenses for the team's participation. The city picked up a large part of the tab, but some community members also pitched in to help financially; the Mothers' Council and Elks' Club contributed $200 each. Even the Sunset Little League, defeated 5-4 by Wilton Manors in the subdistrict tournament, sent a check for $50. Wilton Manors won the state title, beating the Fernandina Beach All-Stars and the Miami Southwest Boys Club and defeating the Clearwater All-Stars in the title game. (Bruce Connolly.)

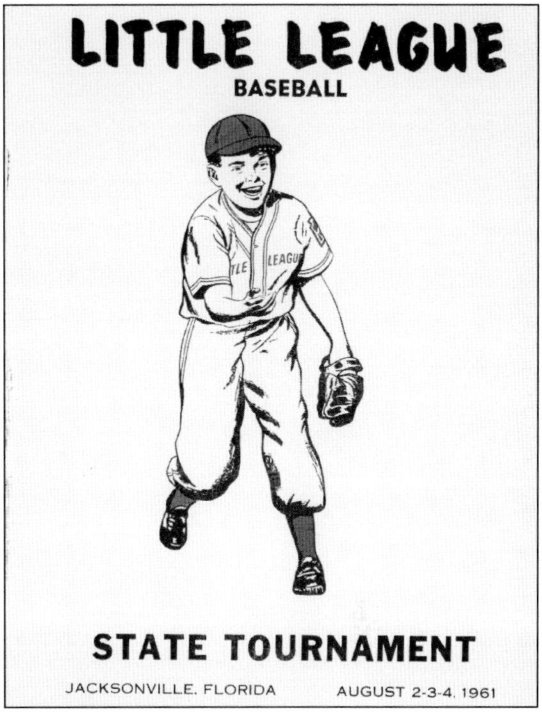


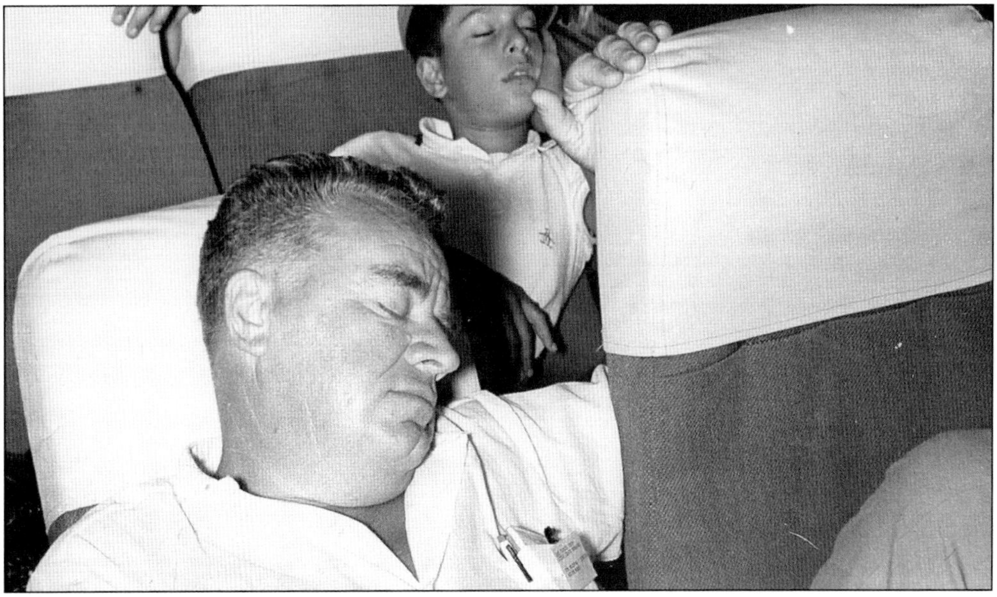

Recreation director Jim McGivern naps on the bus ride home from Jacksonville. The team bus was escorted to city hall by police and fire vehicles, which met the team at the city limits and drove them to a reception attended by more than 200 happy family members, friends, and fans. The 20-foot banner stretched across the twin bays at the fire department read "Welcome Home, Champs." The team went on to compete at the Southeastern Region 3 Championships in Athens, Georgia, where they defeated Clarksville, Tennessee 4-0, but fell a game short of their goal, losing to a team from Charlotte, North Carolina 3-0 in the championship game. (James B. McGivern.)

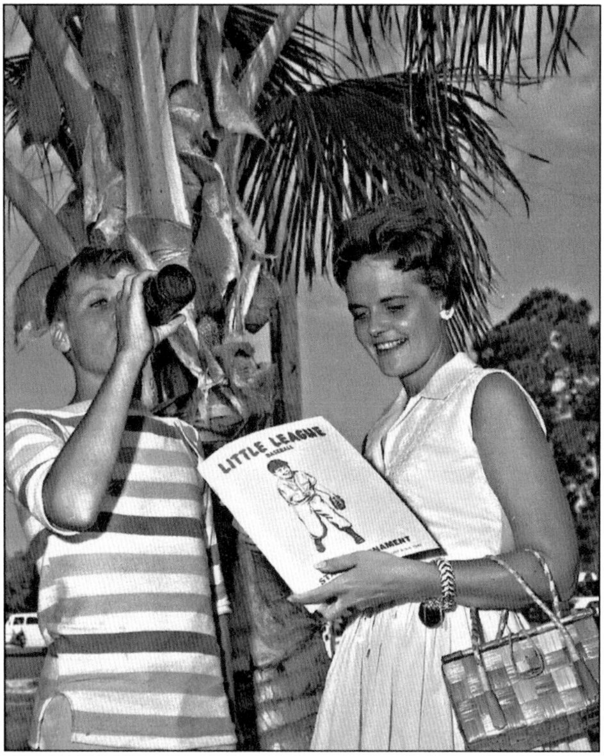


As her son enjoys a cold drink, a Wilton Manors All-Star's mom thumbs through the state championship program upon the team's return from Jacksonville. (Gene Hyde collection, Fort Lauderdale Historic Society, Inc.)

After leaving the recreation department, Jim McGivern went on to operate James Dean's Lauderdale Athletic Club, located on Northeast Fourteenth Avenue, on land now occupied by Wilton Station. Squash was the most popular activity for men there, and in this picture, McGivern, center, watches as a visiting pro demonstrates proper shot-making techniques. Women's facilities, including a workout room, steam cabinets, and Swedish sauna, were on the facility's second floor. (James B. McGivern.)

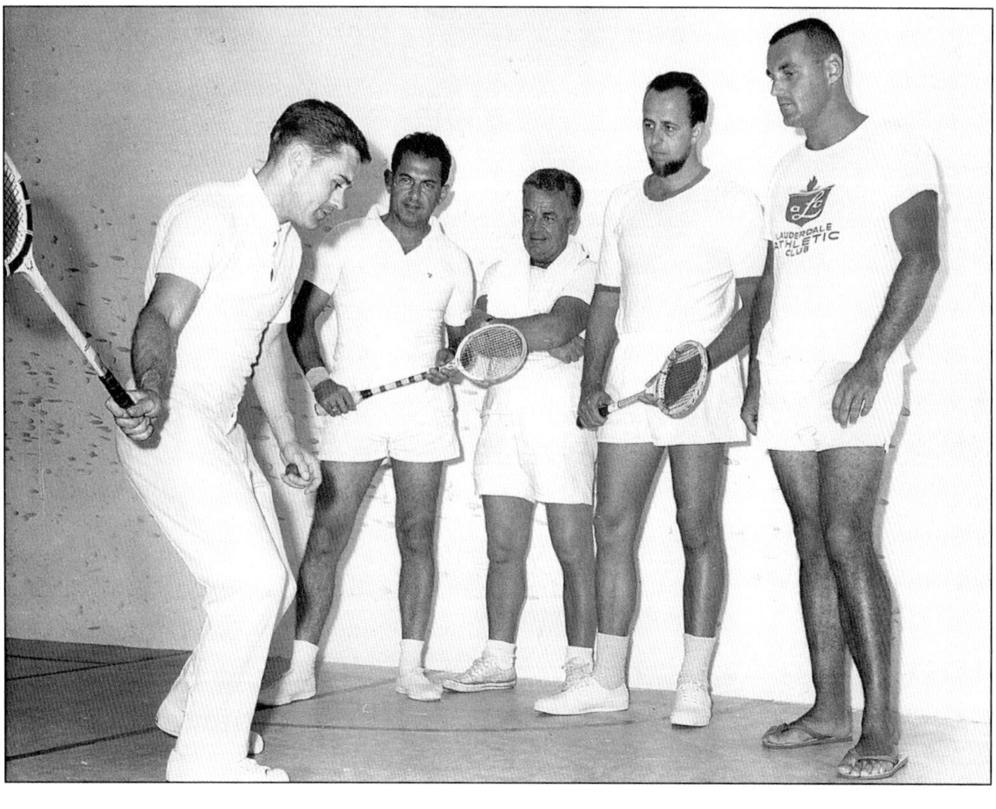

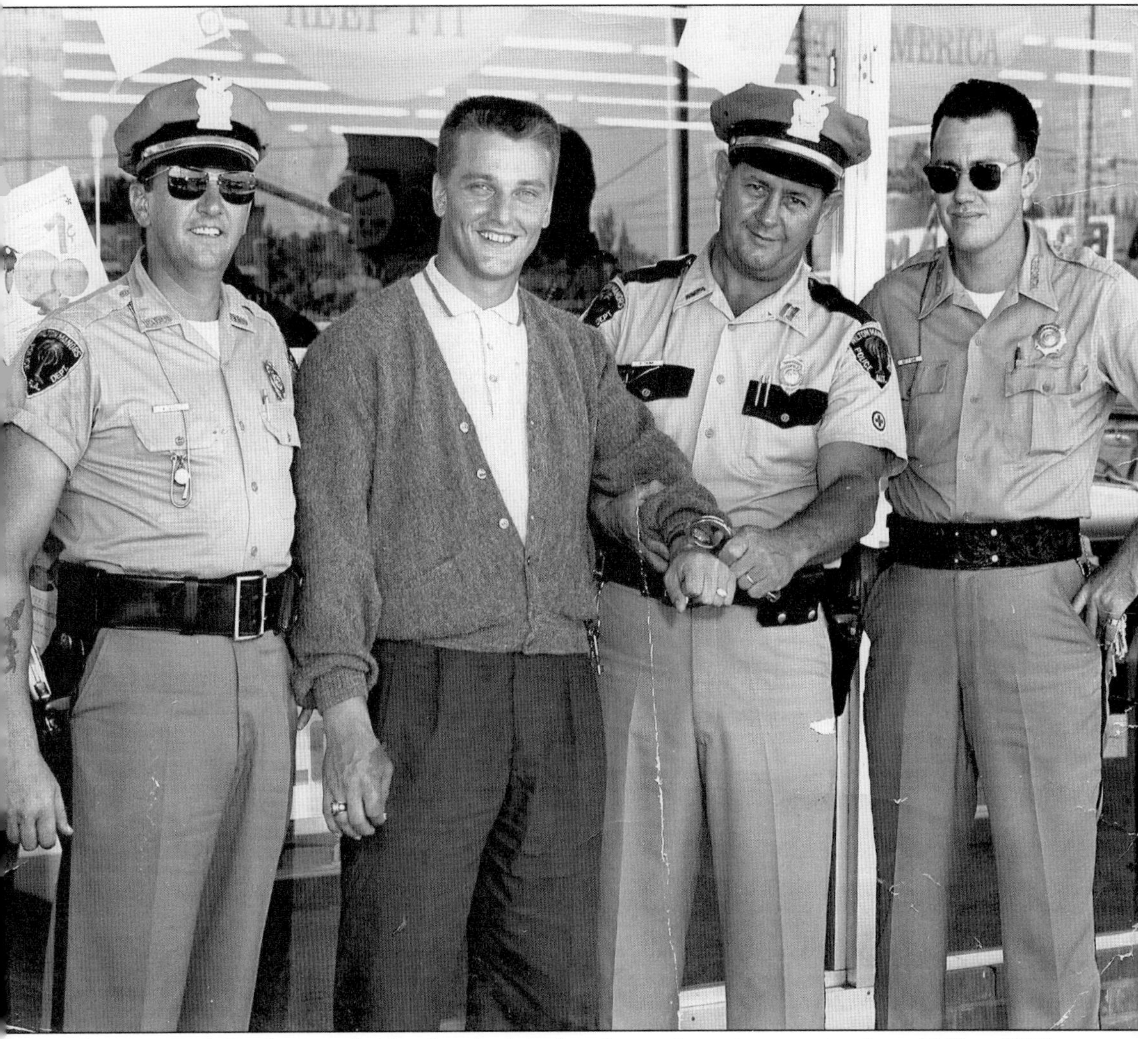

The New York Yankees made Fort Lauderdale their home for spring training from 1962 to 1995. Many of the players rented homes in Oakland Park and Wilton Manors during that period, and residents were sometimes flabbergasted to see players such as Whitey Ford or Tom Tresh shopping in local stores or dining in neighborhood restaurants. In this picture, Wilton Manors police auxiliary captain Tony Thuma playfully pretends to slap handcuffs on slugger Roger Maris outside the Publix Market on Dixie Highway. Officer Bill DeRoo watches on from the left, and Sgt. Frank Cave is on the right.

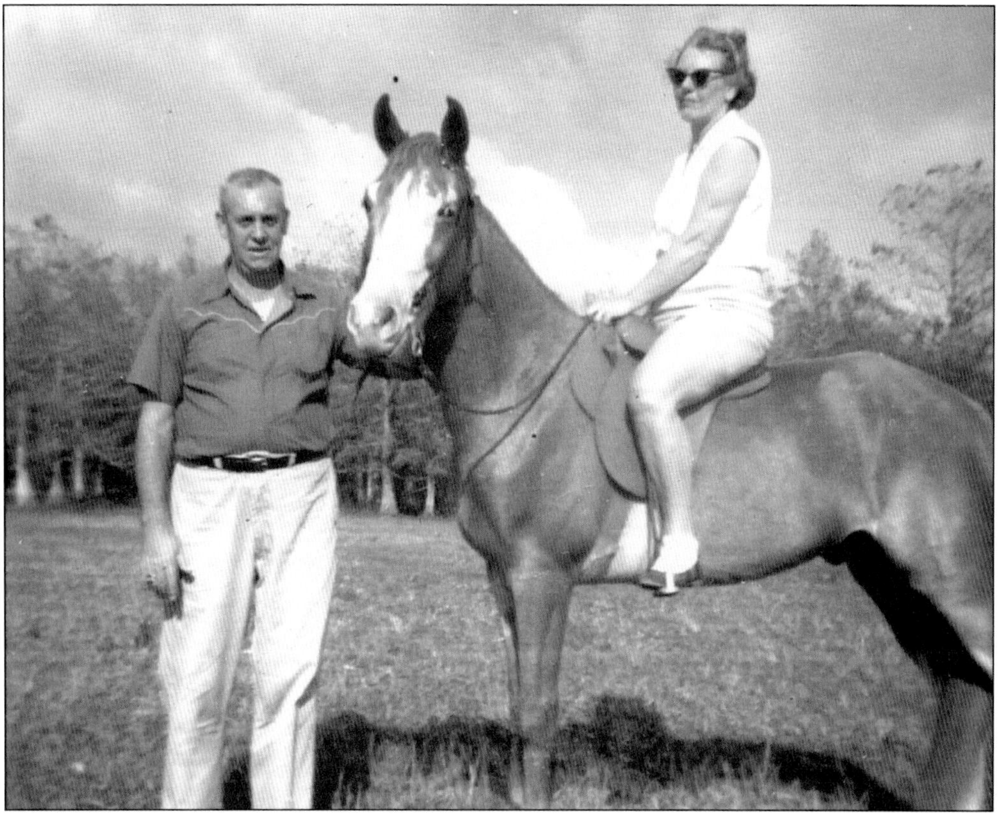

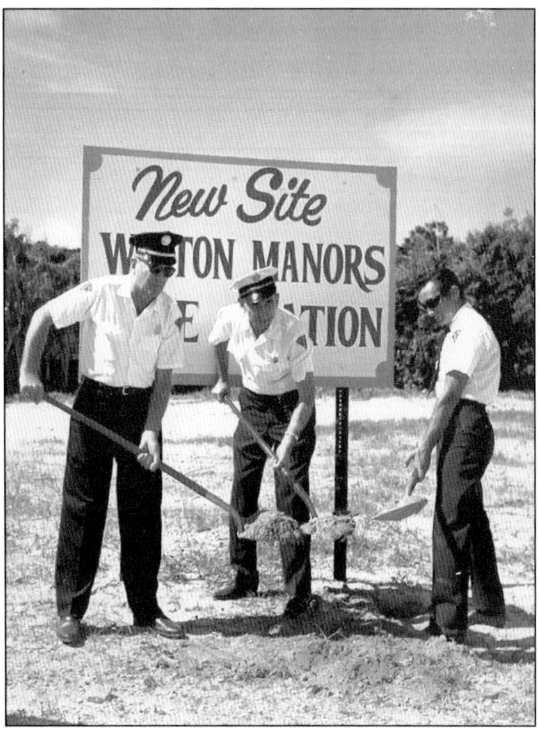


Police Chief Tom Brace, who had a longshoreman's vocabulary but a heart of gold, died in 1961, not long after serving as one of the chaperones of the championship baseball team. Brace, who had become the city's second police chief in 1957, returned from the trip with a bad cough; his condition steadily worsened. He is shown here with his wife, Ethel, riding her prize strawberry roan, Sonny. Brace, an animal lover, also kept a pet raccoon named Willie.

Fire Chief John Miller (center) and other volunteer firefighters help break ground for a new fire station on Northeast Twenty-second Street. (Wilton Manors Historical Society.)

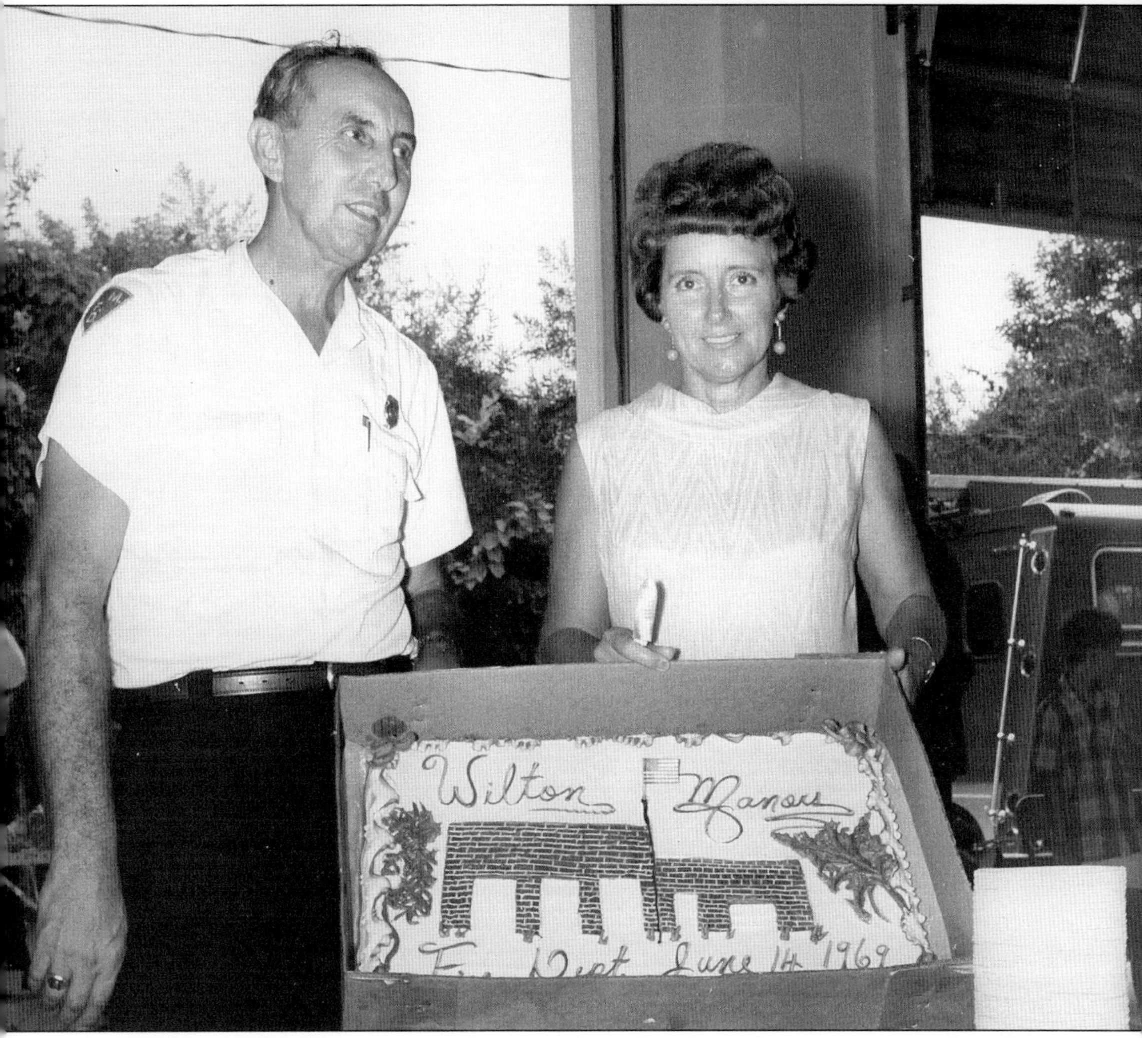


Chief Miller and fire department auxiliary member Edie Alexander prepare to cut the cake at a dedication ceremony for the fire station on June 14, 1969. The spacious new station better fit the needs of the growing community, and when the trucks were pulled out of the bay, the building provided excellent covered space for spaghetti dinners and other social events. (Wilton Manors Historical Society.)

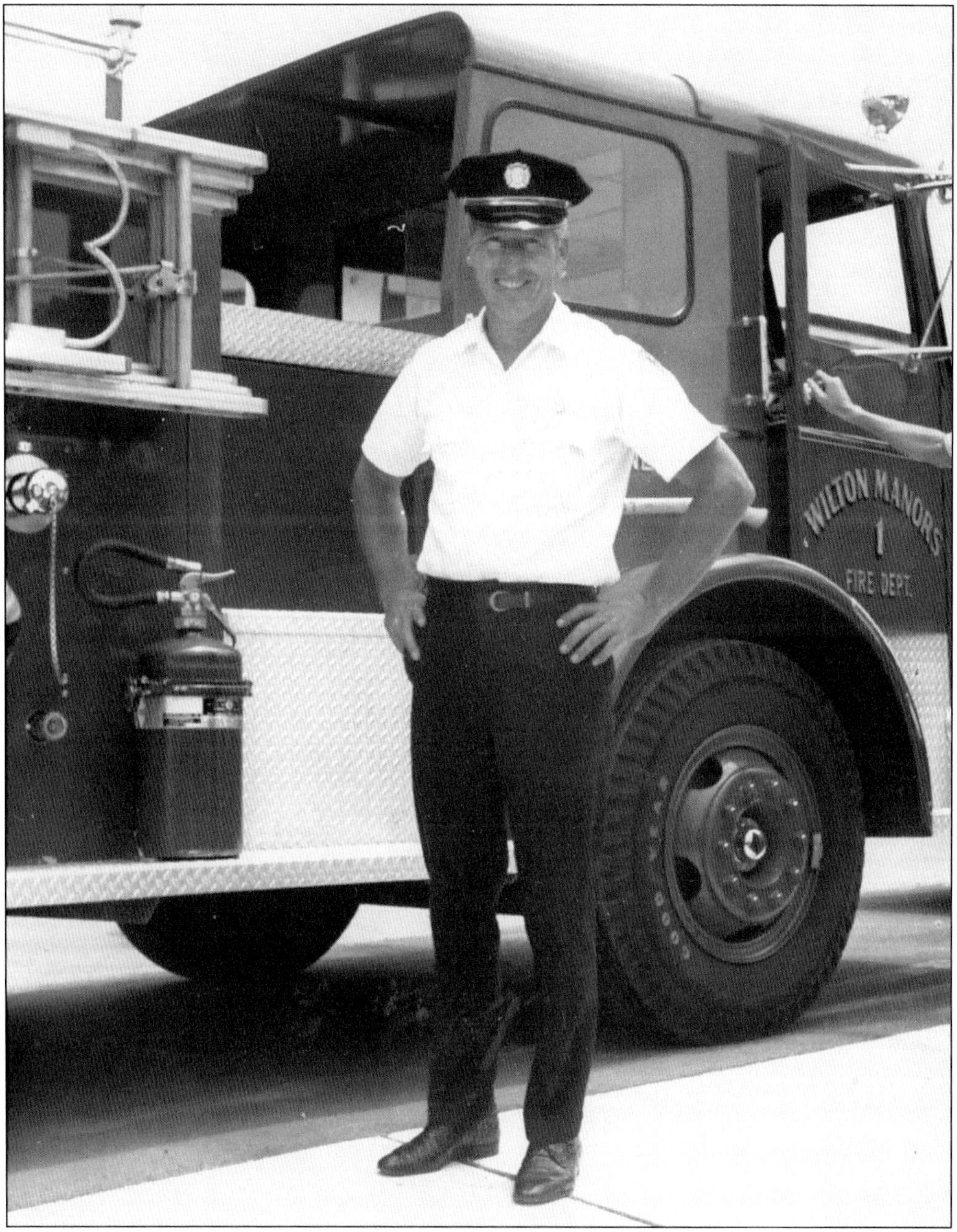


Among the many city fathers who served on the Wilton Manors Volunteer Fire Department was Gerald Thompson. A local bartender and pool contractor, Thompson plunged into city politics and liked it, serving on the city council from 1964 to 1968 and as mayor from 1968 to 1974. He then set his sights on a seat on the Broward County Commission. He not only attained the seat but also served as the commission's chairman and as chairman of the Broward County Expressway Authority, creators of the Sawgrass Expressway. (Wilton Manors Historical Society.)

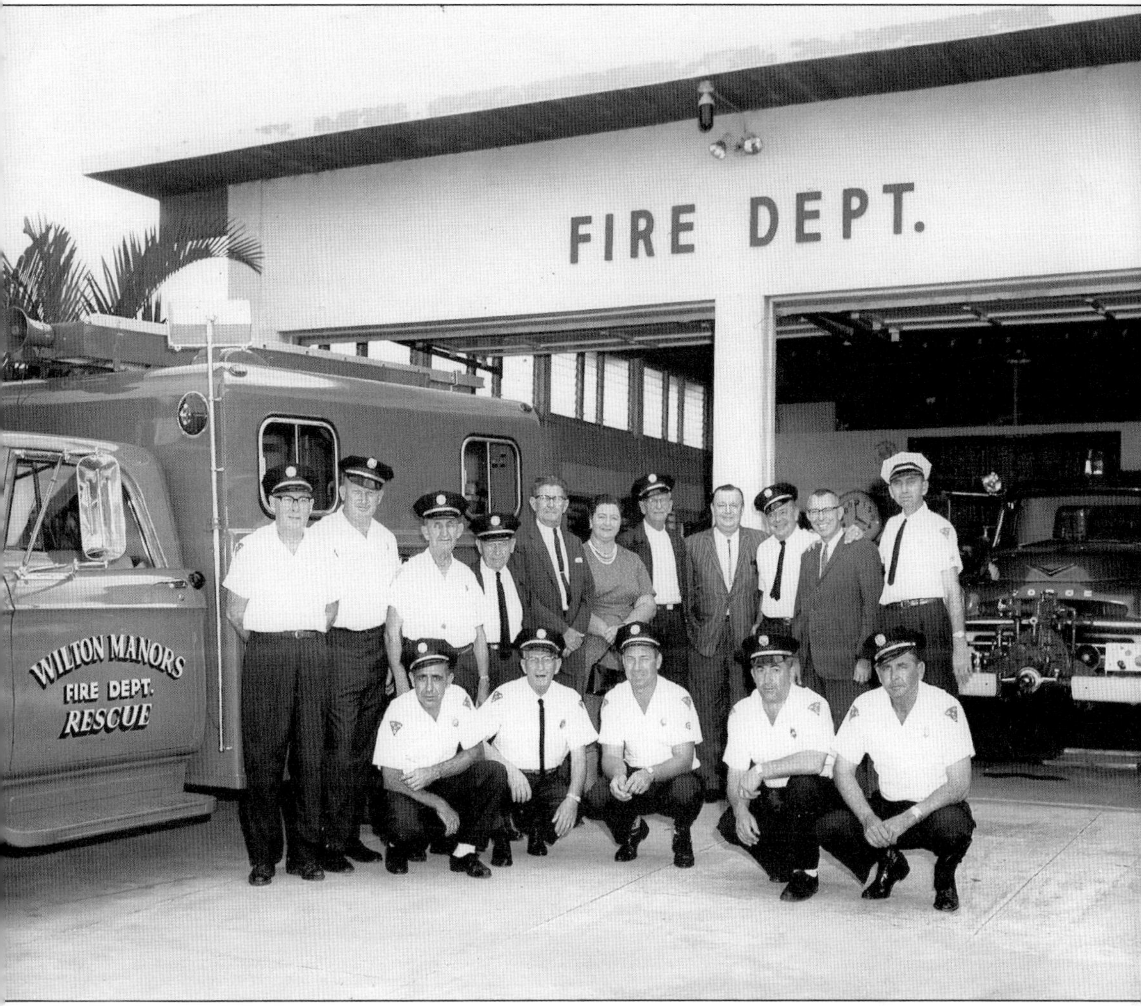


Fire Chief John Miller, at far right in the top row, poses with members of the city council and the city's volunteer firefighters. Marcia Sawyer Stafford, who served eight years as city clerk and 14 on the city council, is the woman in the top row, center. The fire department building where they stand is now part of the commission chambers at City Hall. Miller, who owned a television and radio repair shop, served as chief from 1960 to 1980. Among the members of the department were Fred Haberstich, Carl Alexander, Richard Rothe, Don Cory, Ed Casoria, Danny Kester, Al Walker, Tony Thuma, Richard Beaney, Norman Malcolm, Ralph Smyth, Harry Speck, Harold Price, Jerry Thompson, Clifford Cole, Clarence Sills, Joe Nutero, Dick Boyer, Ed Thomas, Rudy Klippel, Bob Hennen, Charles Saxer, Ray Hamel, Ted Thorstensen, William Pabor, and Bob Perrigo. (The Haberstitch family.)

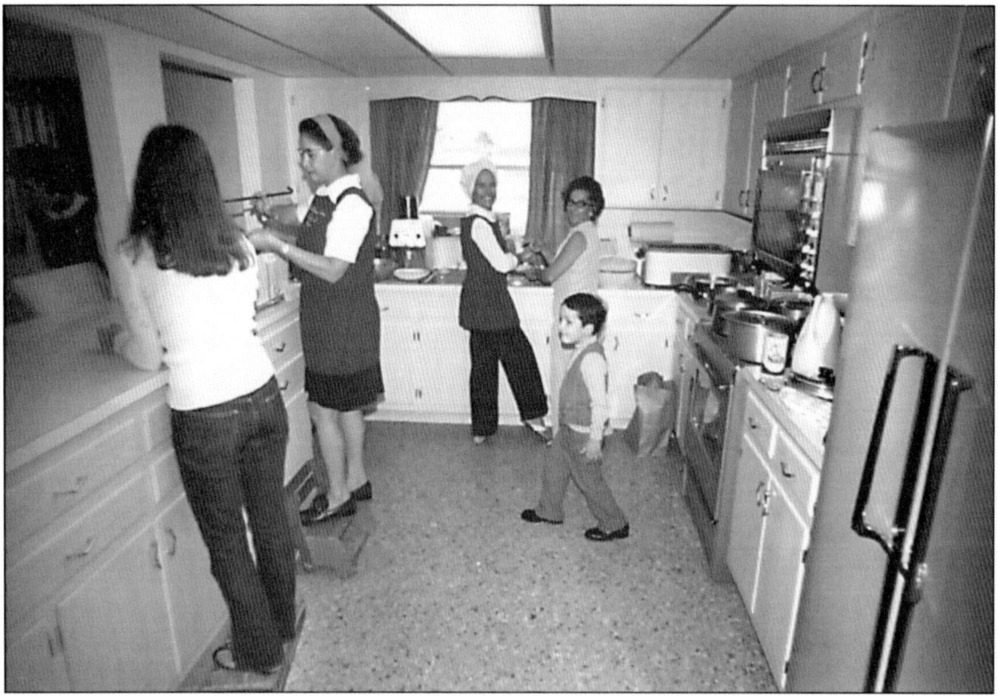

Fund-raising is a constant effort for volunteer fire departments, and Wilton Manors's was no different. The auxiliary was very helpful in coordinating and operating fund-raising activities. In this picture, auxiliary members and the children of firefighters pitch in to help with preparations for the auxiliary's second annual spaghetti dinner in March 1972. (Wilton Manors Historical Society.)

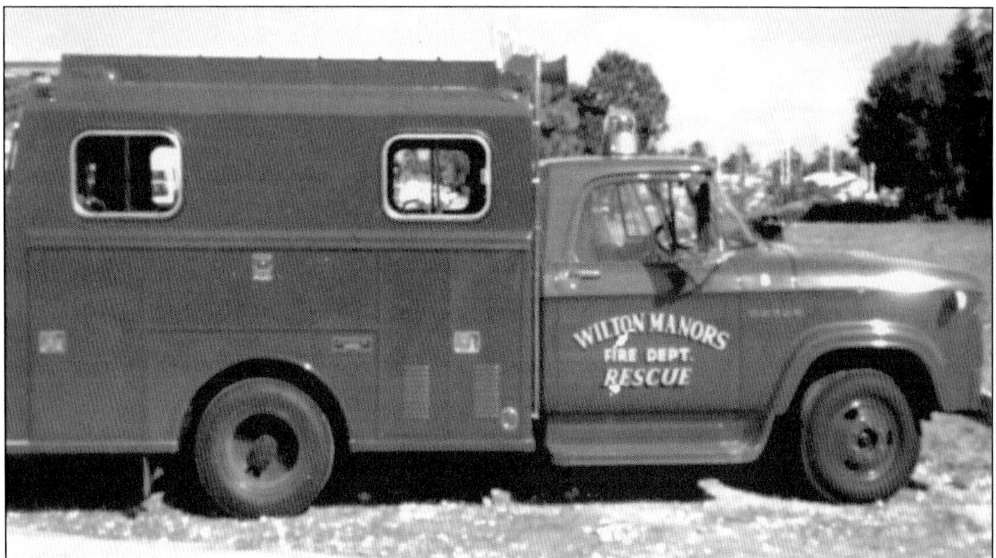


After the days when funeral homes provided ambulance service, but before the days of paramedics and EMT units, fire departments supplied rescue and transportation services. Wilton Manors was able to offer a high quality of emergency service to residents with its well-equipped rescue truck. (Wilton Manors Historical Society.)

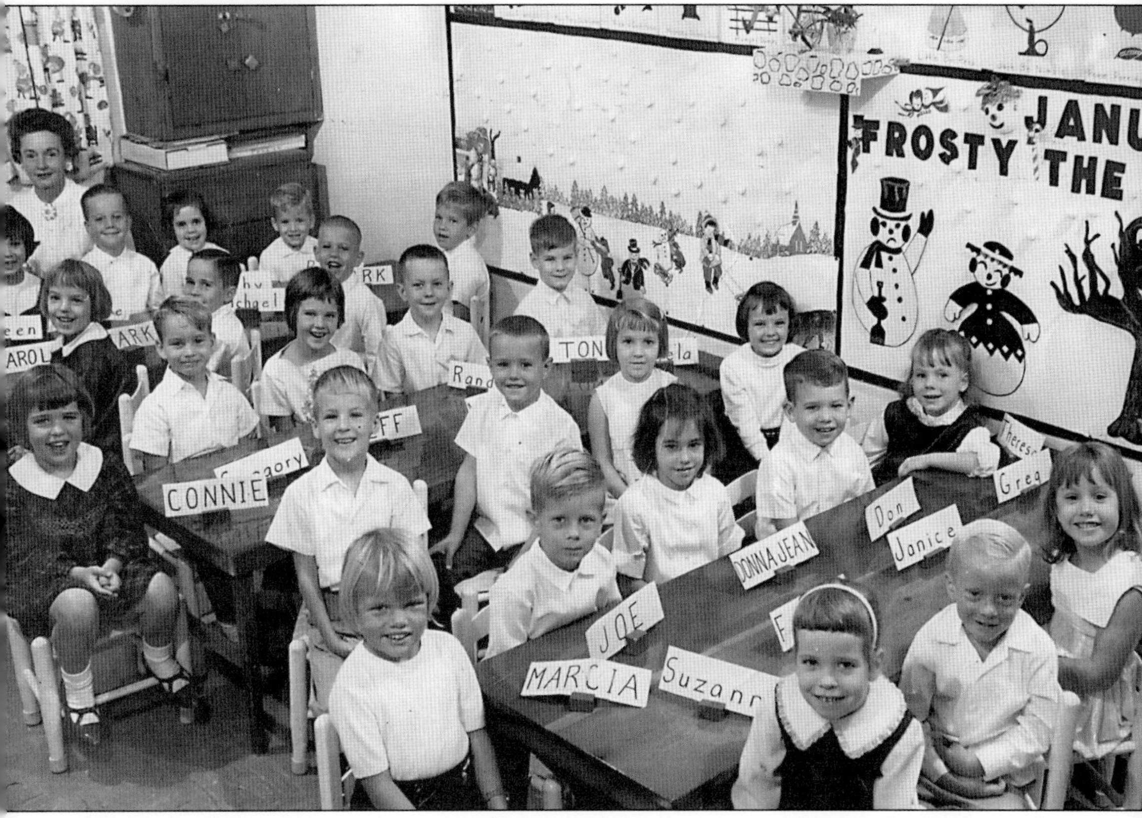


Thousands of the city's youth were well prepared for the rigors of first grade thanks to the efforts of Virginia Von Spreecken, who taught kindergarten at Miss Jordan's School, opened by Margaret Jordan on Northeast Twenty-sixth Street in 1950. When that school closed, Von Spreecken simply moved across the street, becoming director of the Covenant Presbyterian Kindergarten. This is the class of 1966–1967.

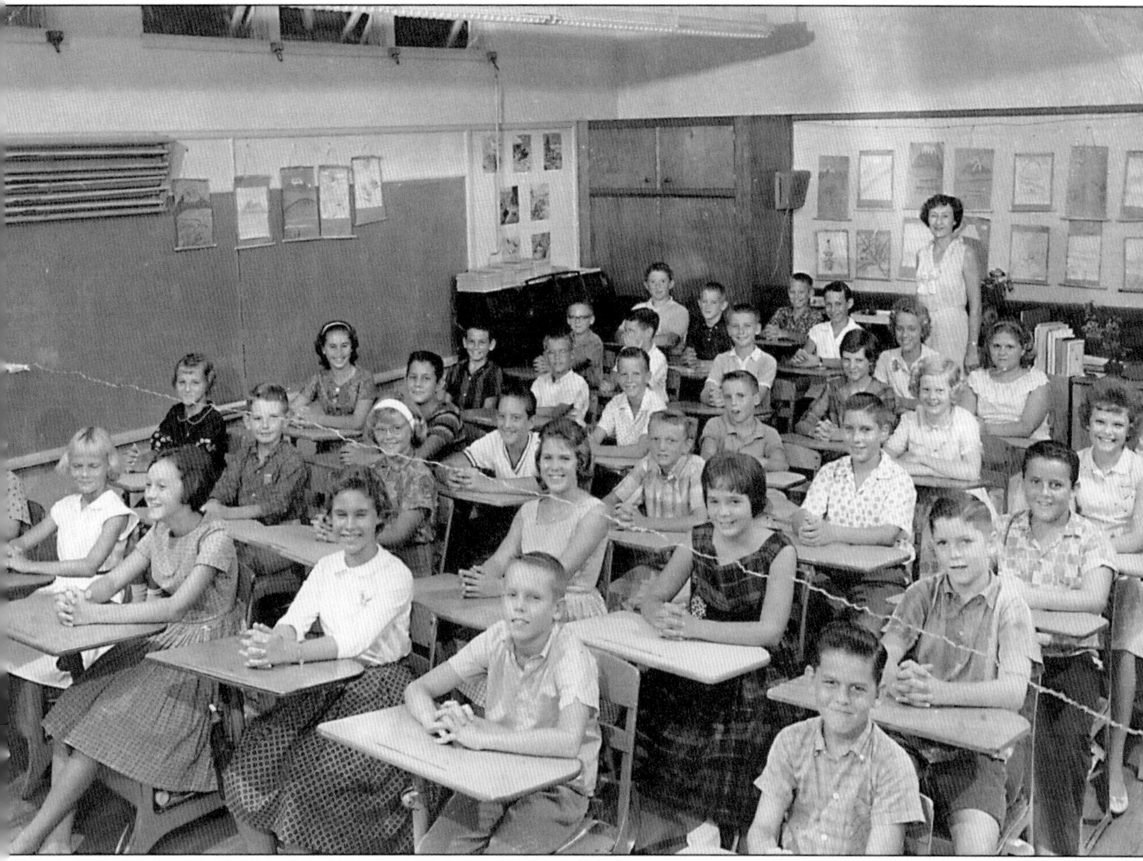

Standing over her classroom of young scholars, Wilton Manors Elementary School sixth-grade teacher Marjorie Elmore Ratliff seemed to know how to bring out the best in each of them. Although she and her husband Hal lived in Lazy Lake, her contributions to Wilton Manors's youth were recognized by the community in 1979, when she and fellow longtime teachers Nell Hudlow Coupanger, Billie K.M. Hooper, and Vada Elder Haun were honored among the city's pioneers. This picture is from the 1962–1963 school year.

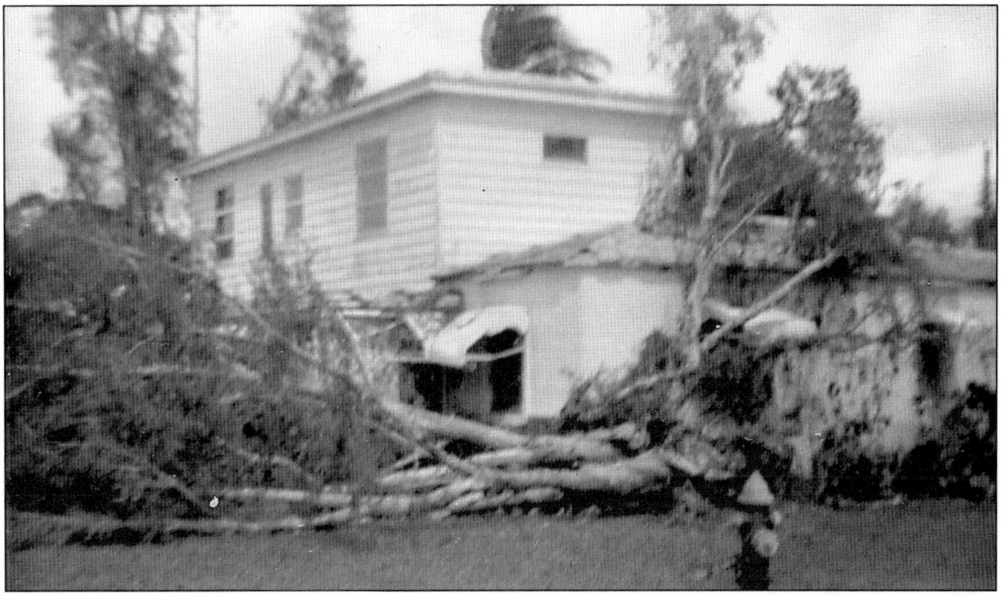

Hurricane Cleo struck Broward County on August 27, 1964. The category 2 storm's eye came ashore at Key Biscayne and moved north along State Road 7 into Broward County, packing winds of 110 miles per hour. Wilton Manors suffered significant horticultural damage and some structural damage. In this photo, the Lund family home on Northeast Twenty-fourth Street suffered some damage after a melaleuca tree brushed it on the way down. (Wilton Manors Historical Society.)

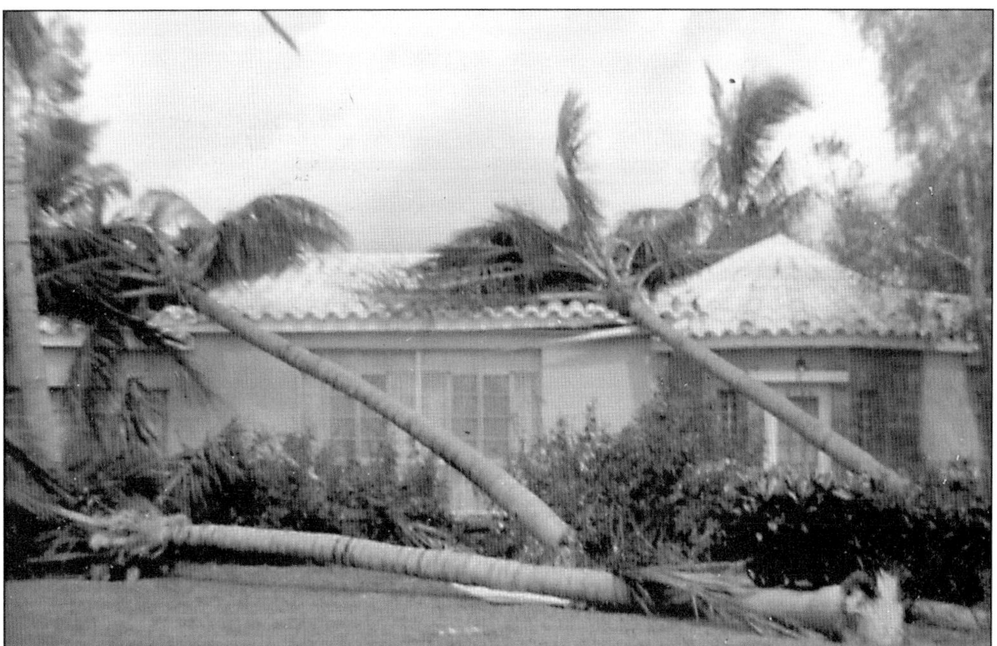

In this photo, coconut trees downed by Hurricane Cleo lie scattered like pick-up sticks at this home at 2125 Northeast Fifth Avenue. (Wilton Manors Historical Society.)

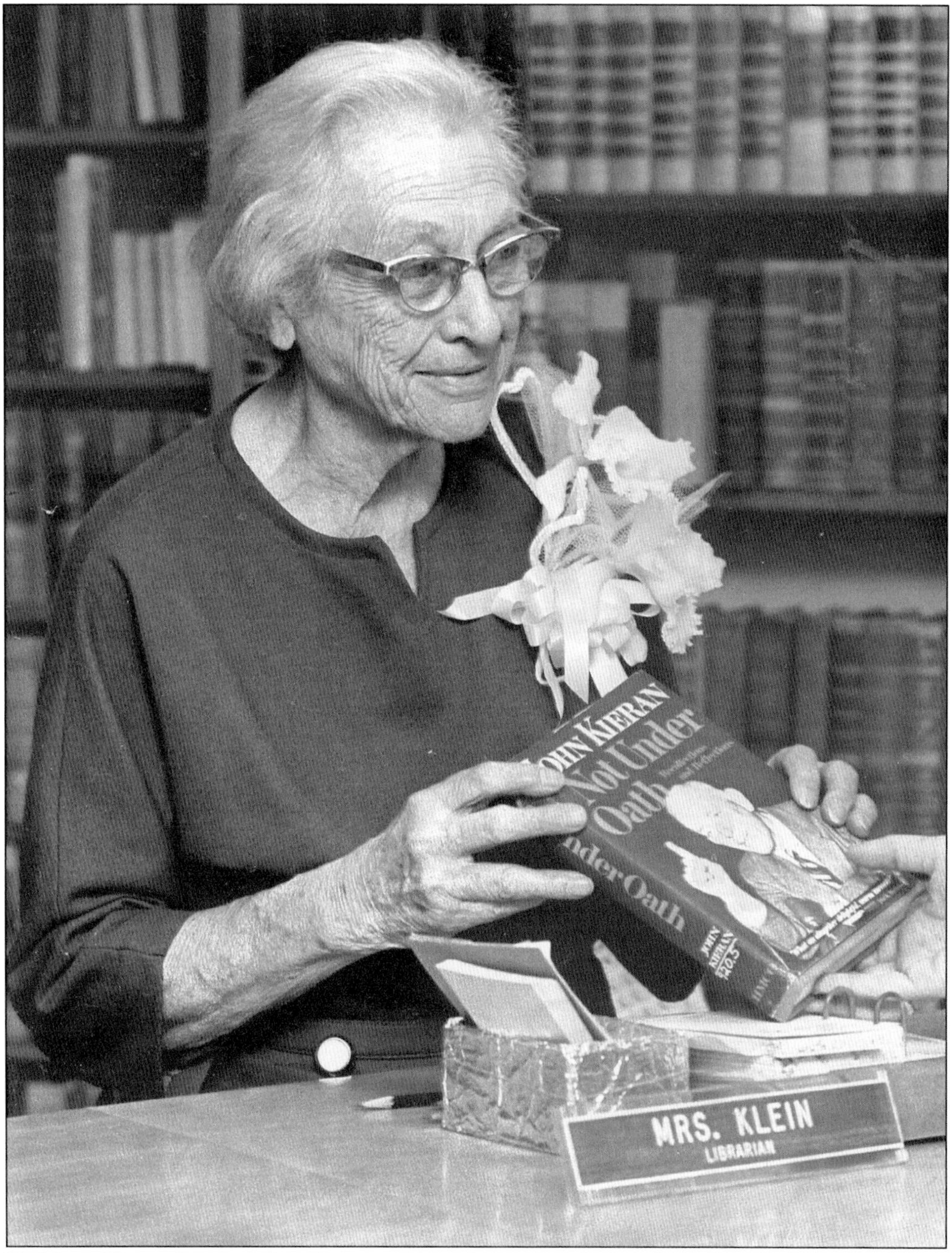


Kathleen Klein, the city's first librarian, retired in 1966. Originally a project of the Jayceettes, the library got its first home when Mayor Frank Starling provided a small shop formerly occupied by a keysmith. The tiny library opened on June 24, 1957, with Kathleen Klein volunteering to serve as its first librarian. The city took over the library in August 1958, hired Klein and moved the library to the original city hall. In 1960, the building was enlarged to double its space. (Wilton Manors Public Library.)

The St. Clement parish continued to grow with the addition of the rectory, completed in 1961 on the north boundary of the parish property. The convent, at the southwest corner, was completed the same year.

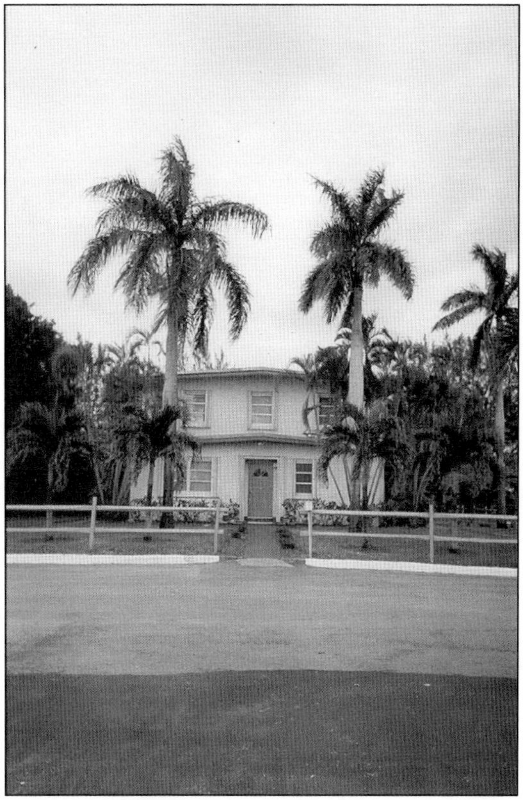

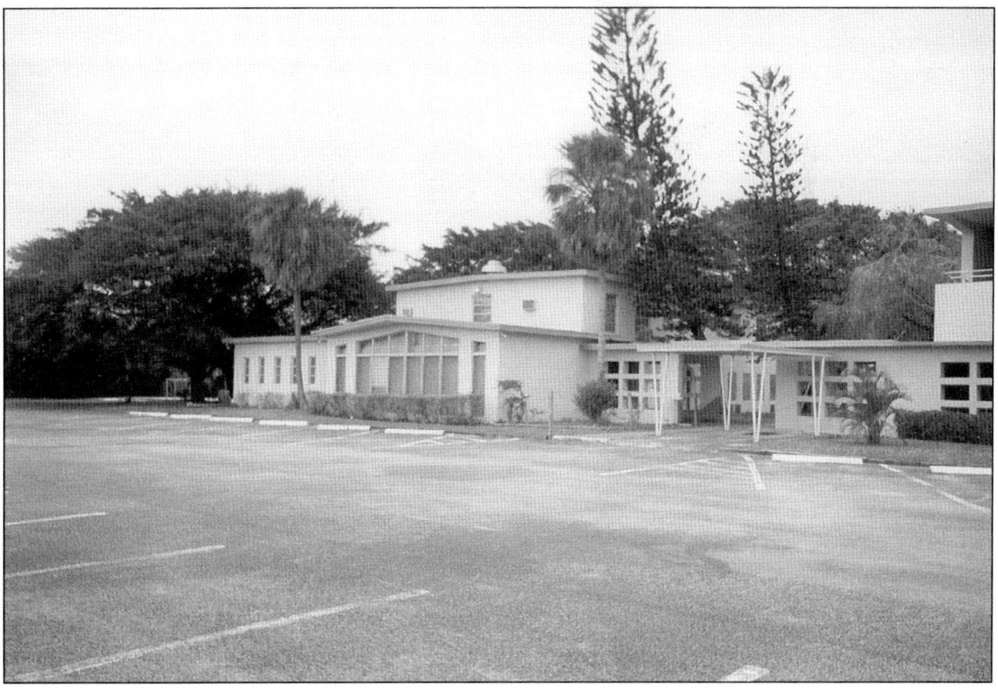

Five sisters of St. Casimir in Chicago were sent to St. Clement parish in 1955. Until completion of the convent in 1961, they lived in a home in Jenada Villas.

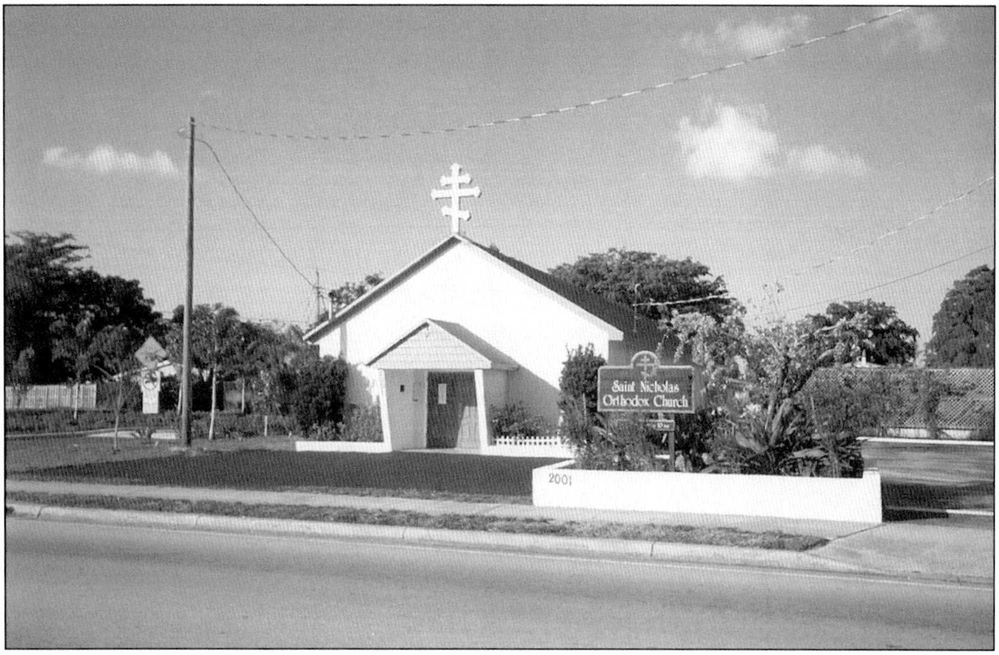


In 1961, a group of retirees of Russian ancestry living in southeastern Florida longed for a place to worship together. They pooled their funds to finance construction of St. Nicholas Orthodox Church. The immigration of Russians to South Florida following the dissolution of the Soviet Union in the early 1990s, as well as the fighting in the Balkans, was felt at St. Nicholas Orthodox Church, which now boasts a diverse congregation of Slavic origin.

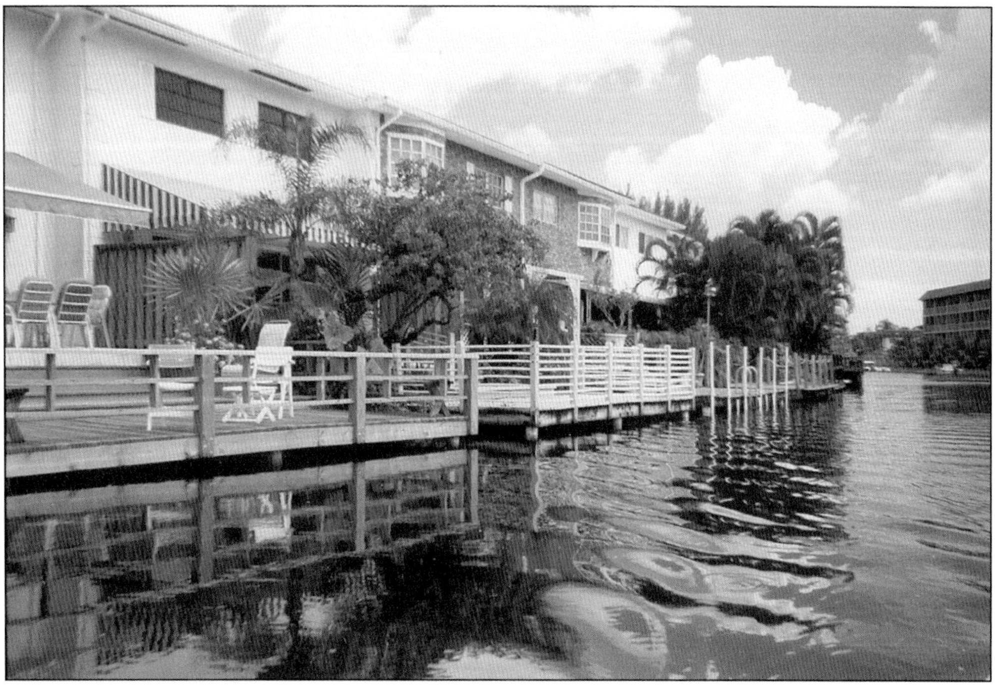

Townhouse Isle is a tiny gem of a community at the city's south border. Its location along the south fork of the Middle River permits dockage at one's backyard.

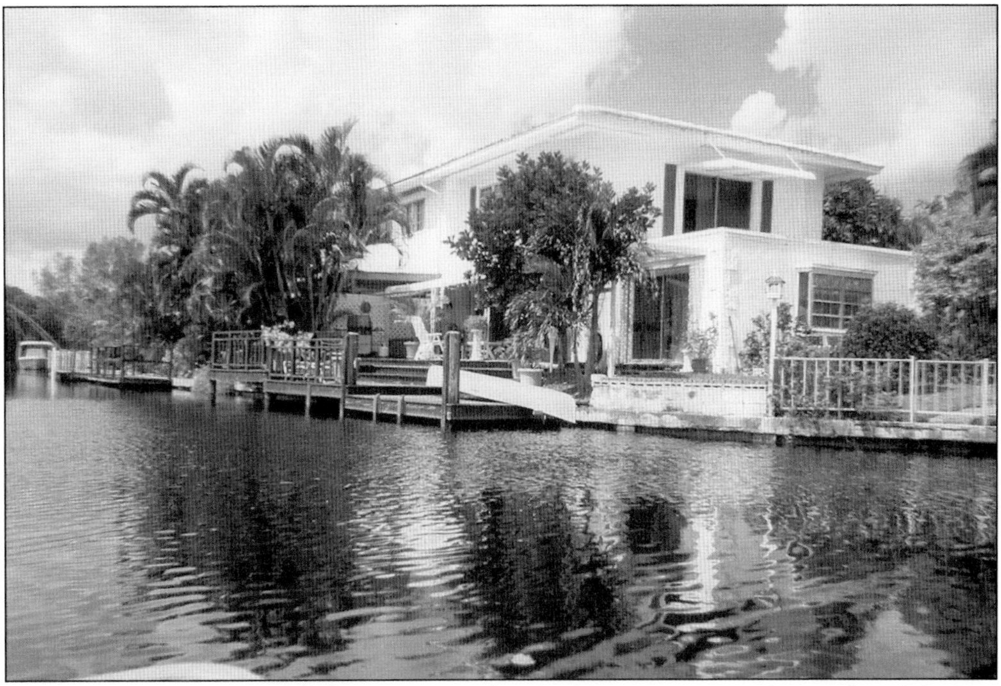

Townhouse Isle's name is slightly a misnomer, because many property owners in the subdivision live in distinctive single-family dwellings.

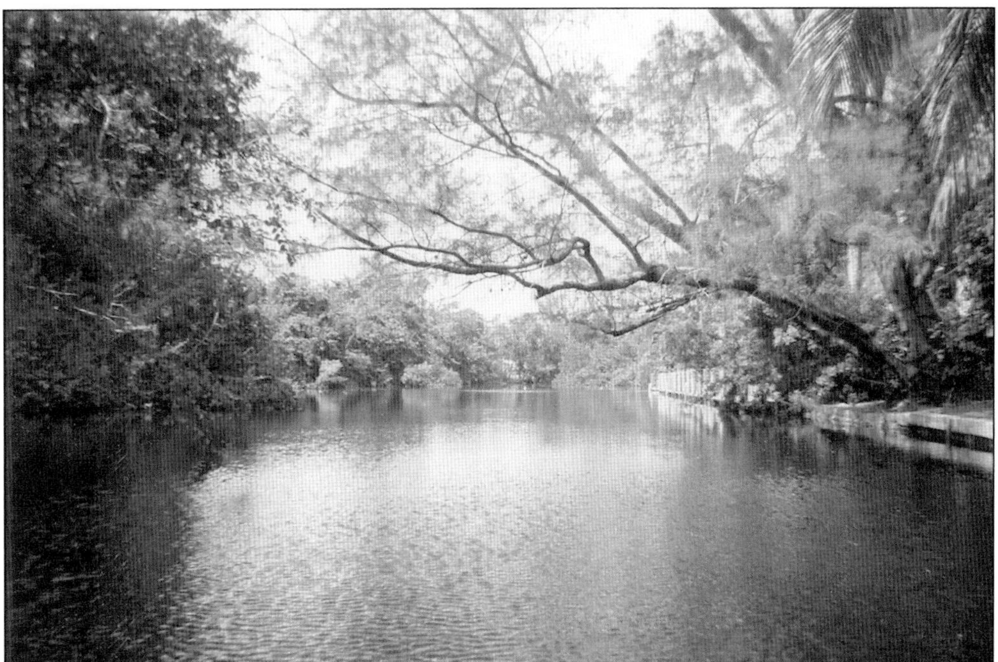

The trip along the south fork of the Middle River offers lots of natural beauties, and Townhouse Isle residents got the chance to enjoy them on a daily basis.

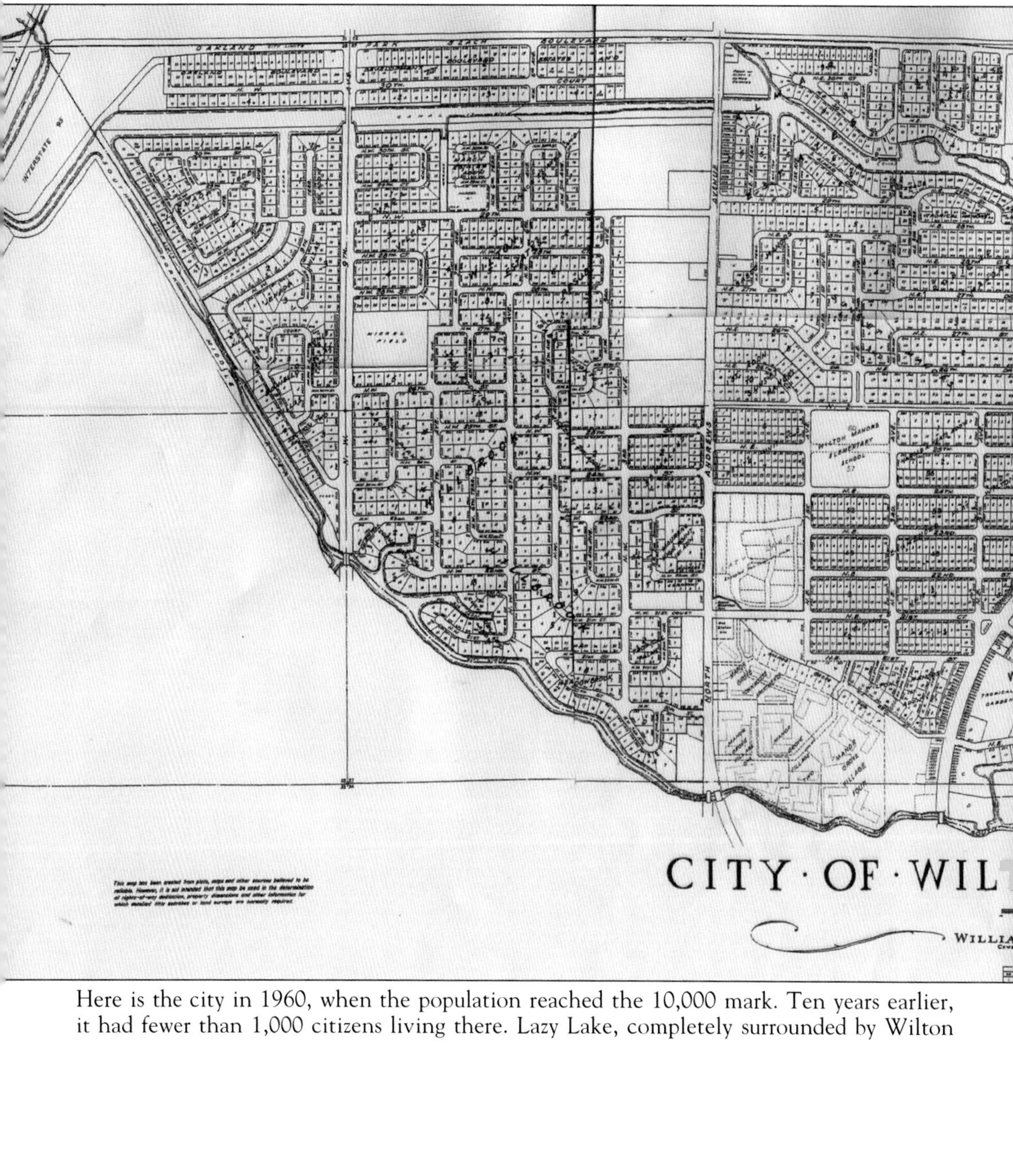


Here is the city in 1960, when the population reached the 10,000 mark. Ten years earlier, it had fewer than 1,000 citizens living there. Lazy Lake, completely surrounded by Wilton

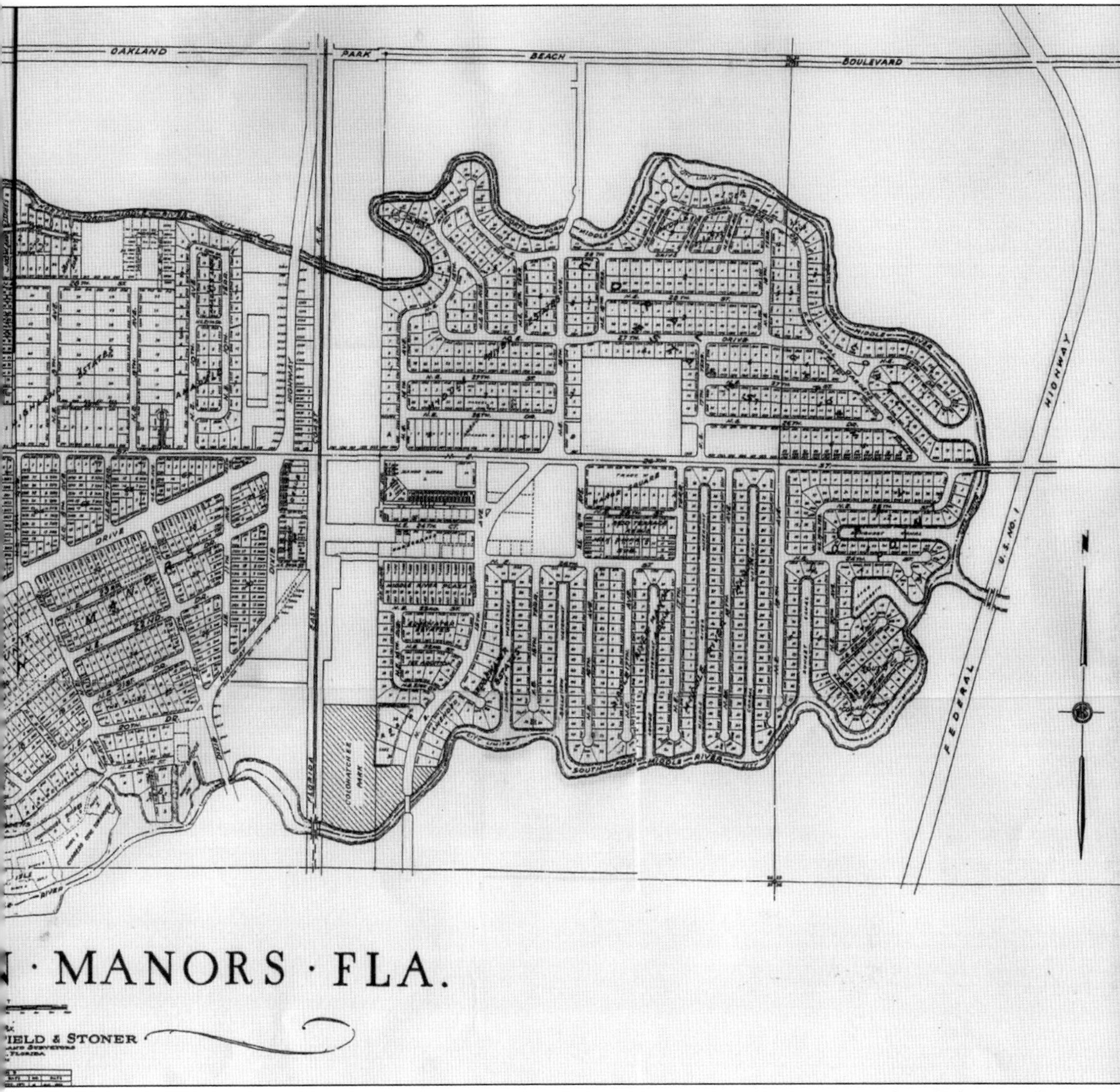


Manors, is just below and slightly to the left of Wilton Manors Elementary School. (City of Wilton Manors.)

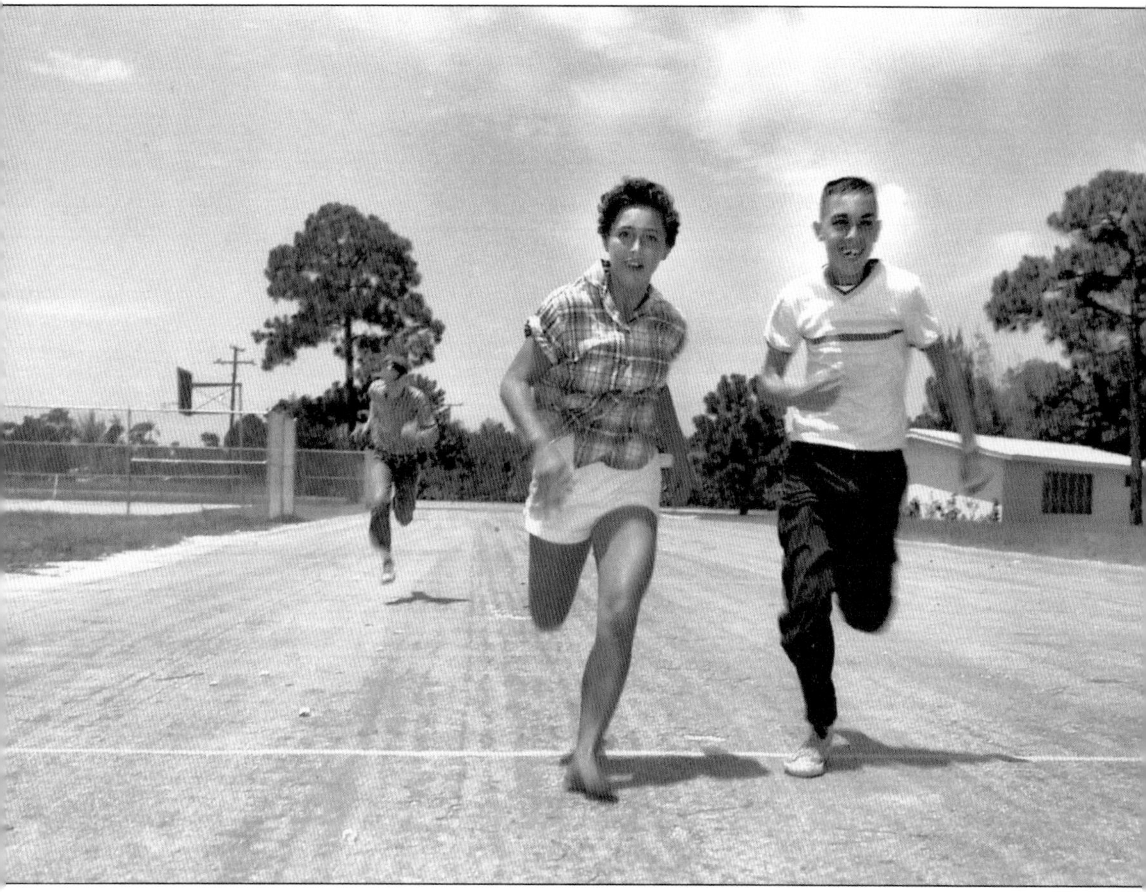

During the 1960s, Wilton Manors earned its stripes as a sports-loving city. Gary Patchen, who had bagged fourth, third, and a pair of second-place finishes in Fort Lauderdale's Soap Box Derby, then held on the Las Olas Boulevard bridge, won the 1961 competition and finished second behind Richard Dawson, of Wichita, Kansas, at the All-American Soap Box Derby in Akron, Ohio. In 1998, Patchen's son, Greg, steered his racer to a second-place finish in the masters division at the 61st derby in Akron. Loren "Duke" Maltby, who played guard for Florida State in 1949 and 1950, built a football powerhouse at Fort Lauderdale High, using many Wilton Manors boys on the Flying L's roster. Maltby's team hosted Melbourne for the Class 2A state championships in 1966, but lost 31-12. After retiring from coaching, Maltby served on the Wilton Manors city council from 1982 to 1984. Much of the athleticism displayed by Wilton Manors youth could be traced back to programs offered by the recreation department and run by top-notch coaches such as Bill Weigle and Madie Davis. In the picture, youths compete in a sprint race at Hagen Park. The Women's Club building is visible on the right. (Gene Hyde collection, Fort Lauderdale Historical Society, Inc.)

# *Five*

# GROWTH SPURT (1970–1979)

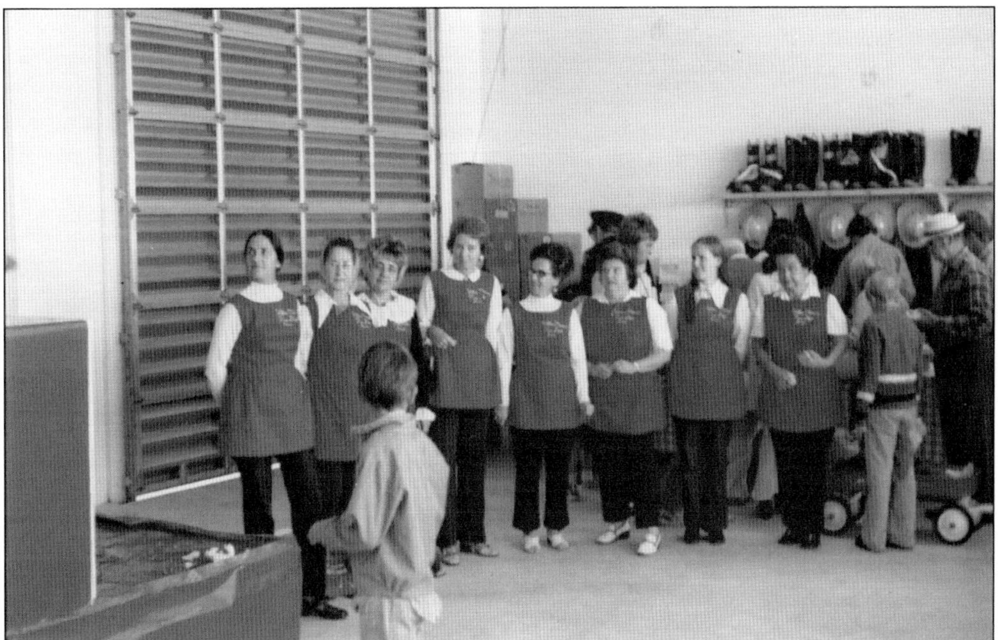

Members of the Wilton Manors Fire Department Auxiliary pose in their new red smocks at the department's 20th anniversary parade and open house. The auxiliary was formed November 16, 1960, with 12 members and dues of $2 annually. The auxiliary members served as hostesses for fire department social events and ran spaghetti dinners, bake sales, potluck suppers, and other fund-raising events. Edie Alexander is fourth from left. Next to her, in glasses, is Ruth Miller. (Wilton Manors Historical Society.)

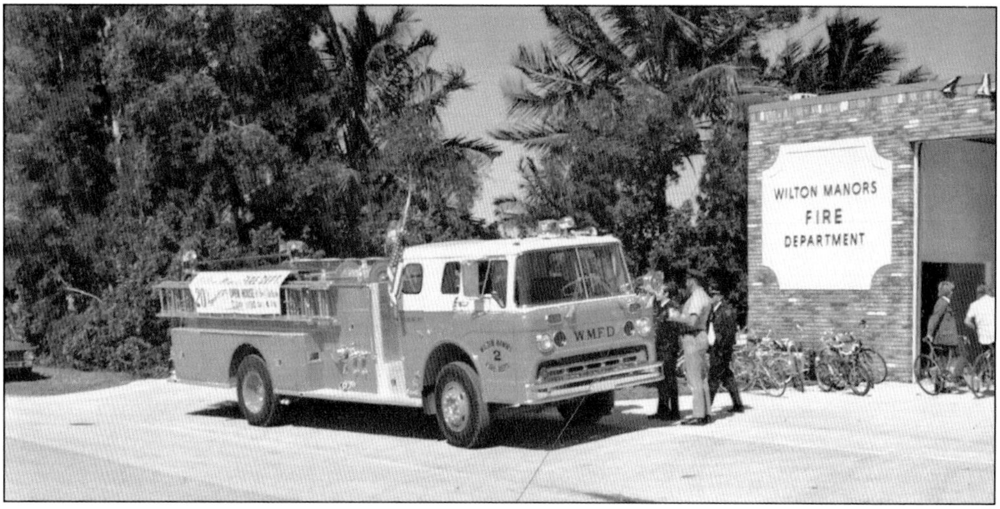


The focal point of the 20th anniversary celebration was the fire department's bright, shiny new yellow truck. All the department's other vehicles were painted red. (Wilton Manors Historical Society.)

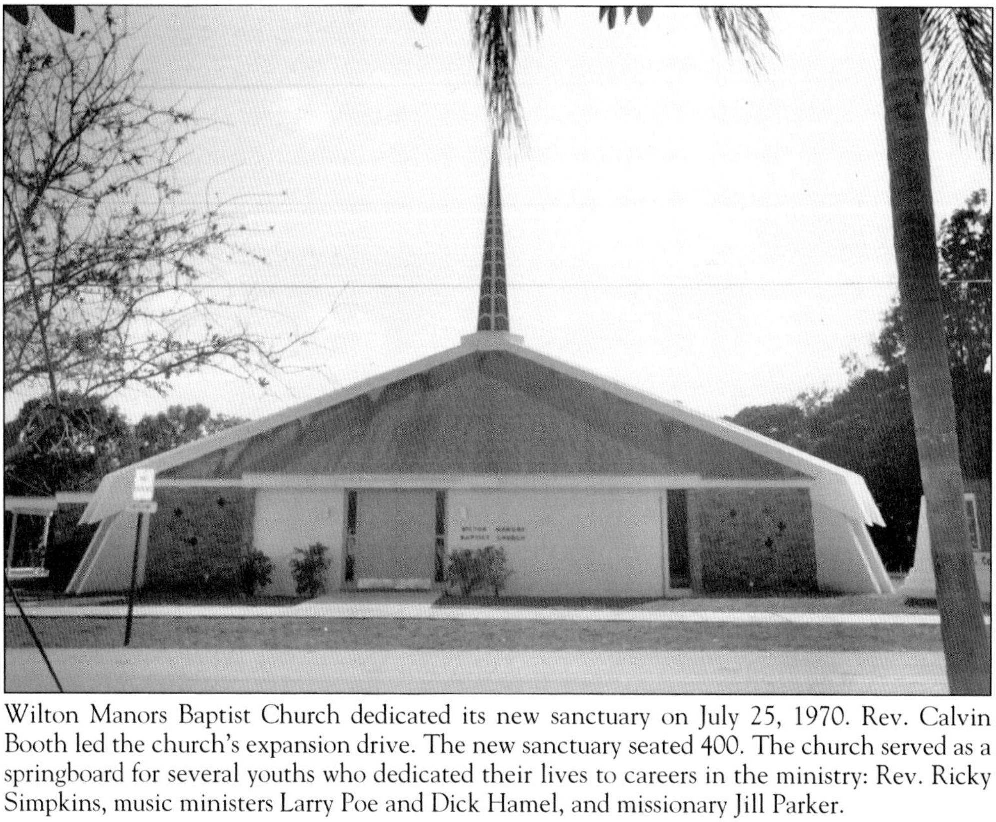

Wilton Manors Baptist Church dedicated its new sanctuary on July 25, 1970. Rev. Calvin Booth led the church's expansion drive. The new sanctuary seated 400. The church served as a springboard for several youths who dedicated their lives to careers in the ministry: Rev. Ricky Simpkins, music ministers Larry Poe and Dick Hamel, and missionary Jill Parker.

St. Clement parish dedicated its new church on November 23, 1970, under the leadership of Rev. Joseph Cronin, who served as pastor from 1963 to 1972.

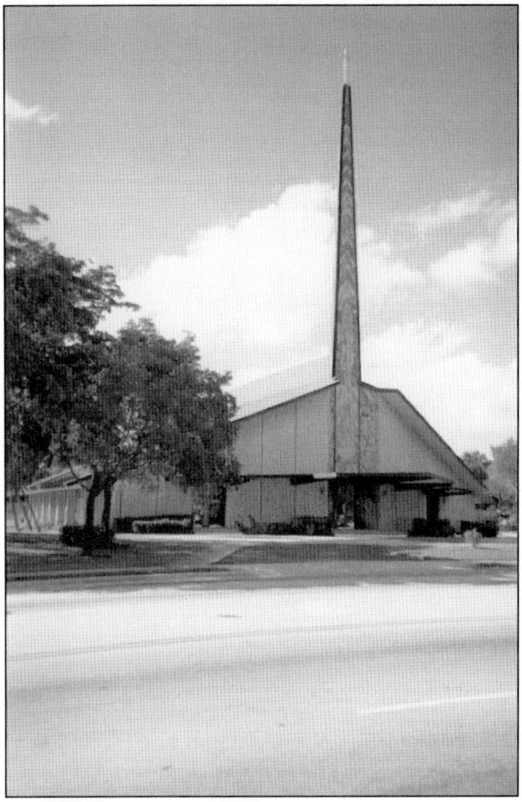

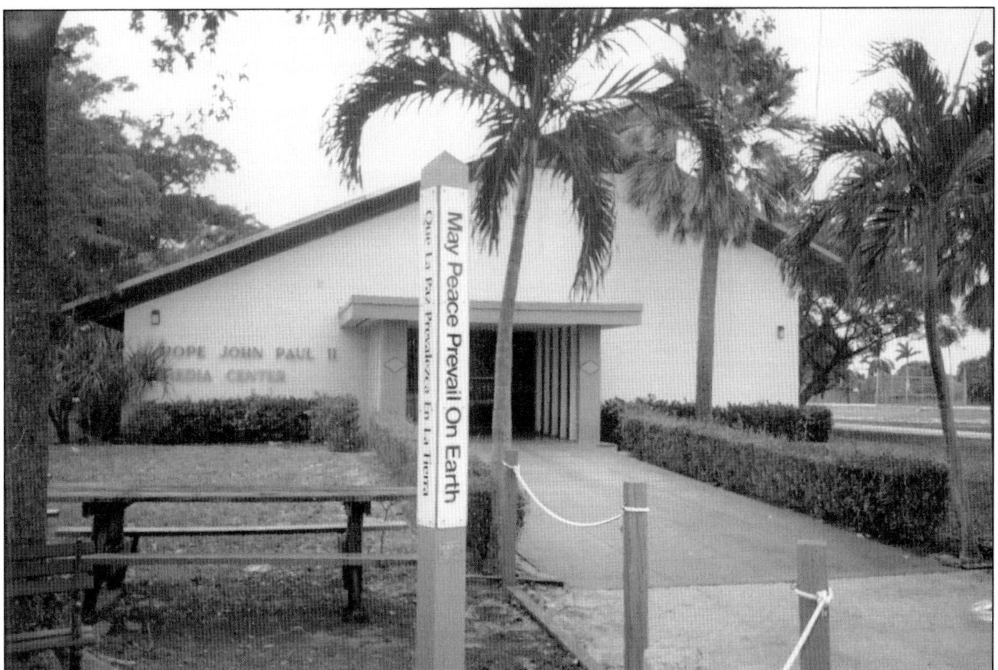


Since the dedication of the new St. Clement Church, the parish has made several additional changes, such as the addition of the Pope John Paul II Media Center.

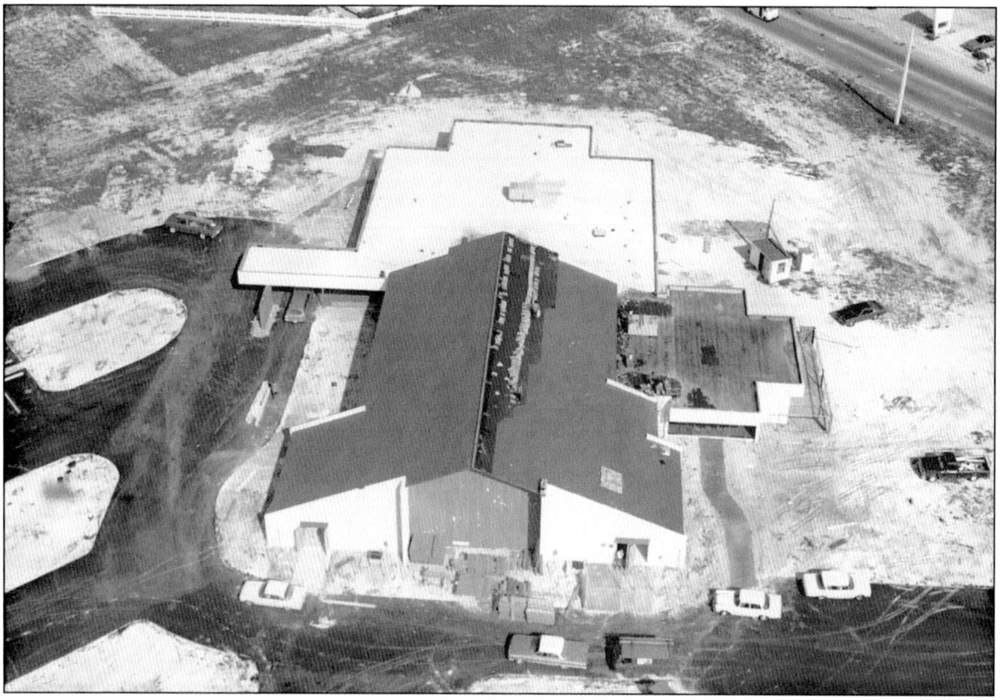

Construction nears completion on the Fort Lauderdale Church of Religious Science, on Northeast Twenty-sixth Street. The church was chartered November 9, 1959, and the congregation met in a storefront building until its permanent edifice was completed in late 1972. (Religious Science Fort Lauderdale.)

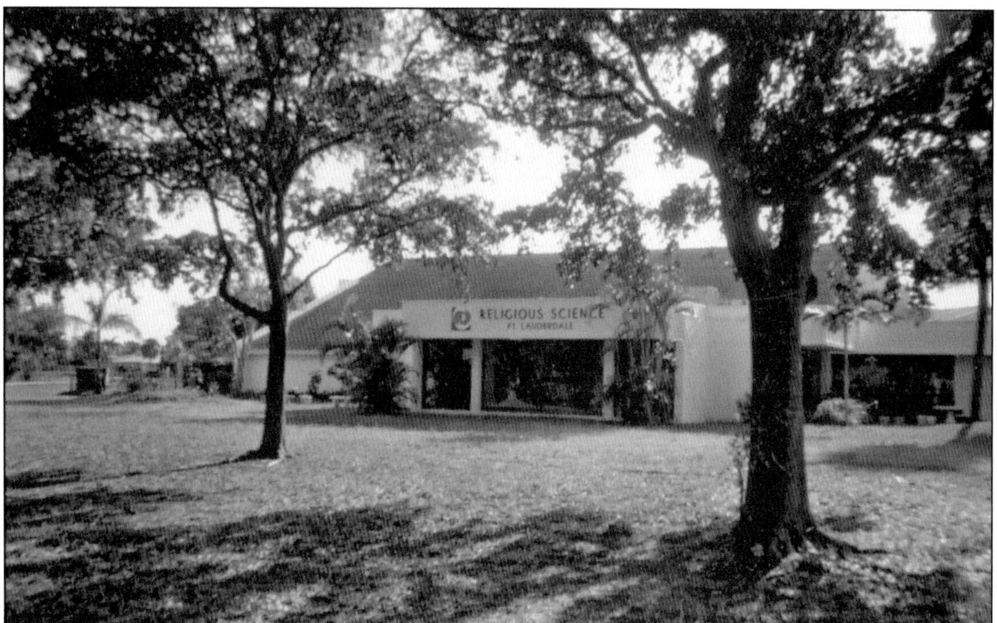


Rev. Ernest Holmes, founder of the International Religious Science movement, personally appointed Revs. Norman and Dorothy Lunde as pastors of the church, now called Religious Science Fort Lauderdale.

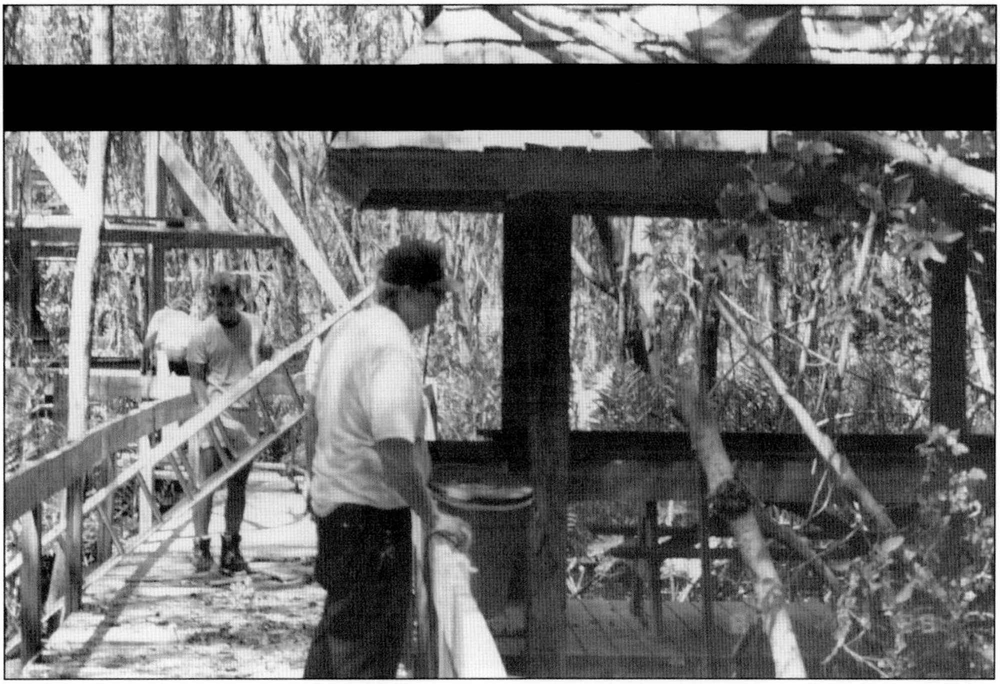

A picnic shelter at 6.5-acre Colohatchee Natural Park takes shape in the mangrove swamp along the Middle River. Land for the park was purchased in 1972, and the park was opened in 1975. The name for the park comes from the first part of early settler William C. Collier's last name and "hatchee," the Seminole word for river. Collier raised orange trees on his land, and the Seminoles often came to barter. The Seminoles named the river after him: Colohatchee, or Collier's River. (City of Wilton Manors.)

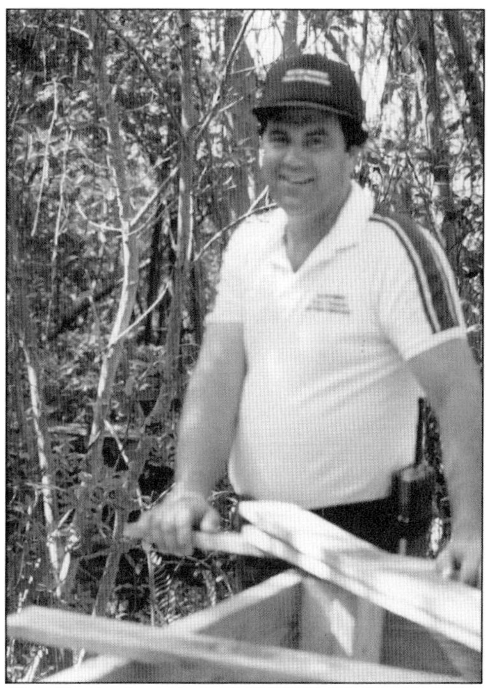

Richard Rothe, the first ranger at Colohatchee Natural Park, moved on to become the parks and facilities director for the city and later, parks and recreation director, until his retirement in 2003. (City of Wilton Manors.)

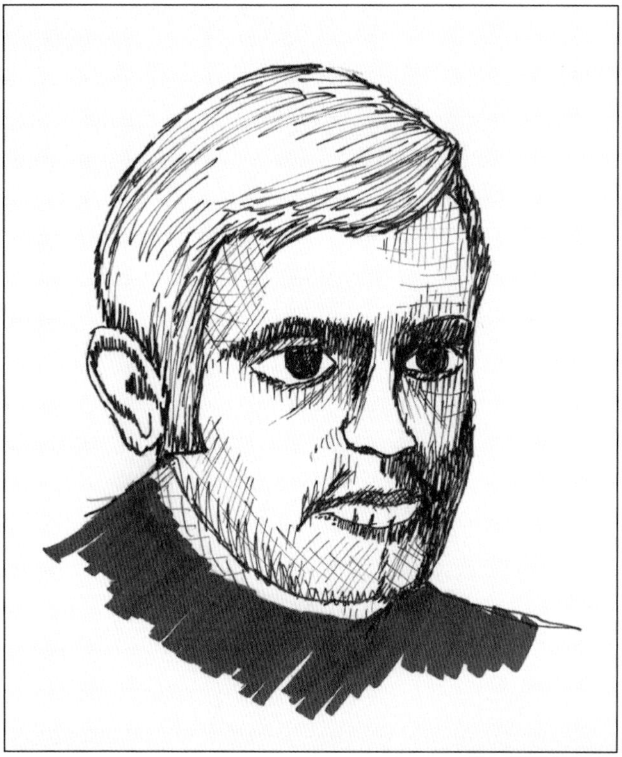

Gerard John Schaefer Jr. was hired by the Wilton Manors Police Department on September 3, 1971, and fired on April 20, 1972. Women had already begun disappearing in Broward County before Schaefer became a police officer, and when he moved north to work for the Martin County Sheriff's Department, the disappearances continued. Before he was sent to the state prison at Starke, Schaefer may have killed as many as 30 women, most of whom were abducted, raped, tortured, and mutilated. Schaefer was murdered in his jail cell on December 3, 1995. Fellow murderer Vincent Faustino Rivera was convicted of the slaying.

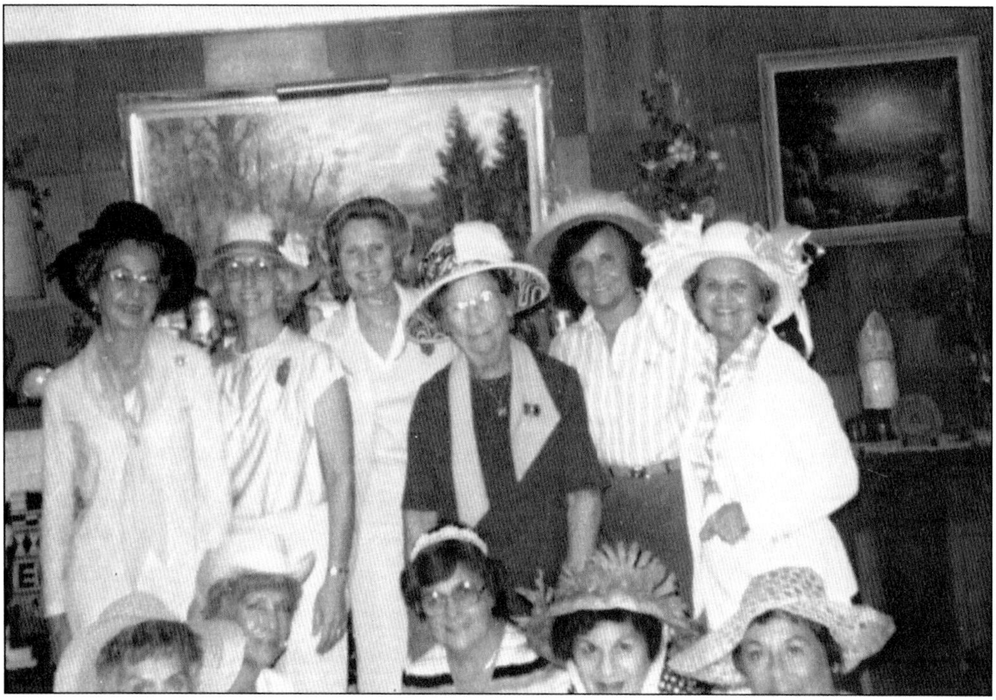

Friends of Easter Lily Gates, Broward County's longtime supervisor of elections, surprised her with a party at her home in Wilton Manors. Everyone wore her favorite chapeau to honor Ms. Gates, whose trademark was her hat. (Ruby Peak.)

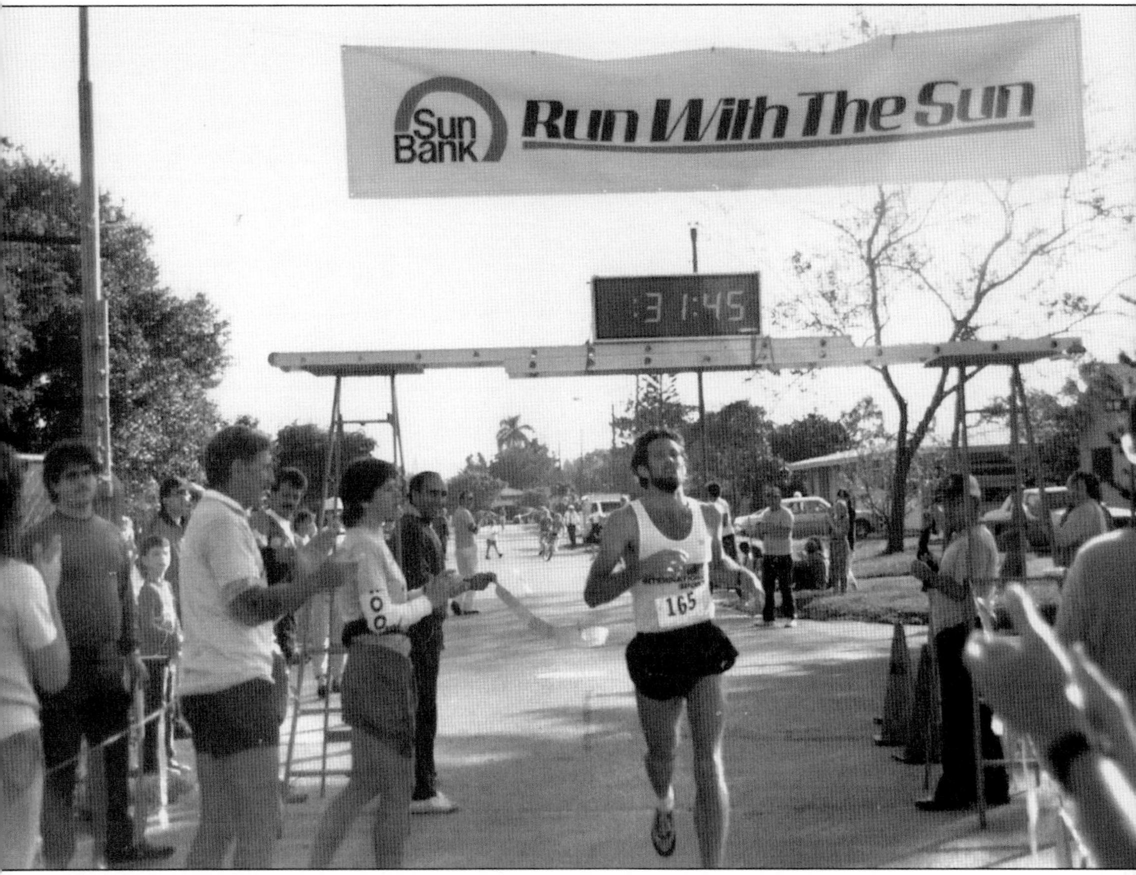


The city hosted the inaugural seven-mile Run for the Sun road race on January 31, 1978. About 600 runners started from Mickel Field and toured the city by foot. Dean Reineke, of Bloomington, Indiana, blew past the field, winning by nearly 45 seconds over the runner-up. (City of Wilton Manors.)

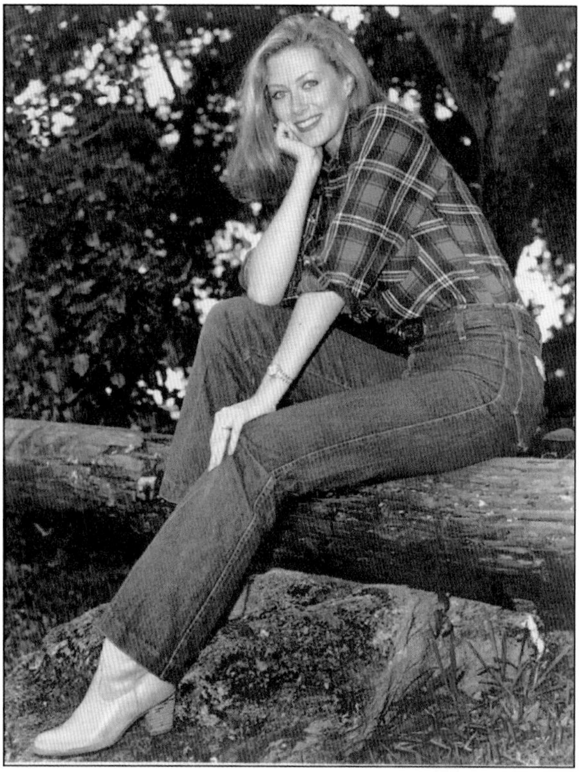

Nancy Stafford, daughter of Les and Marcia Stafford, was named Miss Florida in 1976, which was the start of an illustrious career for her. A journalism graduate of the University of Florida, she went on to become a Ford model and to appear in more than 250 commercials. She went on to acting, earning recurring roles in *Matlock* with Andy Griffith, *St. Elsewhere*, and *Sidekicks*. She has made scores of appearances and has done many specials. Most recently she has acted as host of the syndicated beauty show *Main Floor*.

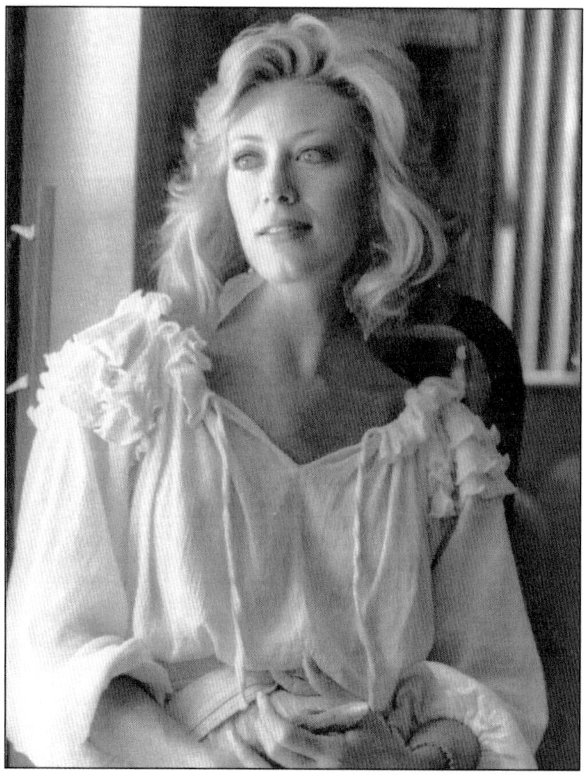

Stafford has shown further versatility in becoming the author of *The Wonder of His Love: A Journey into the Heart of God*, and *Beauty by the Book: Seeing Yourself as God Sees You*. (Broward County Historical Commission.)

# *Six*

# Quality of Life (1980–1989)

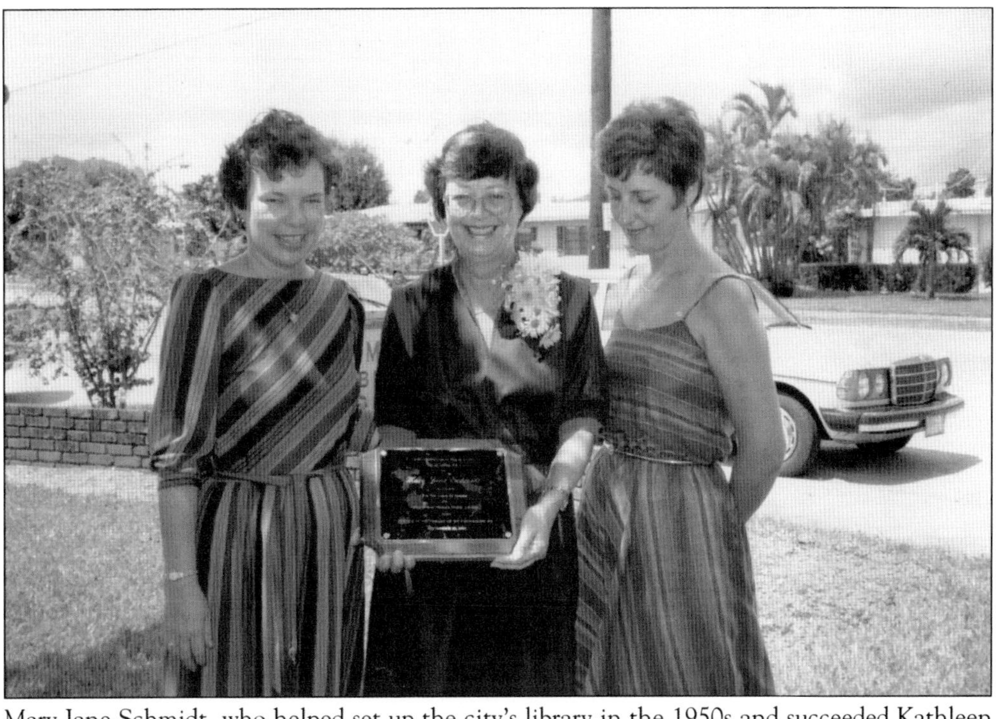

Mary Jane Schmidt, who helped set up the city's library in the 1950s and succeeded Kathleen Klein as librarian, retired in 1983. Marcia Ellington, her successor, and Friends of the Library president Peggy Schumacher, at right, present her with a plaque recognizing her service. (Wilton Manors Public Library.)

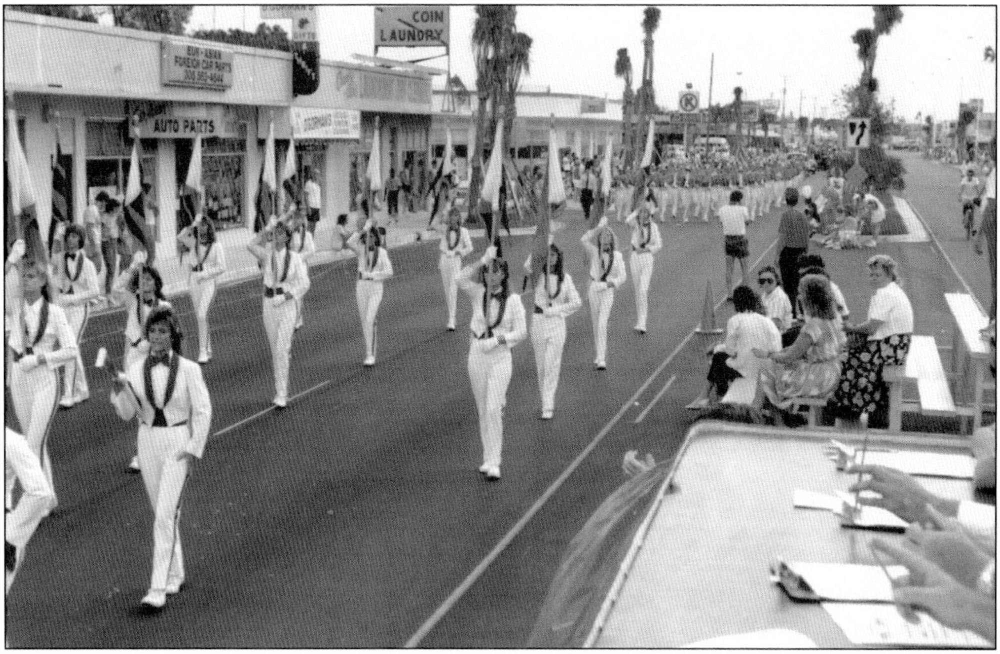


Fort Lauderdale High's Flying L Marching Band and Flag Corps marches down Wilton Drive on October 5, 1985, as part of the dedication ceremonies for the Wilton Drive Improvement Project. The parade celebrated the third construction of the road. It was first built in 1925 as Wilton Boulevard, the focal point of Willingham's development. Willingham had planned for it to be a street of stately residences and lush landscaping. In 1955, it was widened from two to four lanes and drainage was added. (Wilton Manors Historical Society.)

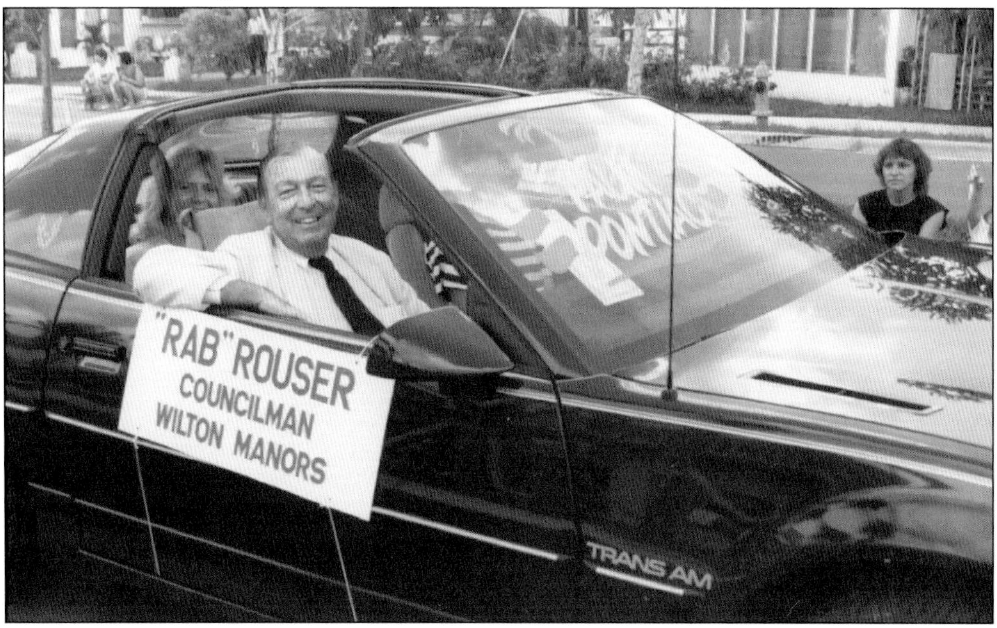


Sherod "Rab" Rouser completed the city council term of Jim Grady, who resigned after serving only part of 1985 on the council. Rouser is all smiles on Wilton Drive at the dedication parade. He later ran to retain the seat but was not elected. (Wilton Manors Historical Society.)

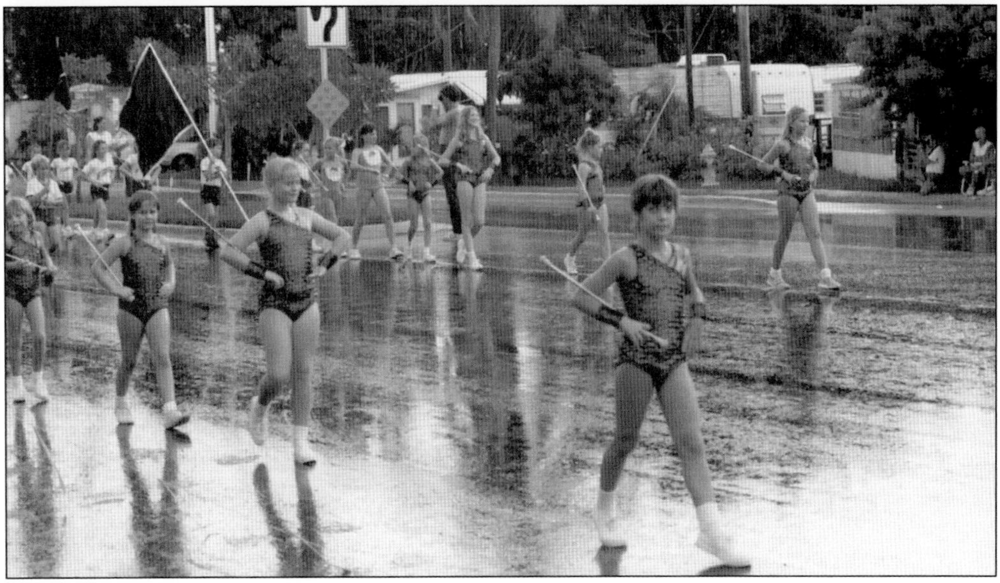

Young twirlers in their sequined costumes strut in style at the parade. Trailer Haven Trailer Park is visible in the background. (Wilton Manors Historical Society.)

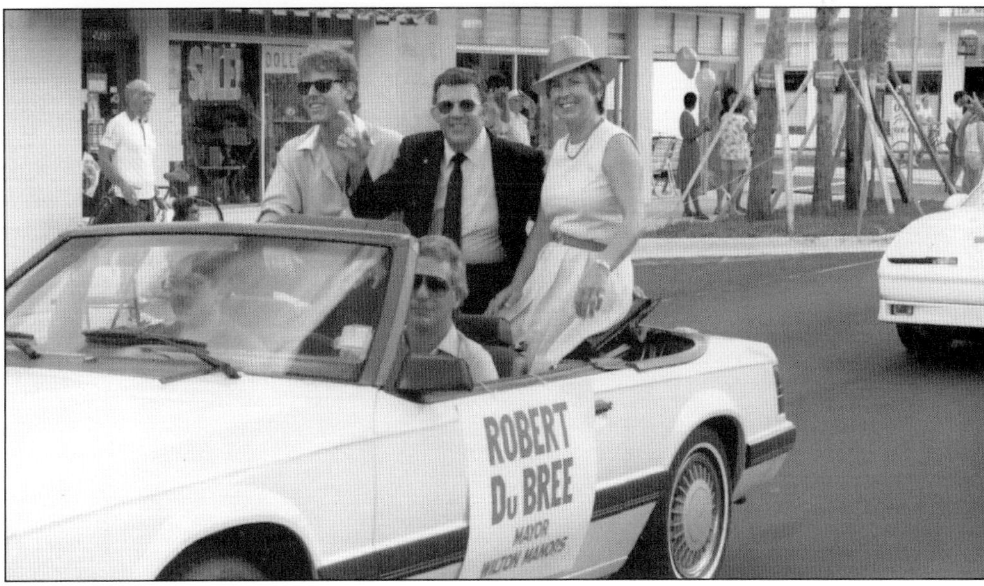


Robert DuBree, who served as mayor from 1984 to 1986, enjoys a lighter moment at the dedication ceremonies. DuBree, who owned the Ponte Rio motel, encountered some curious problems during his term as mayor; once, he negotiated with animal lover Vikki Kittles, who kept a veritable zoo at her home at 1818 Northeast Twenty-seventh Street. Two horses, Mocha and Spider, as well as 3 cats and 39 dogs, lived with her and her 70-year-old mother, Jean Sullivan, in the dwelling. Kittles's neighbors had appeared before the city council numerous times, asking for help in abating the smell and noise from Kittles's squalid home. DuBree and animal protection officer Pat King attempted to get Kittles to move the animals, but she refused. The council then voted to seek a court order to relocate the animals. Judge Brian Kay granted the order, and Kittles, along with her animals, left Wilton Manors. (Wilton Manors Historical Society.)

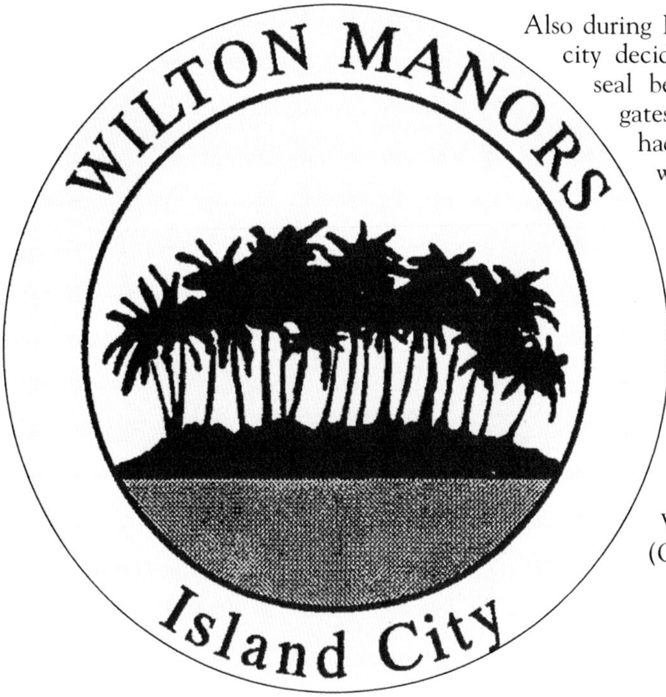


Also during DuBree's tenure as mayor, the city decided to adapt an updated city seal because the Abreu tower and gates depicted on the first seal had been torn down. The seals were to be used on welcome signs at each of the city's 11 bridge entry points. Norma Rollinson, a Wilton Manors resident for three decades and a graduate of the country's best arts college of the day, Pratt Institute in Brooklyn, designed the winning entry. The seal depicts a stand of palm trees in silhouette and reads simply: Wilton Manors—Island City. (City of Wilton Manors.)

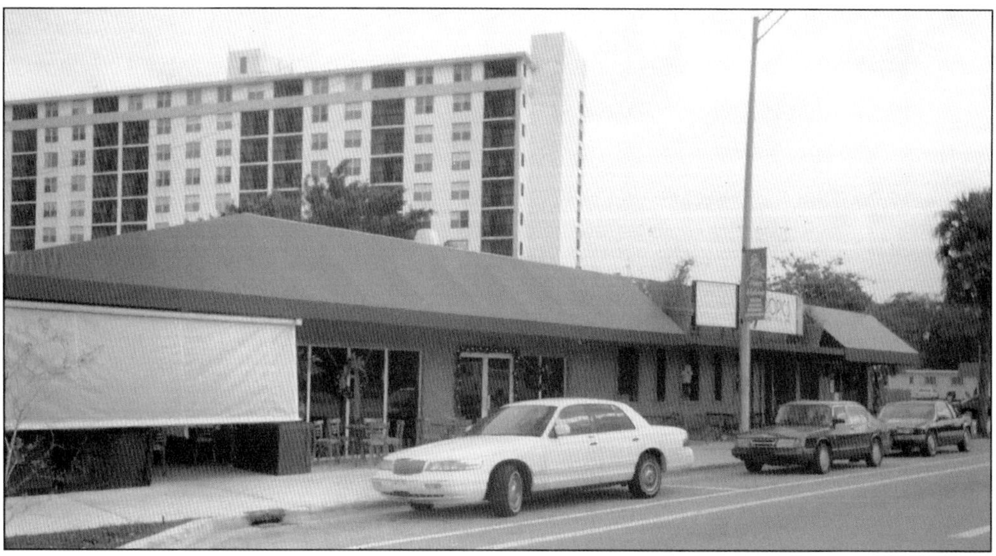

Tropics Restaurant was once divided into several establishments, including Williams Rexall Pharmacy, Kicks Sports Bar, and the Midnight Bottle Club. In the wee hours of September 12, 1987, electric bass guitar great Jaco Pastorius attempted to enter the Midnight Bottle Club, but was turned away by the manager, Luc Havan. Pastorius, whose mental condition and behavior had been spiraling downhill in the days before the episode, attempted to kick down the door of the establishment. Havan confronted him and a fight ensued. Pastorius was beaten senseless, and Havan left him in the parking lot in a pool of blood. Pastorius was taken to Broward General Medical Center where he died on September 21, only 10 days shy of his 36th birthday. Havan was convicted of manslaughter and sent to prison.

# *Seven*

# GOLDEN ANNIVERSARY (1990–1999)

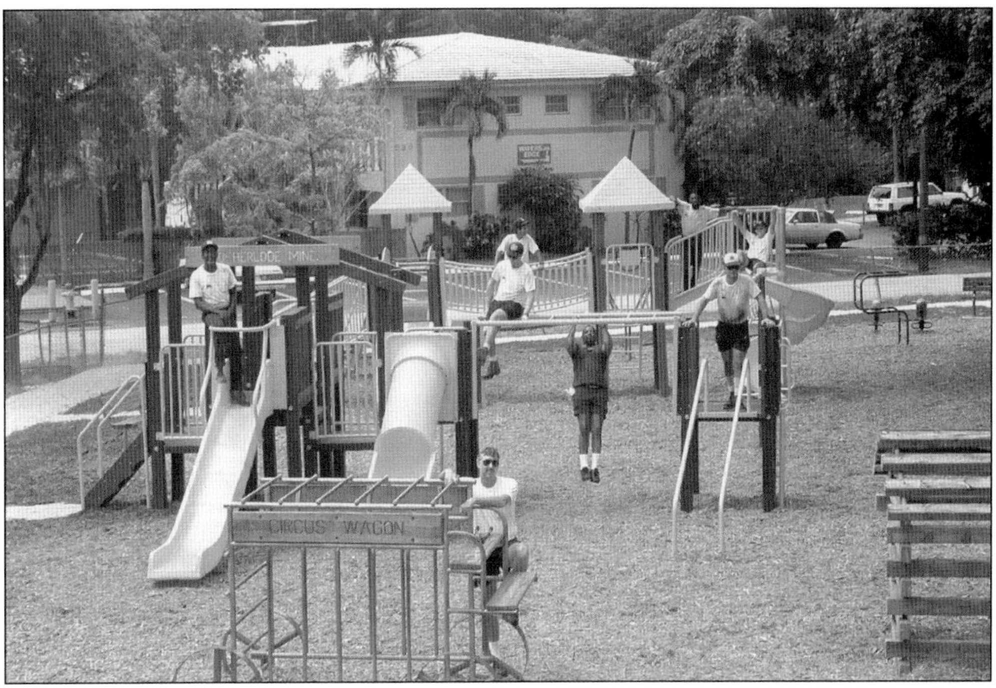


Public works staffers pose on the improved playground at Hagen Park. Improvements included a butterfly garden, fitness trail, and lots of new playground equipment. (City of Wilton Manors.)

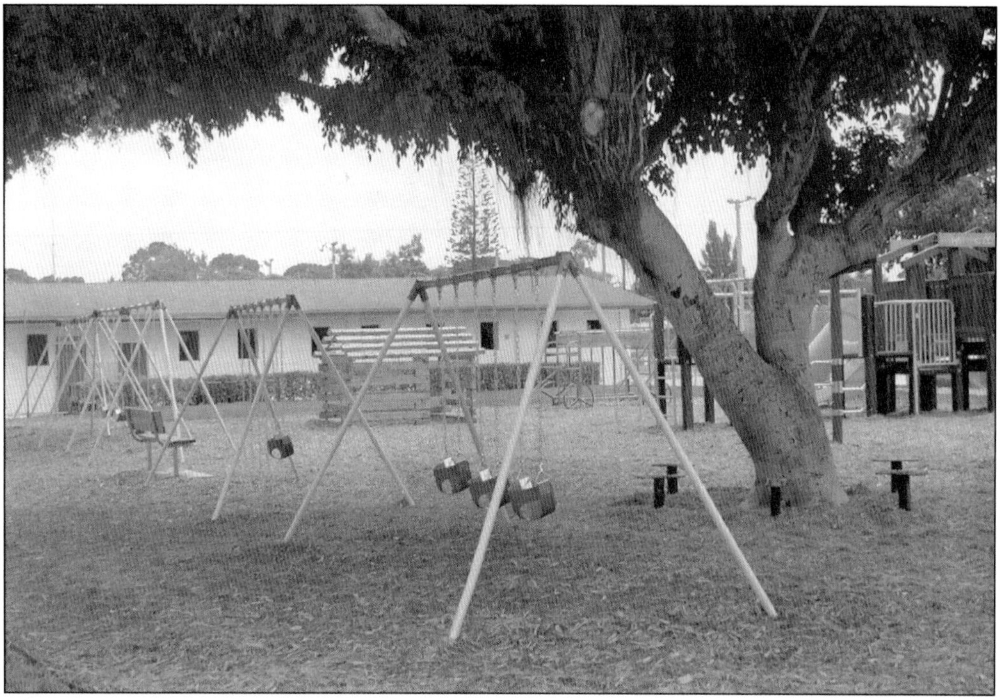

The improvements were put to good use immediately by participants in the city's BASH after-school program. This view of the playground faces north, with the Hagen Park pavilion and offices in the background. (City of Wilton Manors.)

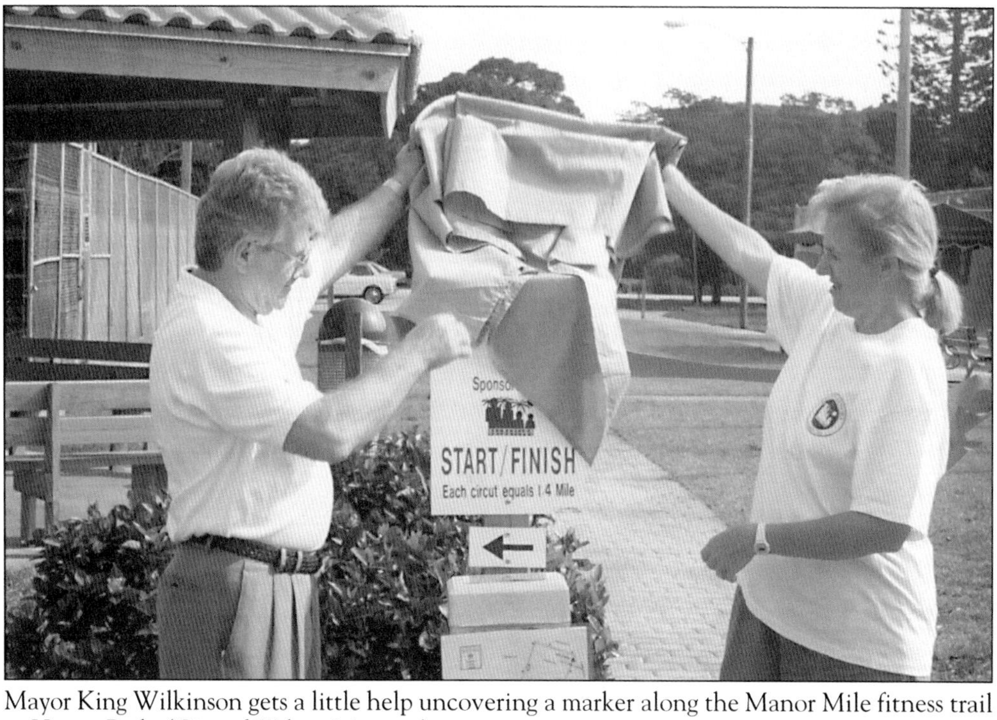


Mayor King Wilkinson gets a little help uncovering a marker along the Manor Mile fitness trail at Hagen Park. (City of Wilton Manors.)

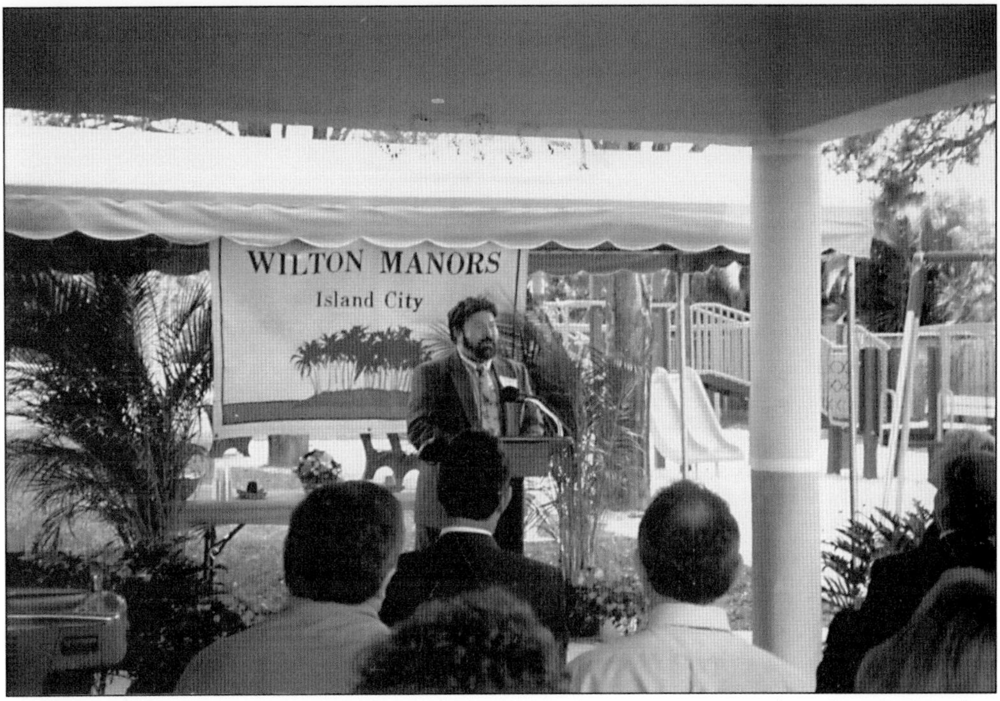


Dr. Robert A. Levy, a Harvard-educated physician who never practiced medicine, served as city manager from 1995 to 1997. Here, he speaks at dedication ceremonies for Kiwanis Park on January 29, 1996. (City of Wilton Manors.)

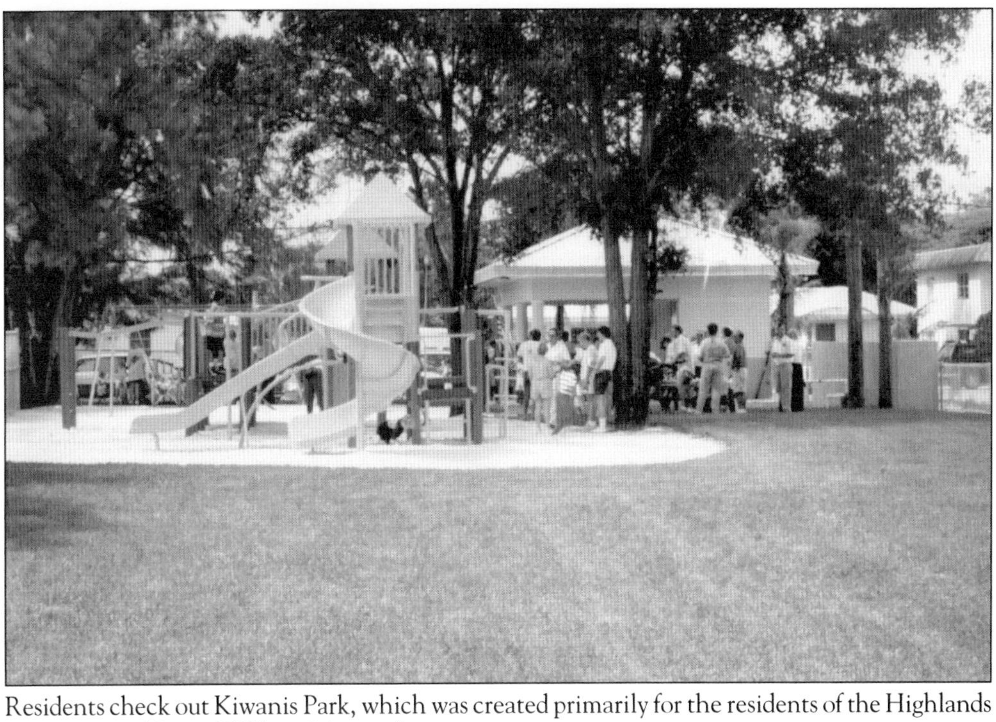

Residents check out Kiwanis Park, which was created primarily for the residents of the Highlands Estates area. (City of Wilton Manors.)

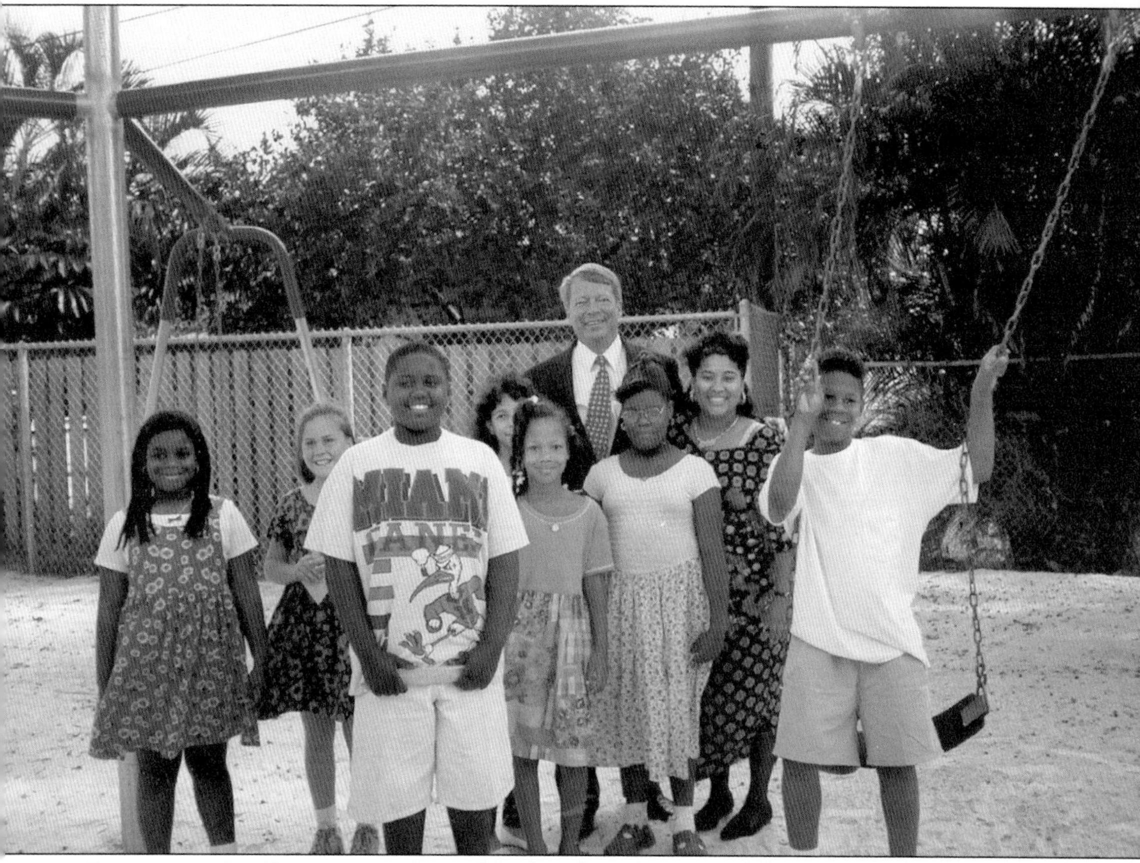


State senator Jim Scott poses with neighborhood youth. Many of the Highlands Estates children had no place to play until the park opened. (City of Wilton Manors.)

During his career with the city, Bernard S. Scott served as a police officer, police chief, and acting city manager. After retirement, he and his wife Marilyn, both St. Louis natives, moved to Georgia.

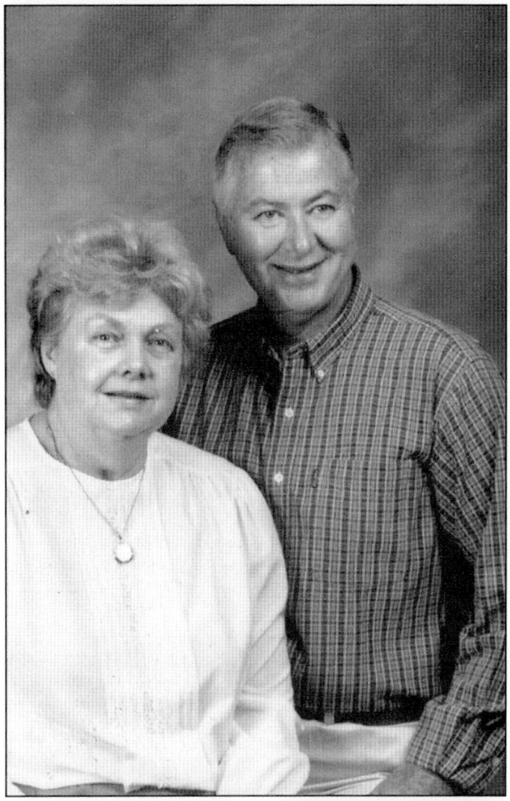

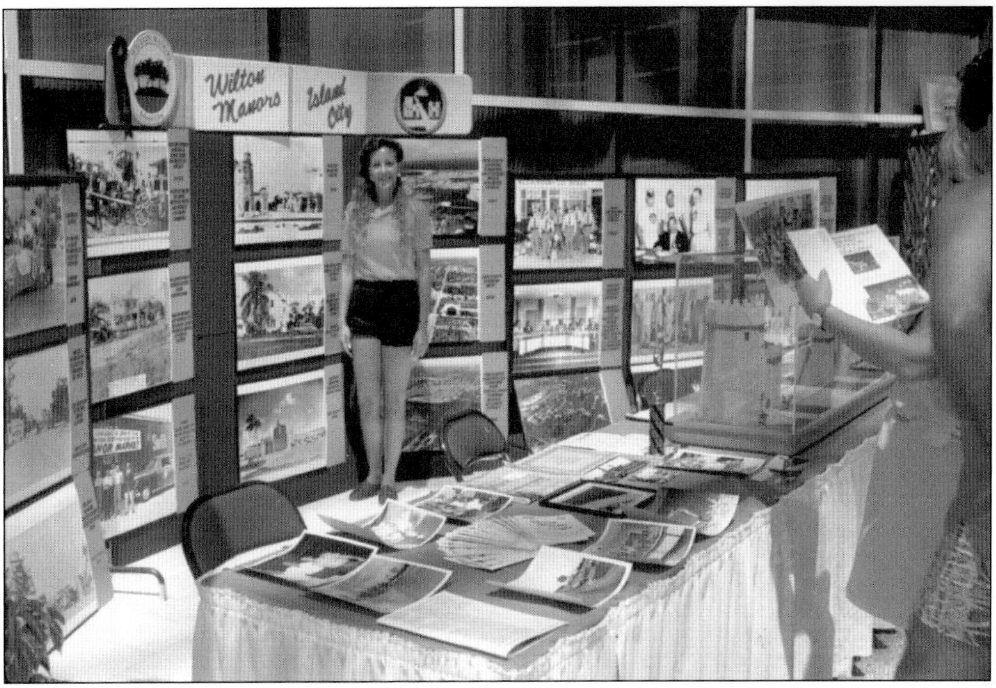


Becky Thacker, longtime assistant recreation director, staffed the city's award-winning exhibit at Broward County Pioneer Days, an event that was started in 1973. (City of Wilton Manors.)

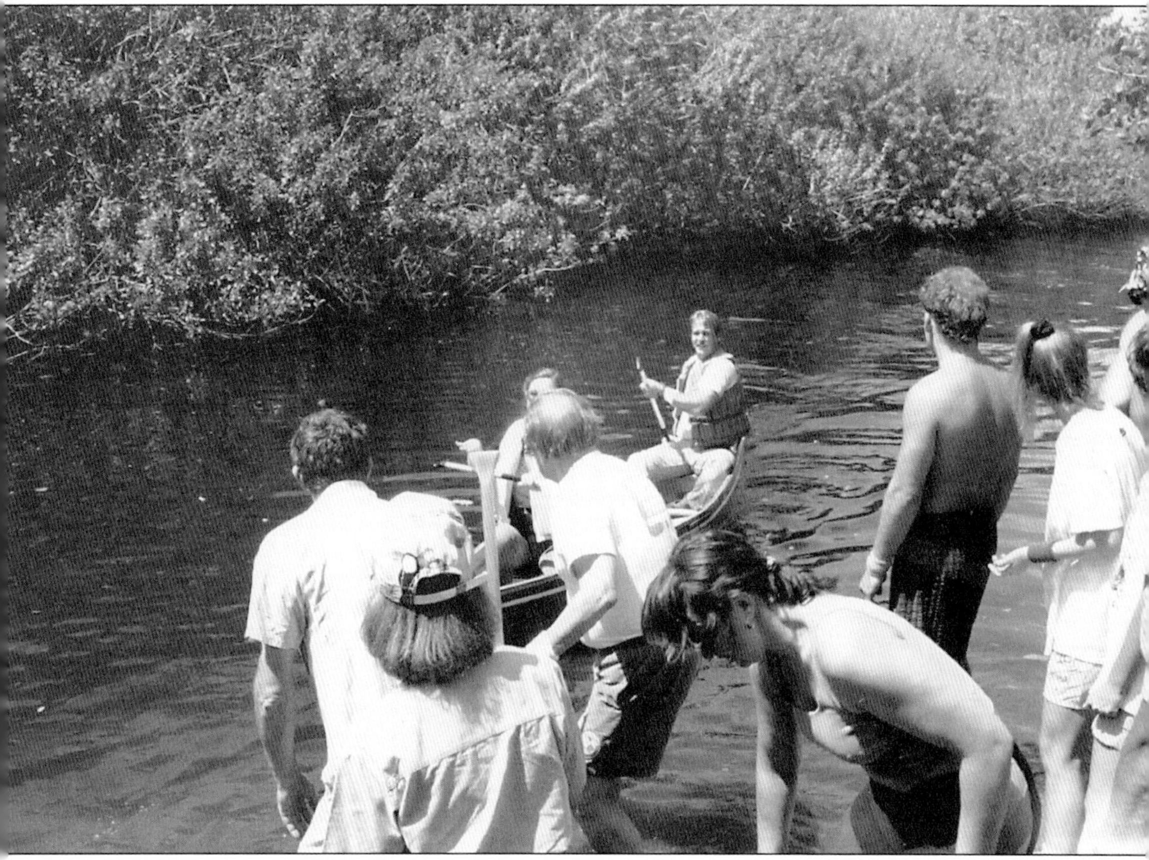

The Island City Canoe Race, in which teams of paddlers cover a 6-mile route to circumnavigate the city, got its start in 1992 and now is an official part of the city's birthday festivities. The race starts and finishes at the Colohatchee Natural Park boat ramp. (City of Wilton Manors.)

CITY OF WILTON MANORS
WILTON MANORS, FLORIDA

# Reflecting on Our Past, Building Our Future

1947 - 1997

DEDICATION OF
THE WILTON MANORS
"TOWERS" AND TIME CAPSULE

Mayor King Wilkinson
Vice Mayor Jack Seller
Council Member John Fiore
Council Member Gloria O'Gorman
Council Member Richard Pratt
City Manager Dr. Robert Levy
Assistant City Manager Daniel W. Keefe

Ron & Ann Lunsford Diane R. Cline
BuilderCoordinator

May 13, 1997
7:00 p.m.

"Reflecting on Our Past, Building Our Future" was the theme of the Island City 50th birthday celebration in May 1997, a nine-day bash with sports events, historical recognitions, a parade, birthday party and street dance, car show, stage and light show, reception, and time-capsule dedication. In short, the celebration provided something for everyone. (Wilton Manors Historical Society.)

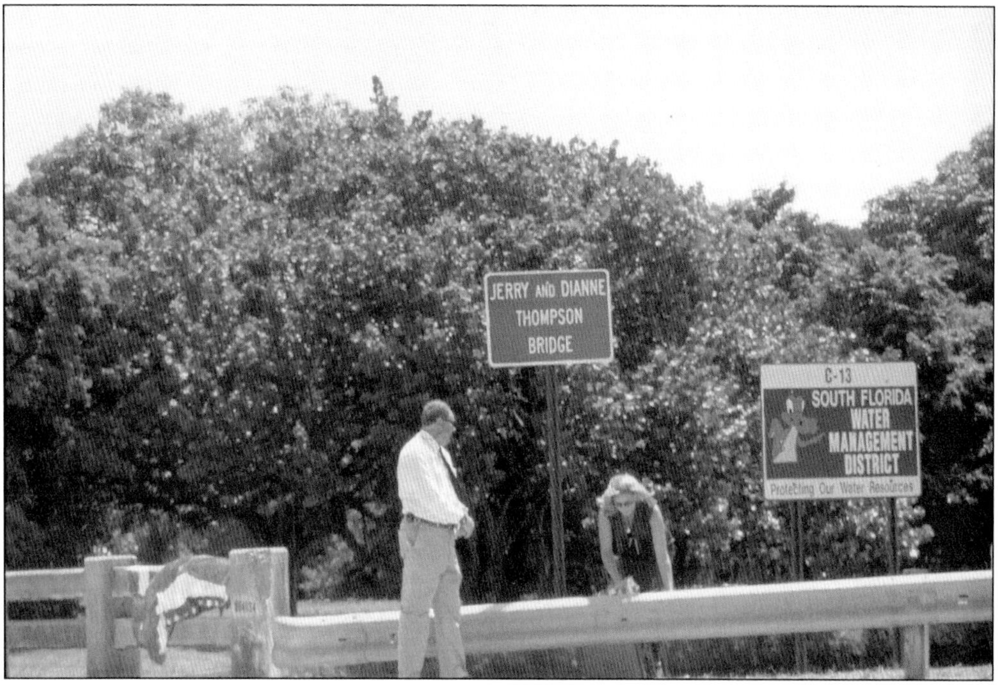


Assistant recreation director Becky Thacker and parks and recreation director Richard Rothe tidy up as they prepare for the dedication of the Jerry and Dianne Thompson Bridge on May 7, 1997. (City of Wilton Manors.)

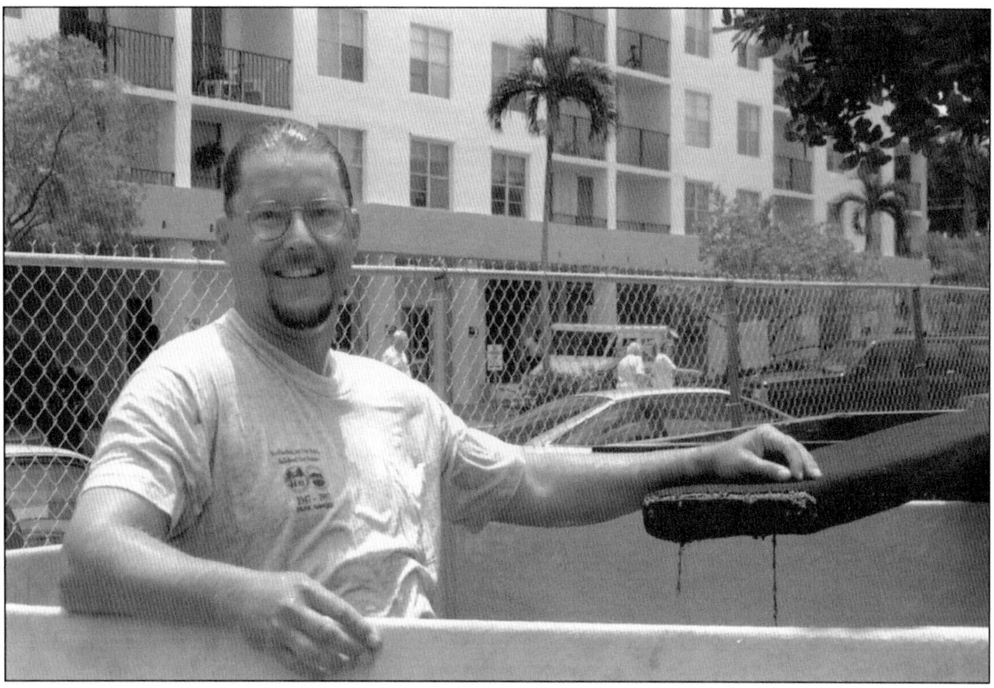

Assistant parks director Bill Wetzel got the chance to cool off as he worked in the dunk tank. (City of Wilton Manors.)

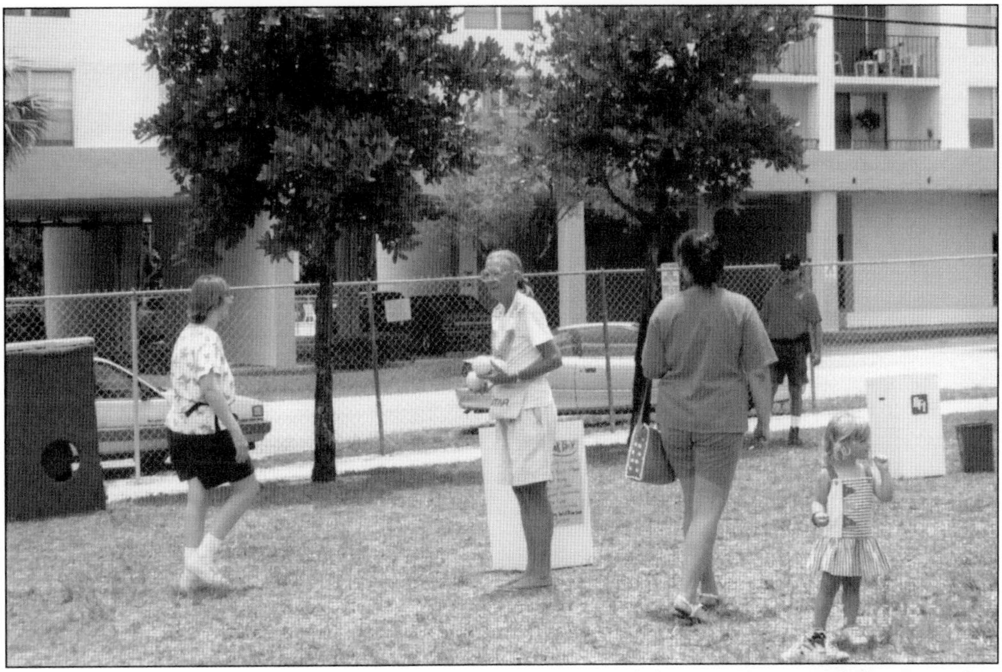

Diane Cline (center, facing left) served on the city council from 1982 to 1986, has served as president of Main Street and the Wilton Manors Historical Society, and has contributed in many other ways. Here, she rounds up throwers for the dunk tank. (City of Wilton Manors.)

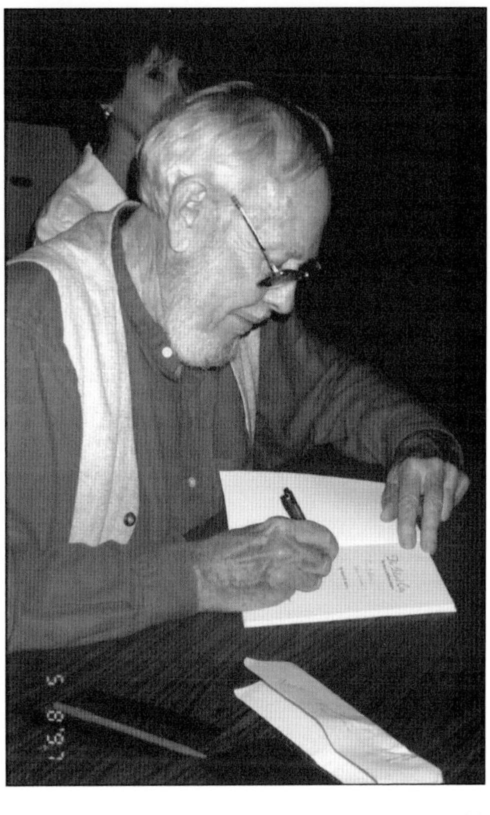

Historian and author Stuart McIver signs a copy of *The Island City: The Story of Wilton Manors*, which he wrote for the city's 50th birthday. (City of Wilton Manors.)

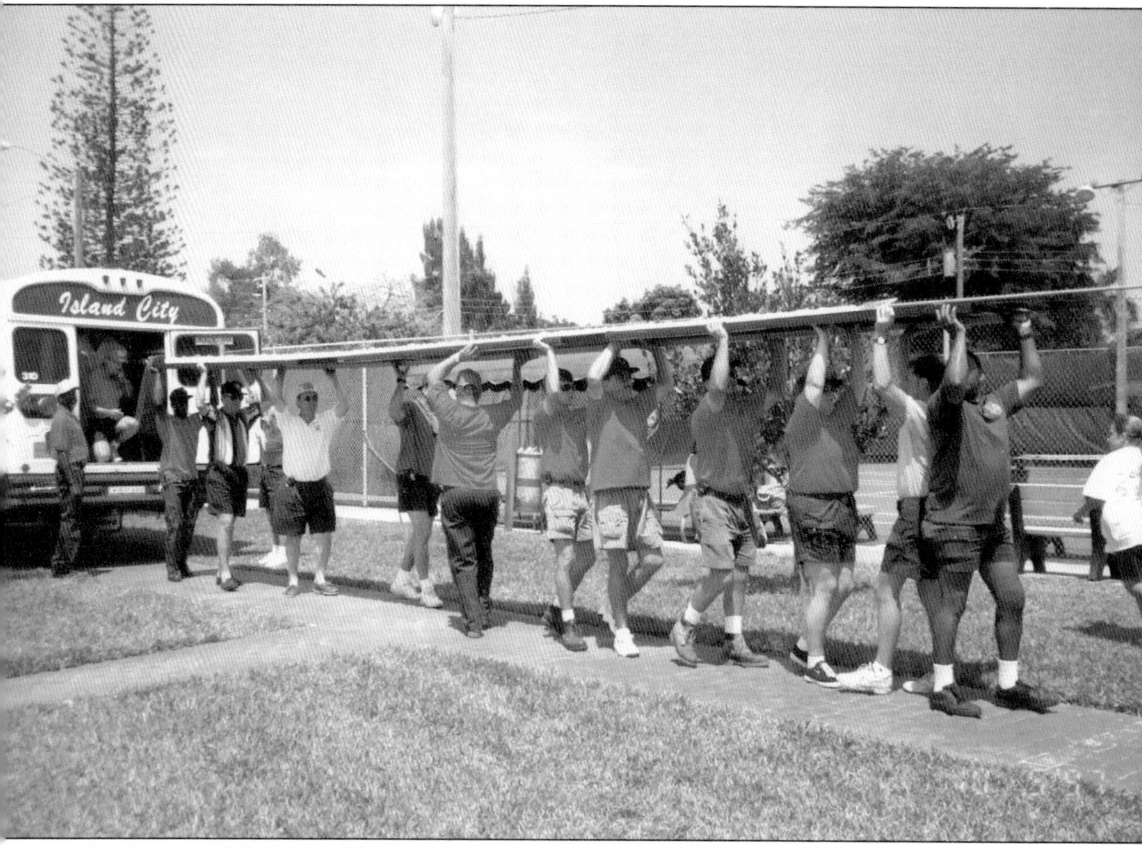


Workers carefully unload the city's 50-foot birthday cake, created by the Publix Market bakery at Five Points for the celebration. (City of Wilton Manors.)

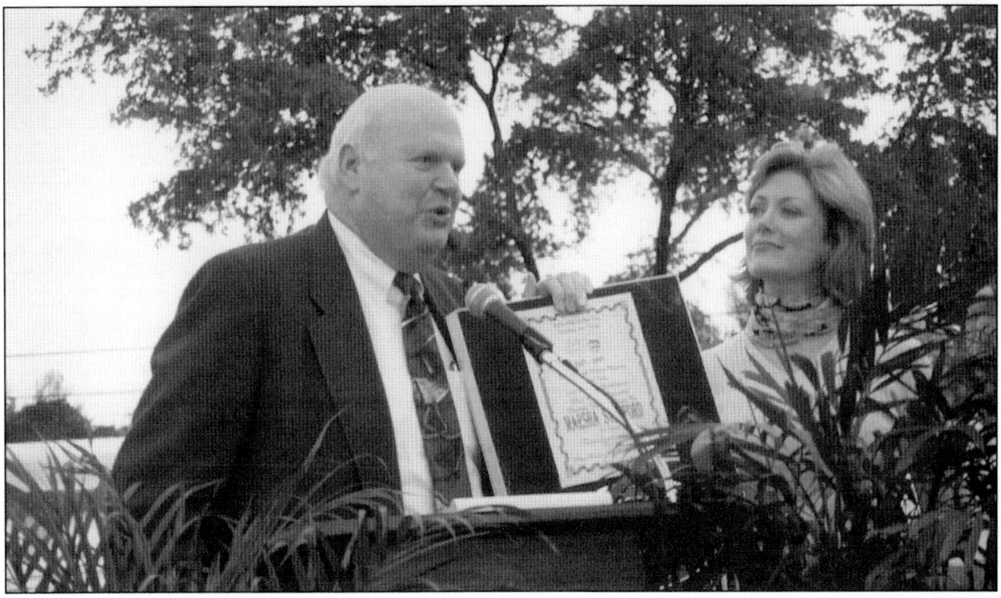

Tracy and Nancy Stafford accept an award on behalf of their mother, Marcia. Marcia Stafford stepped down from the city council in 1975, the year Tracy was elected to the council. He served as council member for six years and mayor for four before running for the Florida legislature. He served District 92 in the legislature for 10 years. (City of Wilton Manors.)

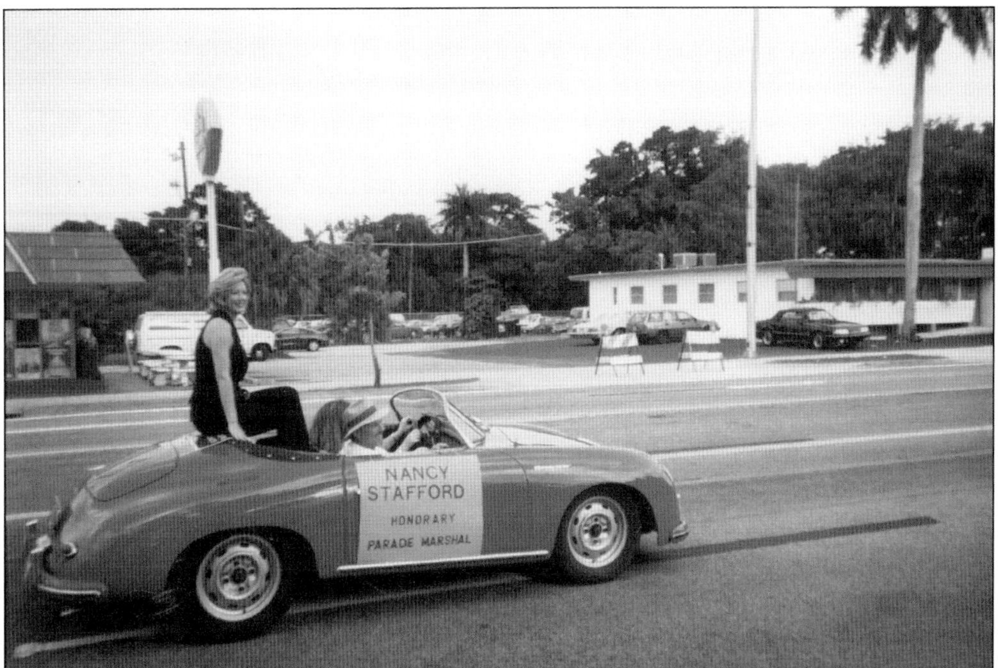


Nancy Stafford did double duty at the celebration, also serving as an honorary parade marshal. Although she and husband, Rev. Larry Myers, live in Southern California, Stafford still makes time to visit her childhood home a few times a year. (Marilyn Menchini.)

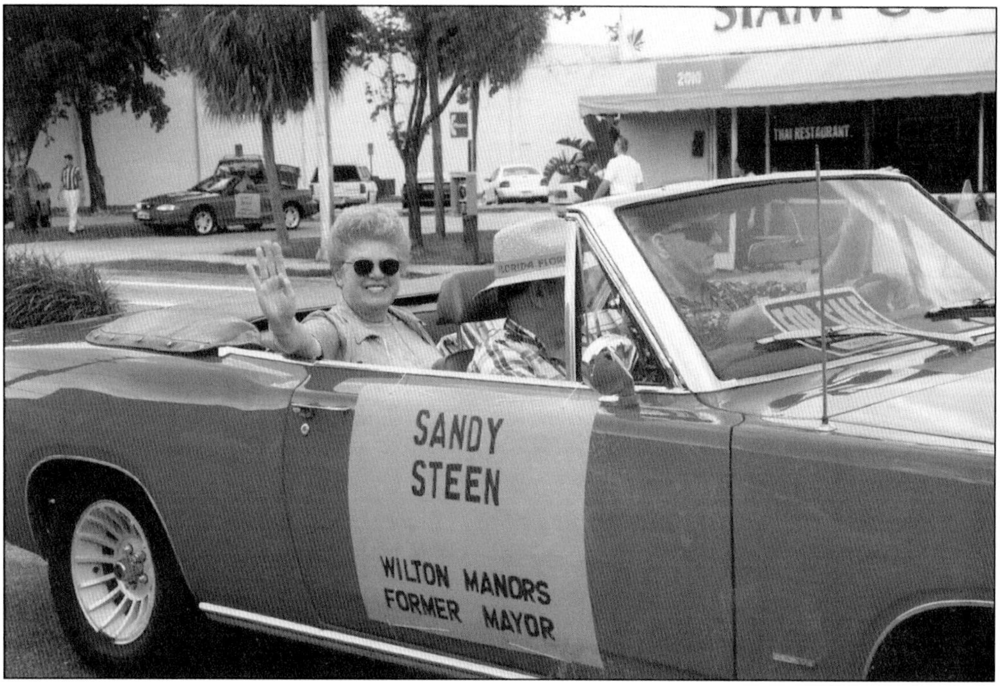


Sandy Jedlicka Steen served on the city council for 12 years and served four years as the city's first female mayor. She chaired the blue-ribbon committee for the 50th birthday celebration. (Michael Murphy.)

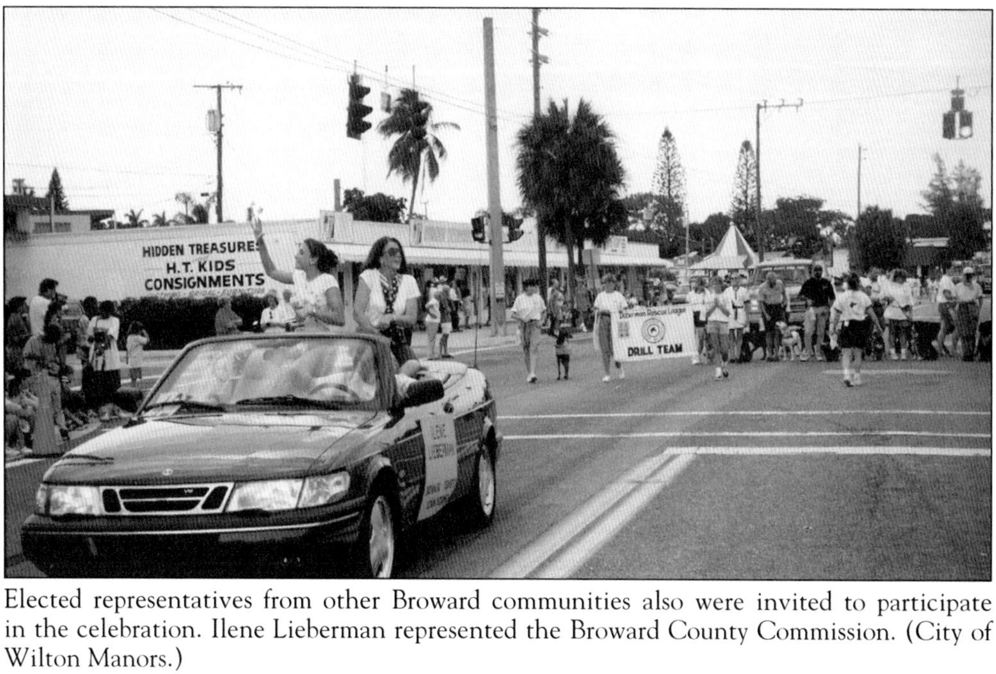


Elected representatives from other Broward communities also were invited to participate in the celebration. Ilene Lieberman represented the Broward County Commission. (City of Wilton Manors.)

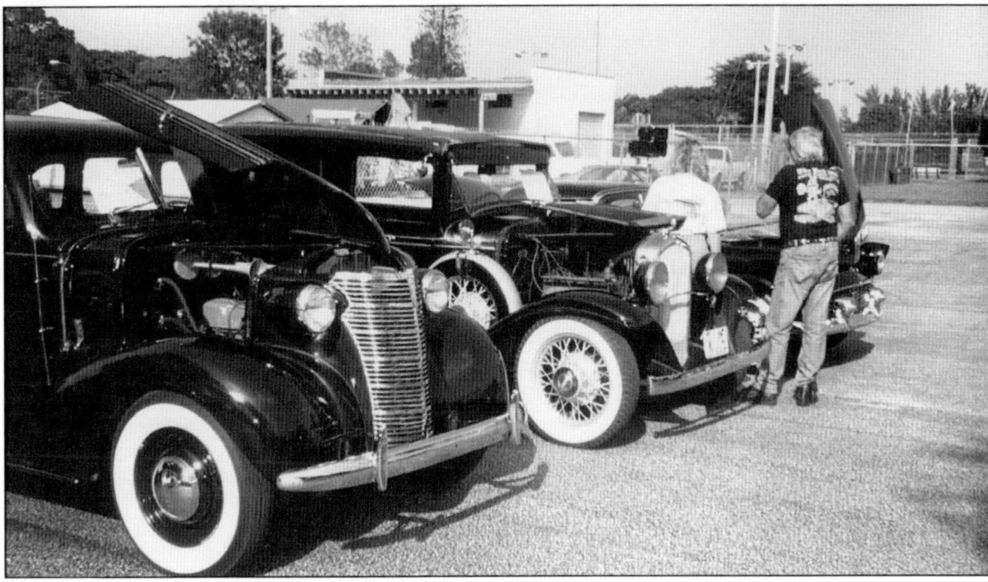

A vintage car show at the Hagen Park parking lot caught the eyes of many of the birthday celebrants. (City of Wilton Manors.)

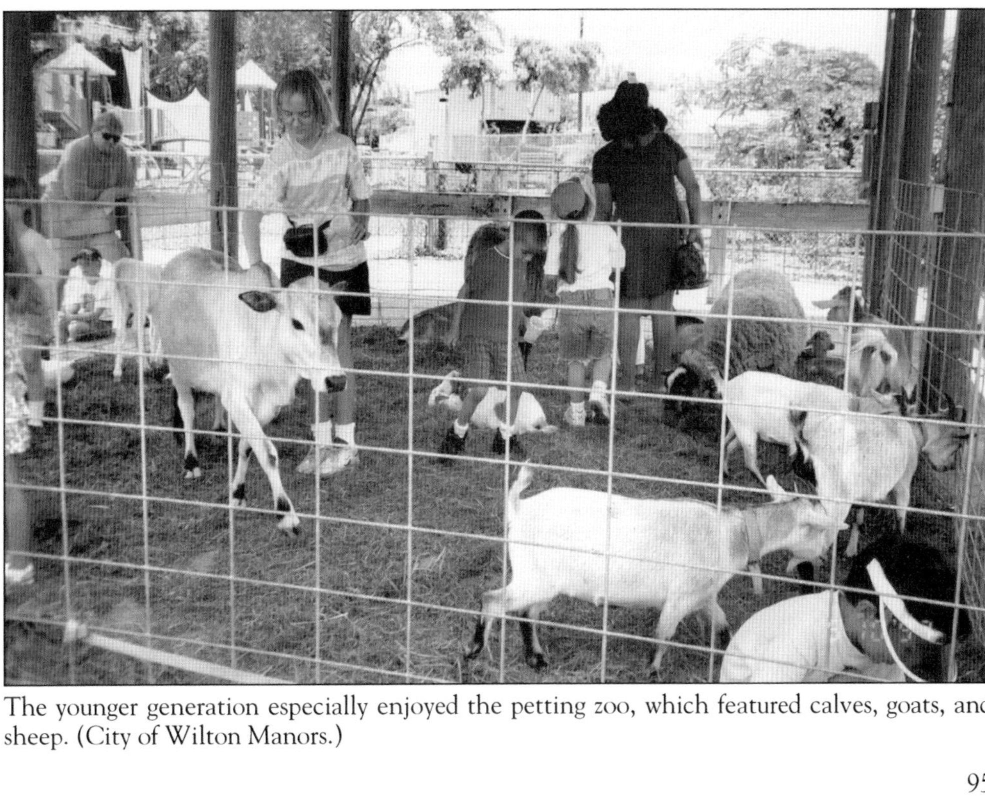

The younger generation especially enjoyed the petting zoo, which featured calves, goats, and sheep. (City of Wilton Manors.)

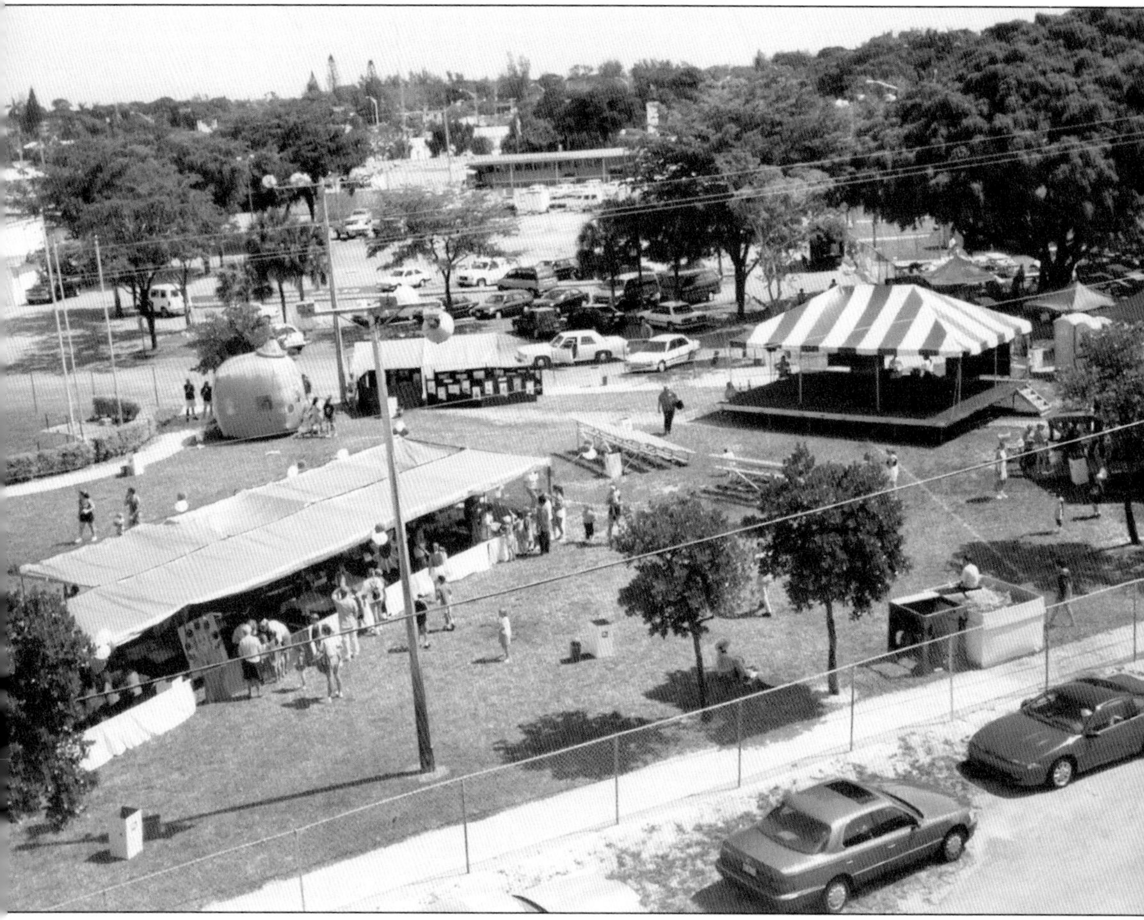

A picture shot from Wilton Towers apartments shows some of the activities on the Children's Day in the Park, part of the 50th birthday celebration on May 10, 1997. (Marilyn Menchini.)

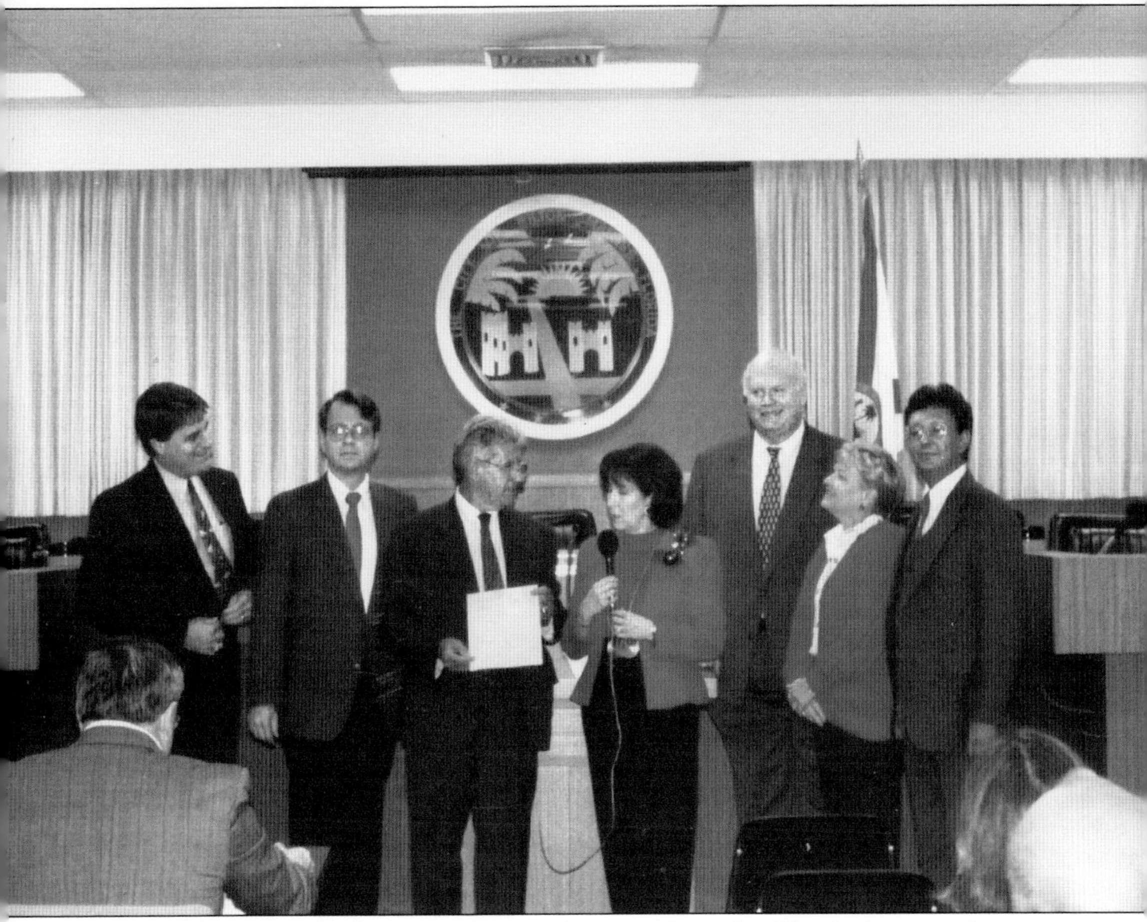

Debby Sanderson, with the microphone, who served in the Florida house and senate for a combined 20 years, brings birthday wishes from Tallahassee, along with native son Rep. Tracy Stafford, who stands behind Sanderson's left shoulder. Also pictured from left to right are council members Jack Seiler and Richard Pratt, along with Mayor King Wilkinson. To Sanderson's left are council members Gloria O'Gorman and John Fiore. (City of Wilton Manors.)

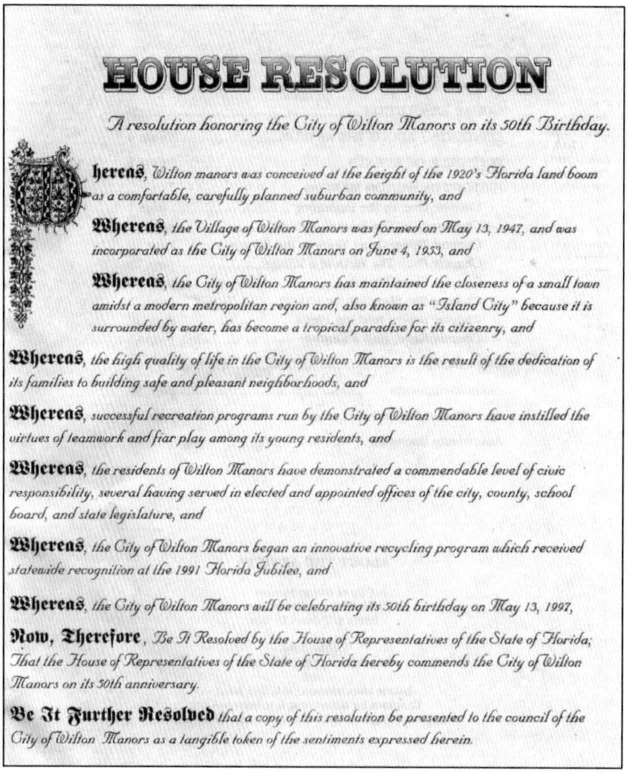

# HOUSE RESOLUTION

*A resolution honoring the City of Wilton Manors on its 50th Birthday.*

**Whereas**, *Wilton manors was conceived at the height of the 1920's Florida land boom as a comfortable, carefully planned suburban community, and*

**Whereas**, *the Village of Wilton Manors was formed on May 13, 1947, and was incorporated as the City of Wilton Manors on June 4, 1953, and*

**Whereas**, *the City of Wilton Manors has maintained the closeness of a small town amidst a modern metropolitan region and, also known as "Island City" because it is surrounded by water, has become a tropical paradise for its citizenry, and*

**Whereas**, *the high quality of life in the City of Wilton Manors is the result of the dedication of its families to building safe and pleasant neighborhoods, and*

**Whereas**, *successful recreation programs run by the City of Wilton Manors have instilled the virtues of teamwork and fiar play among its young residents, and*

**Whereas**, *the residents of Wilton Manors have demonstrated a commendable level of civic responsibility, several having served in elected and appointed offices of the city, county, school board, and state legislature, and*

**Whereas**, *the City of Wilton Manors began an innovative recycling program which received statewide recognition at the 1991 Florida Jubilee, and*

**Whereas**, *the City of Wilton Manors will be celebrating its 50th birthday on May 13, 1997,*

**Now, Therefore**, *Be It Resolved by the House of Representatives of the State of Florida; That the House of Representatives of the State of Florida hereby commends the City of Wilton Manors on its 50th anniversary.*

**Be It Further Resolved** *that a copy of this resolution be presented to the council of the City of Wilton Manors as a tangible token of the sentiments expressed herein.*

The Florida House of Representatives commemorated the 50th birthday celebration with a resolution. (City of Wilton Manors.)

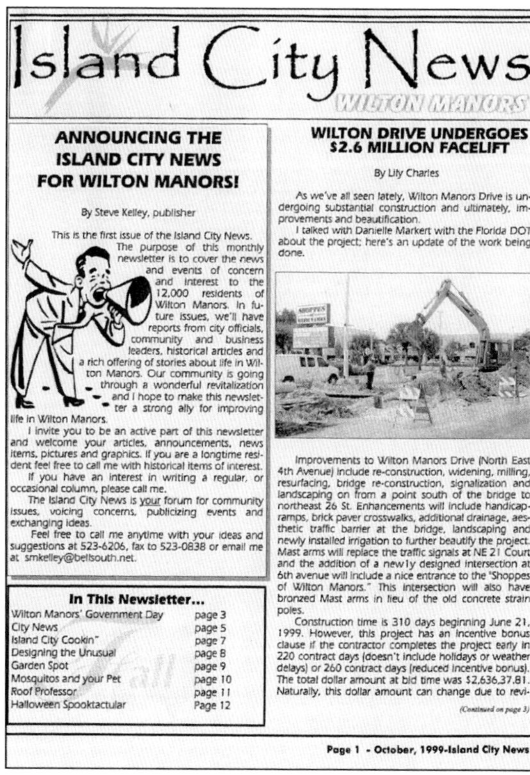

# Island City News

WILTON MANORS

## ANNOUNCING THE ISLAND CITY NEWS FOR WILTON MANORS!

By Steve Kelley, publisher

This is the first issue of the Island City News. The purpose of this monthly newsletter is to cover the news and events of concern and interest to the 12,000 residents of Wilton Manors. In future issues, we'll have reports from city officials, community and business leaders, historical articles and a rich offering of stories about life in Wilton Manors. Our community is going through a wonderful revitalization and I hope to make this newsletter a strong ally for improving life in Wilton Manors.

I invite you to be an active part of this newsletter and welcome your articles, announcements, news items, pictures and graphics. If you are a longtime resident feel free to call me with historical items of interest.

If you have an interest in writing a regular, or occasional column, please call me.

The Island City News is your forum for community issues, voicing concerns, publicizing events and exchanging ideas.

Feel free to call me anytime with your ideas and suggestions at 523-6206, fax to 523-0838 or email me at smkelley@bellsouth.net.

**In This Newsletter...**



## WILTON DRIVE UNDERGOES $2.6 MILLION FACELIFT

By Lily Charles

As we've all seen lately, Wilton Manors Drive is undergoing substantial construction and ultimately, improvements and beautification.

I talked with Danielle Markert with the Florida DOT about the project; here's an update of the work being done.

Improvements to Wilton Manors Drive (North East 4th Avenue) include re-construction, widening, milling, resurfacing, bridge re-construction, signalization and landscaping on from a point south of the bridge to northeast 26 St. Enhancements will include handicap-ramps, brick paver crosswalks, additional drainage, aesthetic traffic barrier at the bridge, landscaping and newly installed irrigation to further beautify the project. Mast arms will replace the traffic signals at NE 21 Court and the addition of a new1y designed intersection at 6th avenue will include a nice entrance to the "Shoppes of Wilton Manors." This intersection will also have bronzed Mast arms in lieu of the old concrete strain poles.

Construction time is 310 days beginning June 21, 1999. However, this project has an incentive bonus clause if the contractor completes the project early in 220 contract days (doesn't include holidays or weather delays) or 260 contract days (reduced incentive bonus). The total dollar amount at bid time was $2,636,37.81. Naturally, this dollar amount can change due to revi-

(Continued on page 3)

Page 1 - October, 1999-Island City News

In October 1999, Steve Kelley, publisher of several neighborhood newsletters, began publishing the *Island City News*, again giving the city a publication to call its own. (Steve Kelley.)

*Eight*

# A Municipal Renaissance (2000–2005)

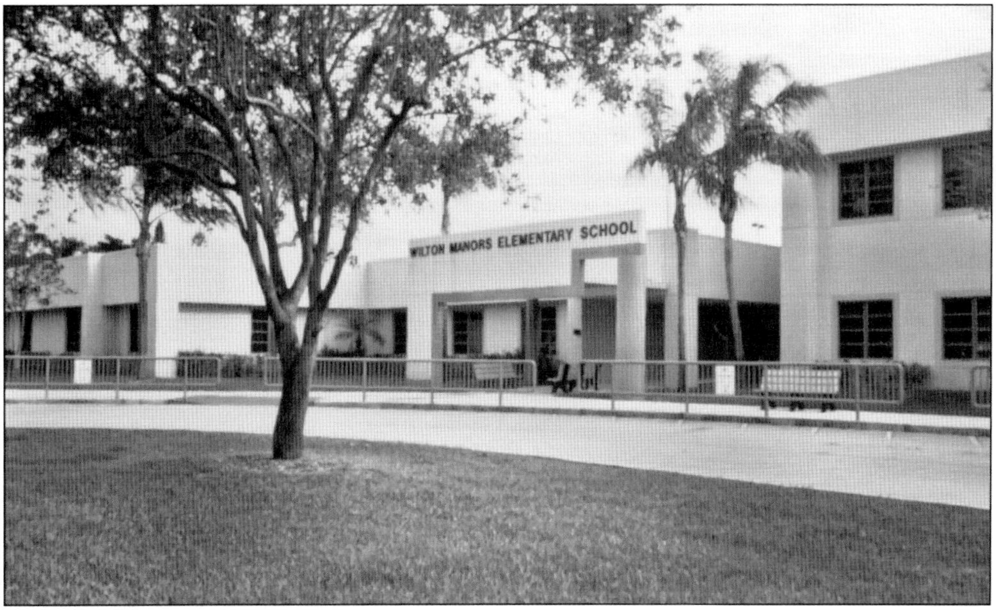


After more than 50 years of service to the community, Wilton Manors Elementary School earned a makeover, but a series of misfortunes dragged the reconstruction of the school out for seven years. The 50th anniversary celebration and rededication of the school was held on March 22, 2002.

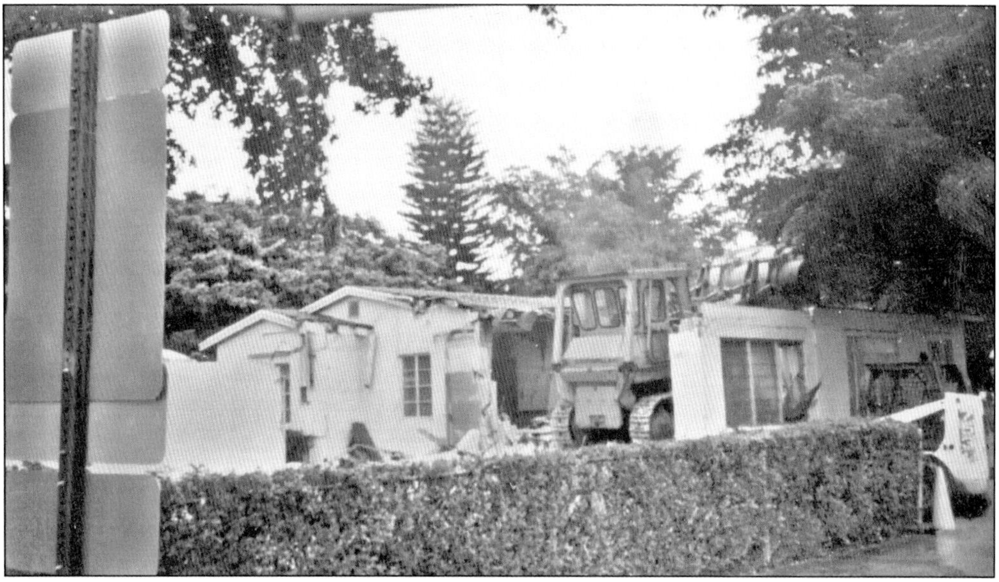

The Wilton Manors Public Library broke ground for its new home on December 29, 2001. To facilitate that expansion, a house behind the building was demolished. That is usually not a formidable undertaking, except that the property also was the home of a thick-walled nuclear fallout shelter built during the Kennedy administration. (Wilton Manors Public Library.)

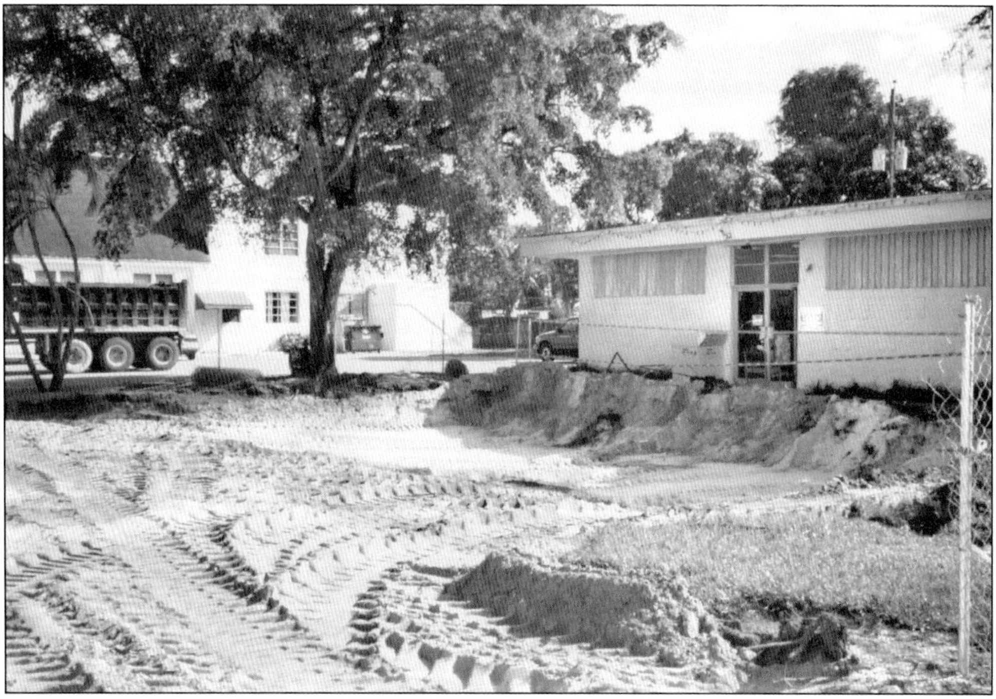

Site clearance work preceded demolition of the old library building. To keep the library functional during construction, books and other materials were moved to a trailer on the other side of Covenant Presbyterian Church. (Wilton Manors Public Library.)

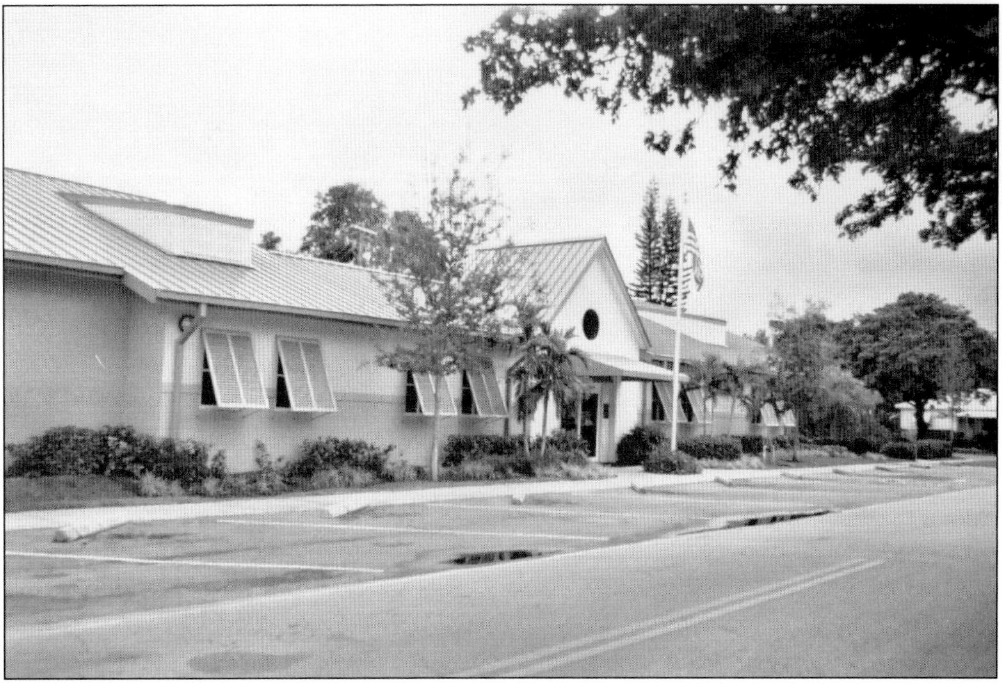

After the shell of the new building was completed, workers moved the books back and shelved them again. The new library was dedicated and opened on March 14, 2003.

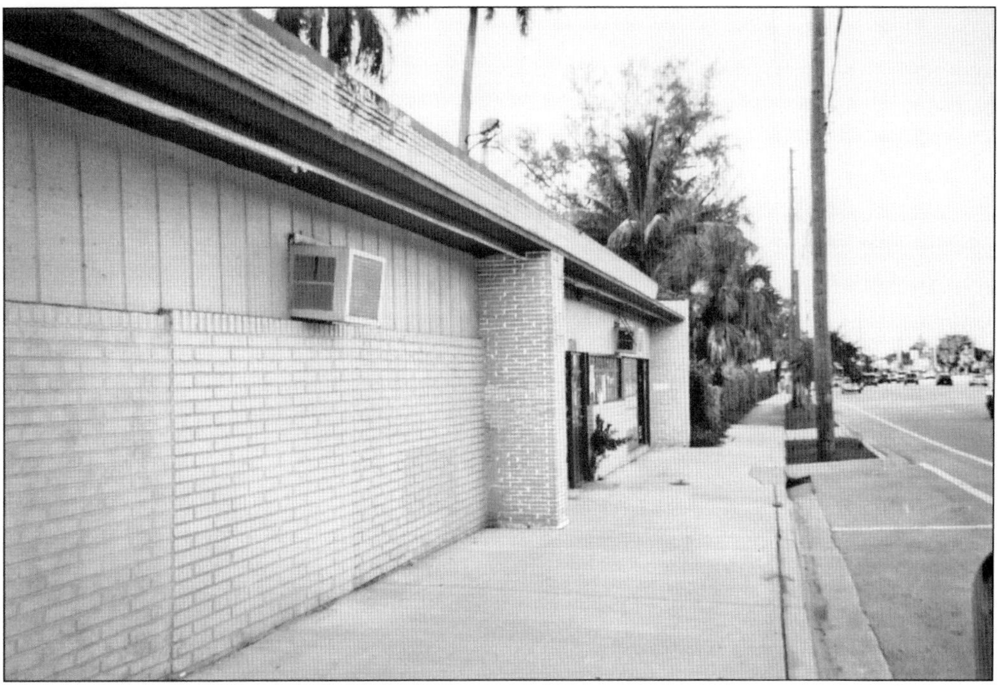

The city's acquisition of the Richardson family estate on July 9, 2002, brought it a historical and recreational treasure but a challenge as well. One of the first tasks was removal of an old commercial building along Wilton Drive. Over the years, the building had served as home to a religious bookstore, an attorney's office, and a real estate company, among others.

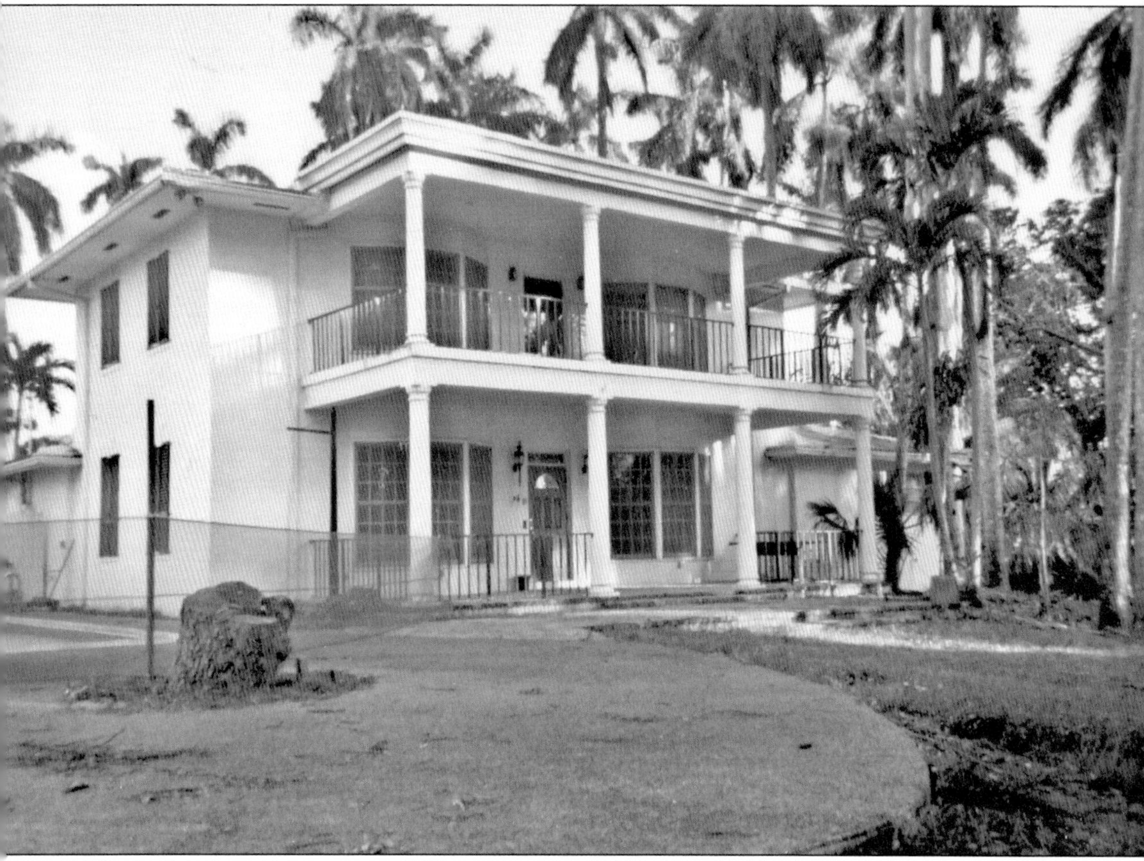

The Richardson estate, acquired for use as a park and historical center, begins its metamorphosis. The family home, built in 1938, will be used for a variety of purposes. The $3.85 million cost of the estate and its 4.5 acres of land came from a unique funding arrangement by the Broward County Commission, Florida Communities Trust, and city funds from a 1998 parks bond fund.

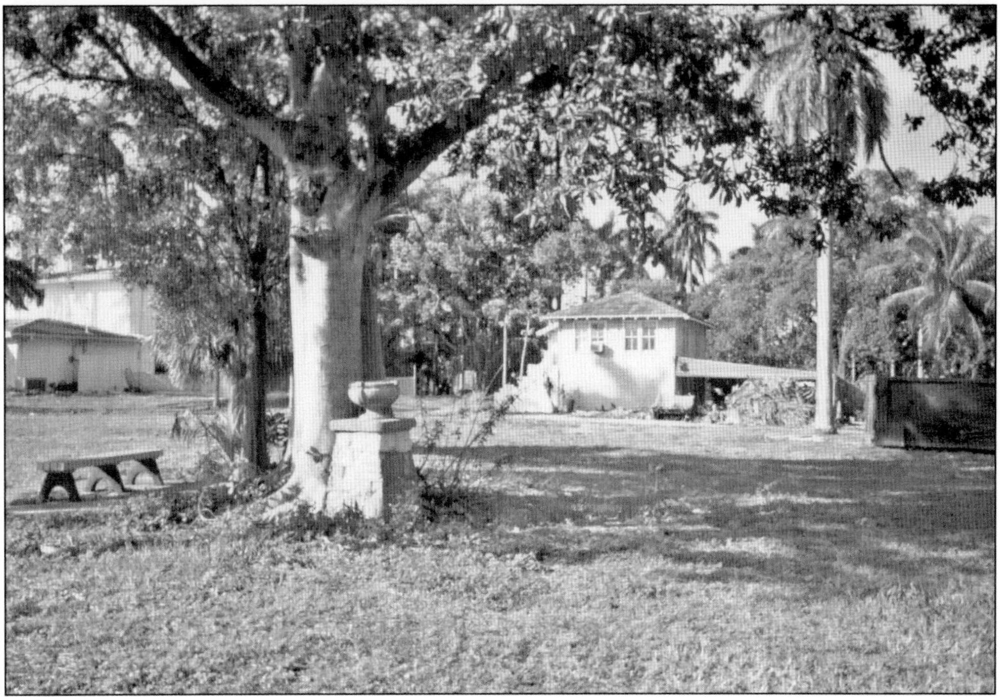

The Wilton Manors Historical Society has particular interest in restoring the 1925 vernacular carriage house, the oldest building on the property and the one with the most historic appeal, although the building is in severe disrepair.

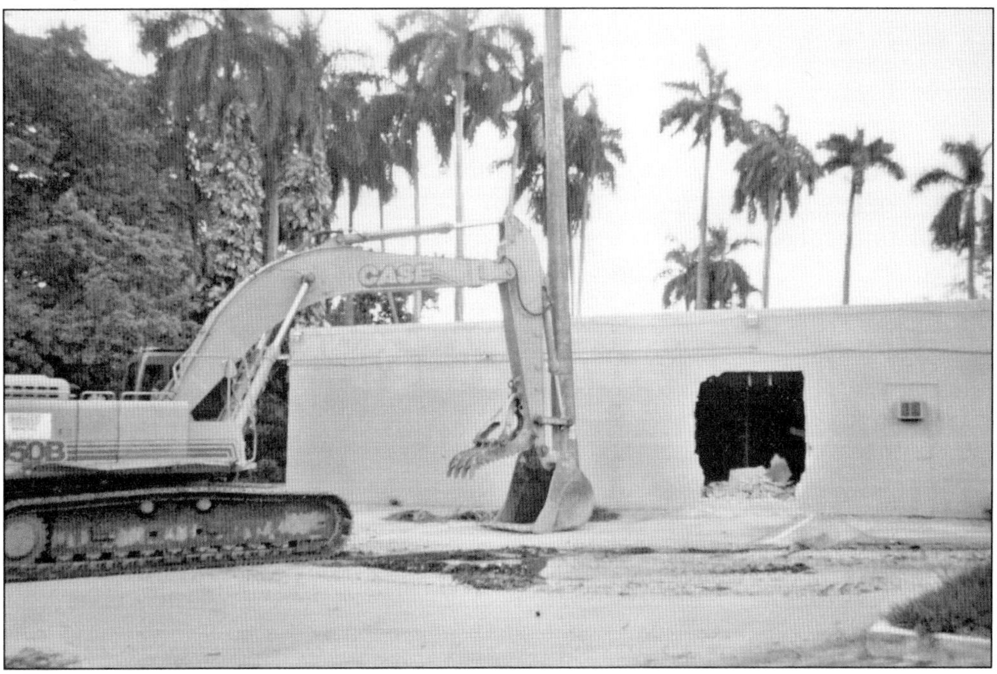


Demolition crews reduced the commercial buildings on the property quickly and efficiently. Later, an archaeological study undertaken along the waterway nearby confirmed the site possessed bones, pottery fragments, and other artifacts of interest.

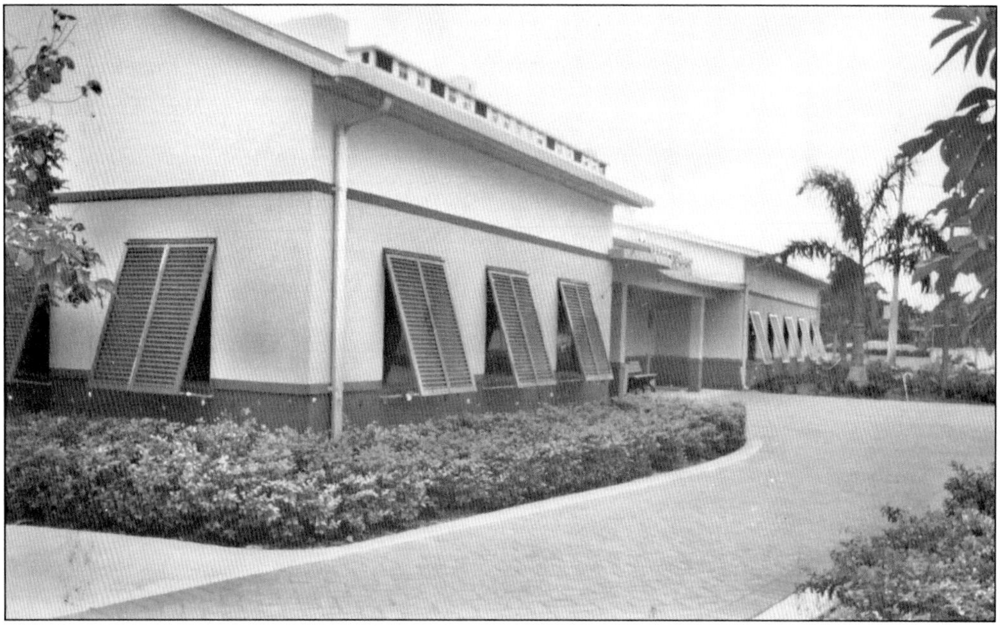

Guests entering the Hagen Park rededication on November 21, 2003, were given a tiny votive candle in a glass holder, in keeping with the event's theme of "Lighting the Way to a Better and Brighter Future." Hagen Park's renovations started on July 12, 2002.

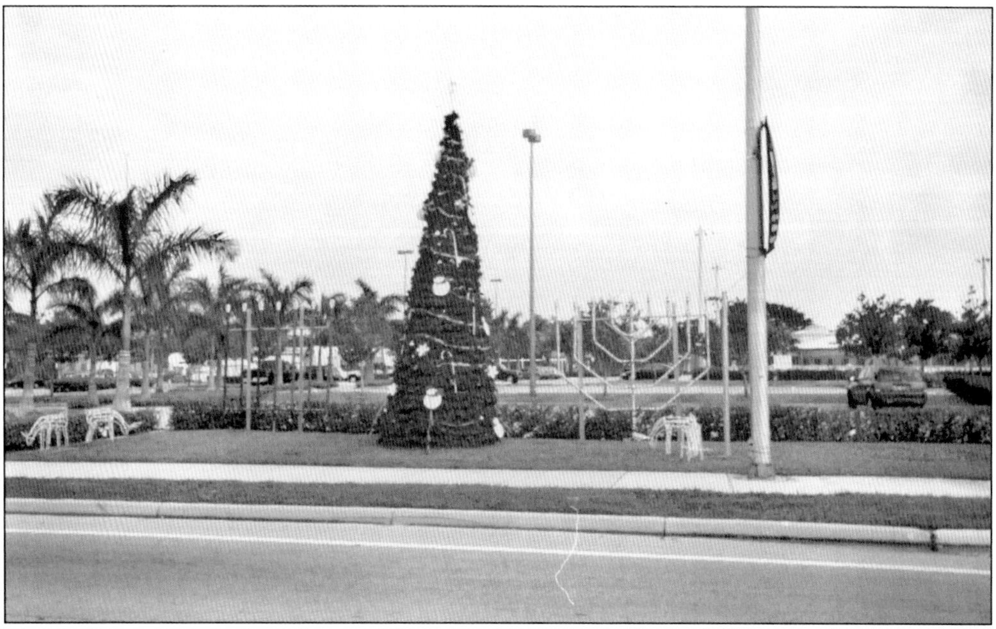

The holiday display, featuring a Christmas tree, menorah, and Kwanzaa kinara, erected along Wilton Drive, is a reminder of the city's diversity. The land on which it is placed was formerly occupied by a Food Fair market. After the market closed, Broward County used it for administrative offices. After the county left, the city had planned to make it the Island City Arts Center and use it for the performing and visual arts. Instead, the land was used for the Hagen Park expansion, particularly the street hockey rink, and for much needed parking in the downtown area.

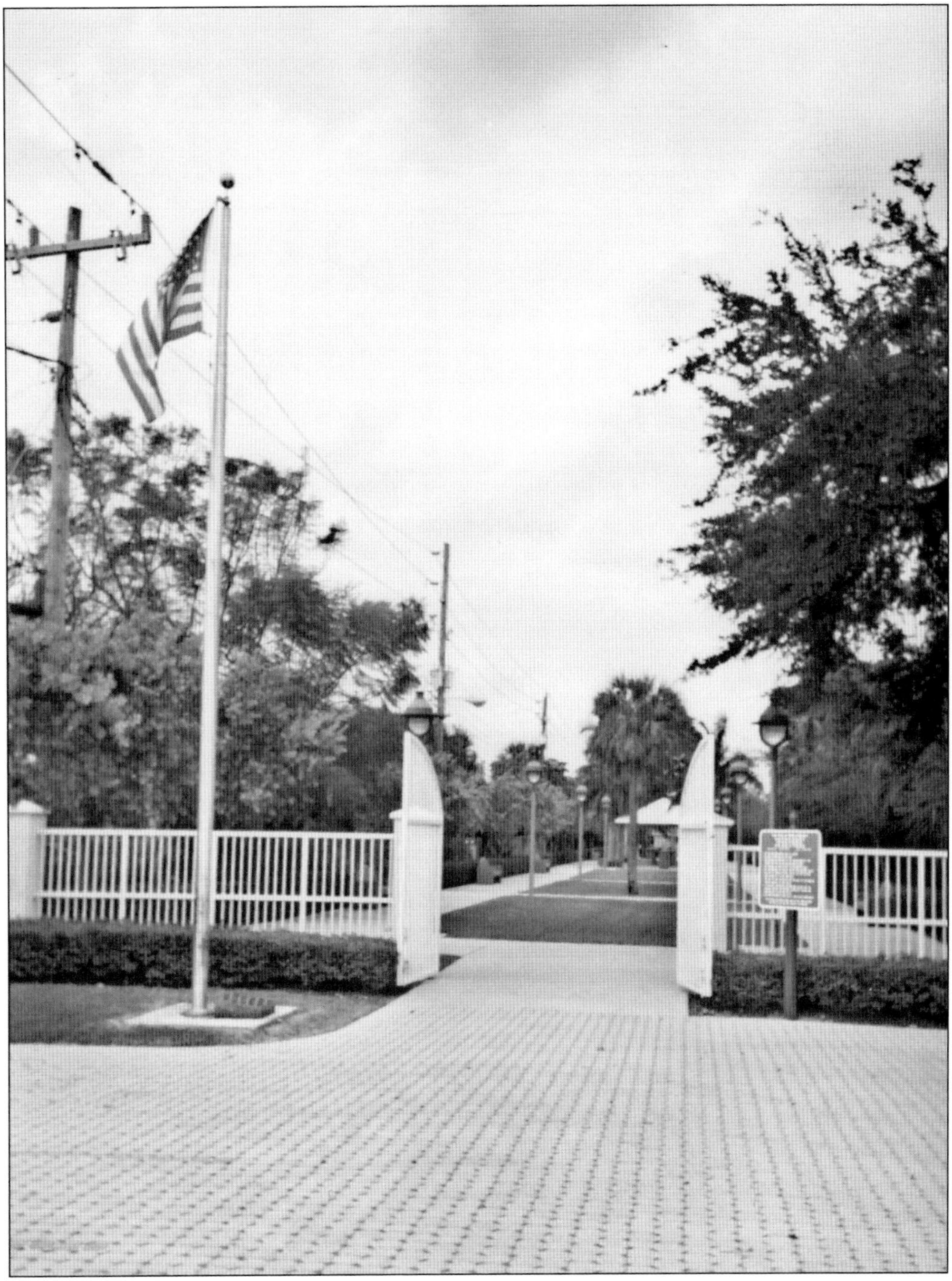

Donn Eisele Park, dedicated in 2000, is a .9-acre linear park that offers a picnic shelter, benches, and a dock on the north fork of the Middle River.

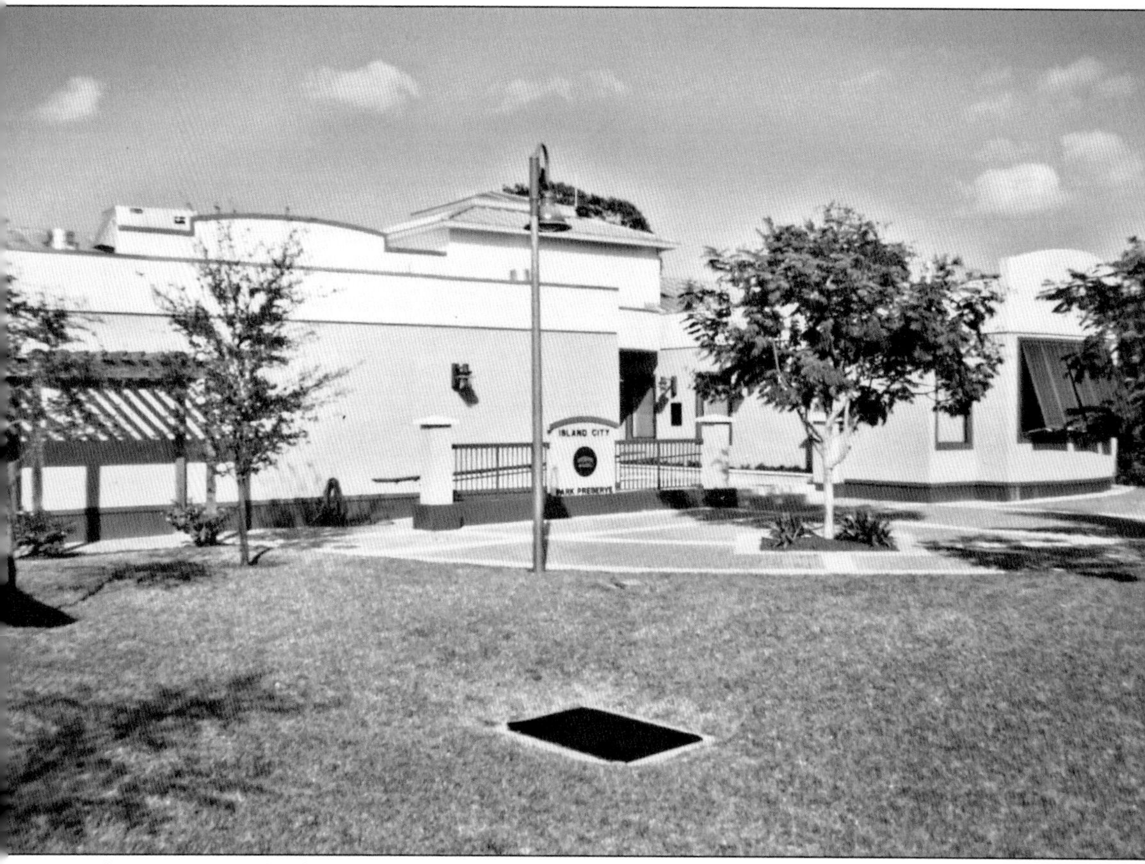


The 3.15-acre Island City Park Preserve, dedicated on September 29, 2003, is adjacent to Kiwanis Park and provides a recreational facility for Highland Estates residents that celebrates the Island City's beautiful waterways.

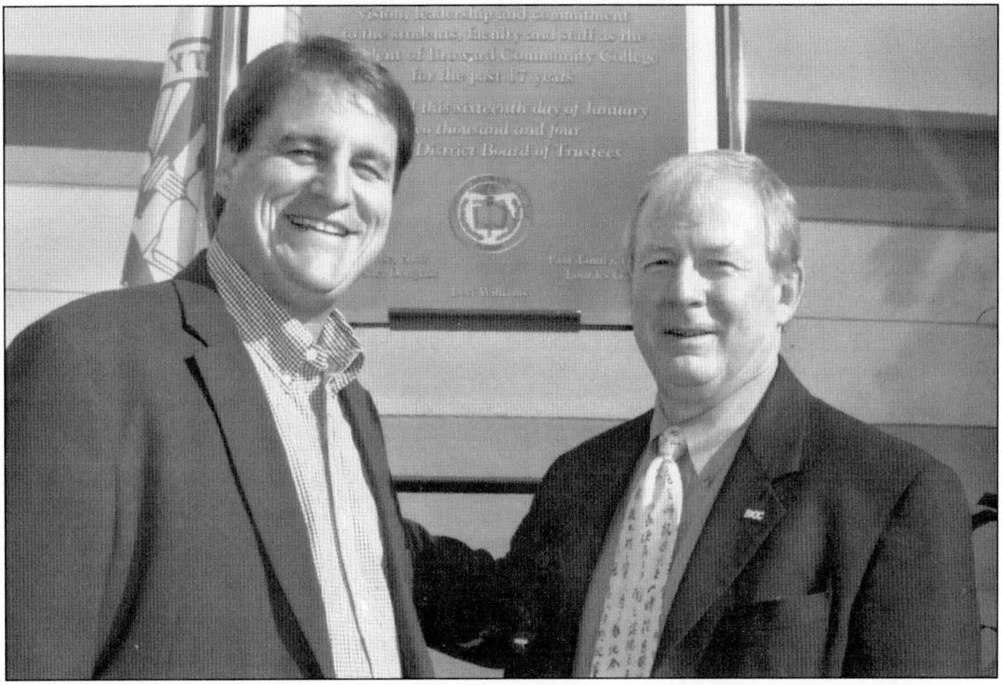

Rep. Jack Seiler and Broward Community College president Will Holcombe are all smiles at Holcombe's retirement party in 2003. (Broward Community College.)

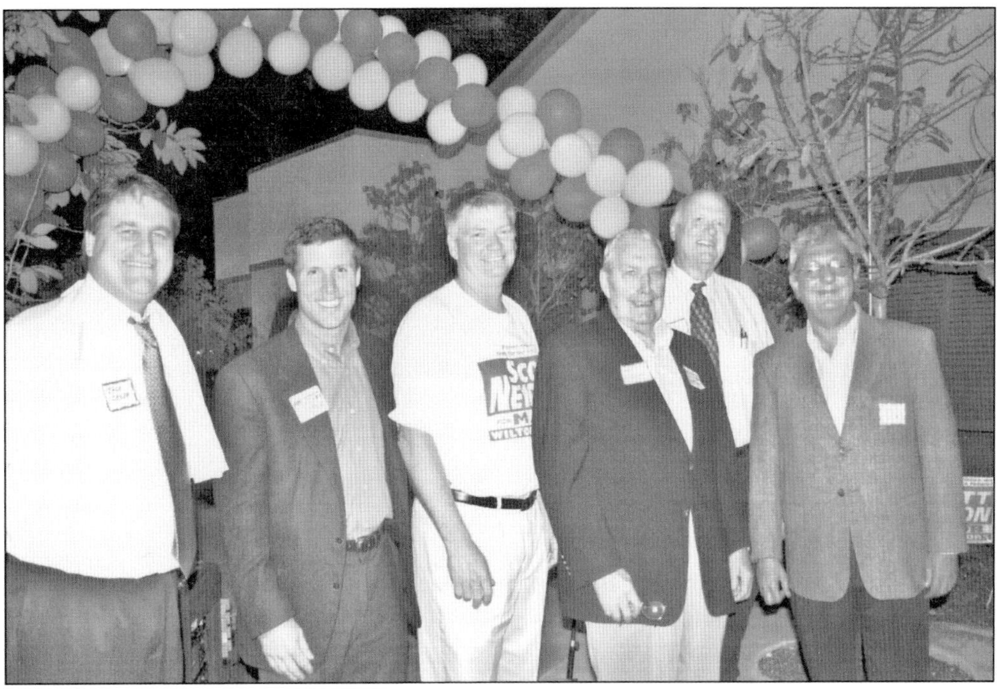

A group of the Island City's mayors posed for a picture at a 2003 event. From left to right are Jack Seiler, Jim Stork, Scott Newton (who was running for the post at the time of the picture), Arthur Welling, Tracy Stafford, and John Fiore. (Poco French.)

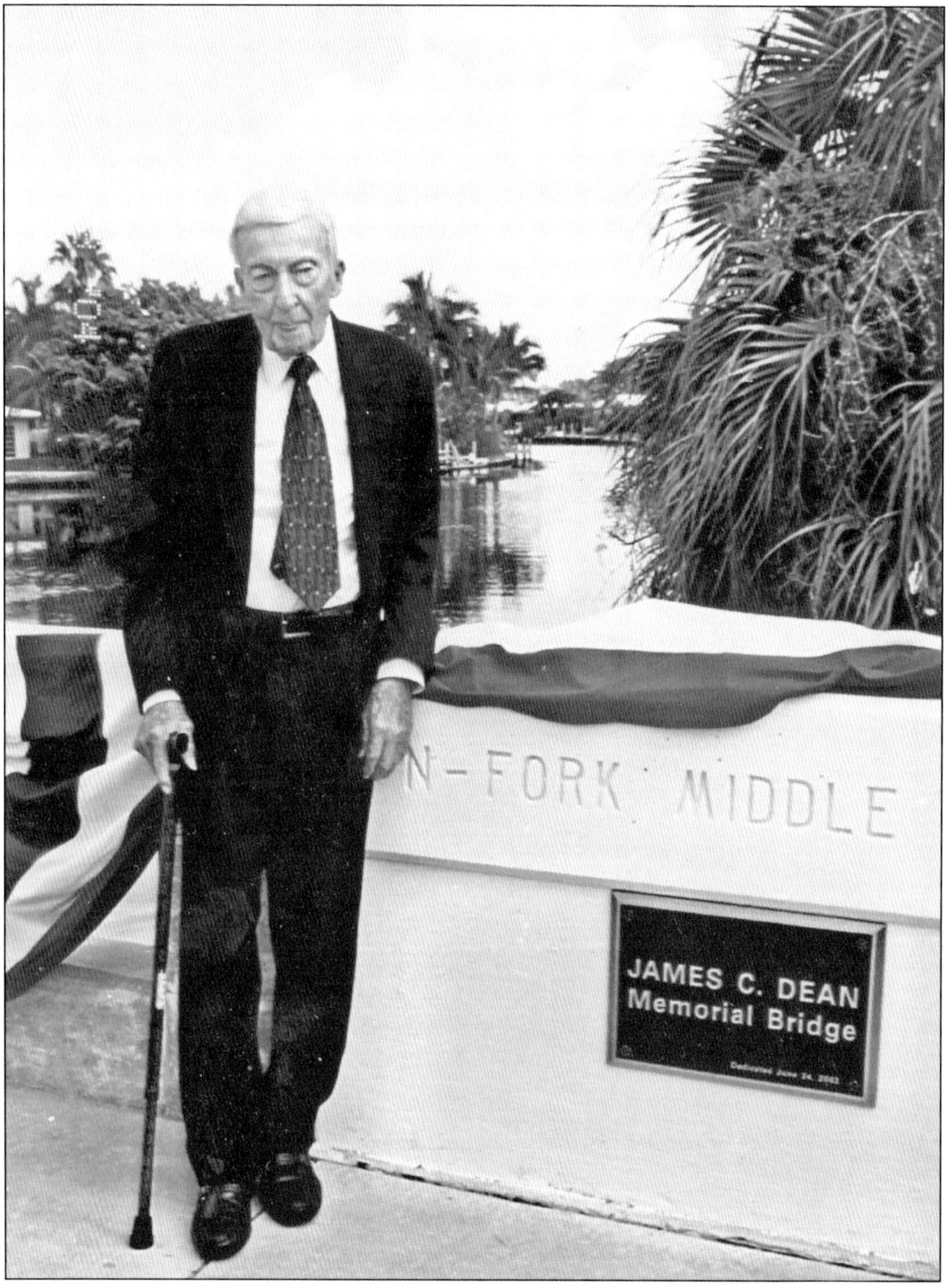


Pioneer James Dean stands beside the plaque honoring him on Northeast Twenty-sixth Street near Federal Highway at the north fork of the Middle River. A group of men—Dean, a principal in the Middle River Estates development, Dave Turner, Bob Roberts, Coral Ridge Properties developers Joseph Taravella and James Hunt (who were developing Coral Point), and Coral Gardens developers Joe Schmitt and Charles Dalton—financed plans to build a $20,000 bridge over the north fork of the Middle River to extend Northeast Twenty-sixth Street to meet Federal Highway. More than 2,000 people turned out when the bridge was dedicated on December 20, 1952. Fifty-two years later, in August 2004, the bridge was named in Mr. Dean's honor. (Sharon Kerwick.)

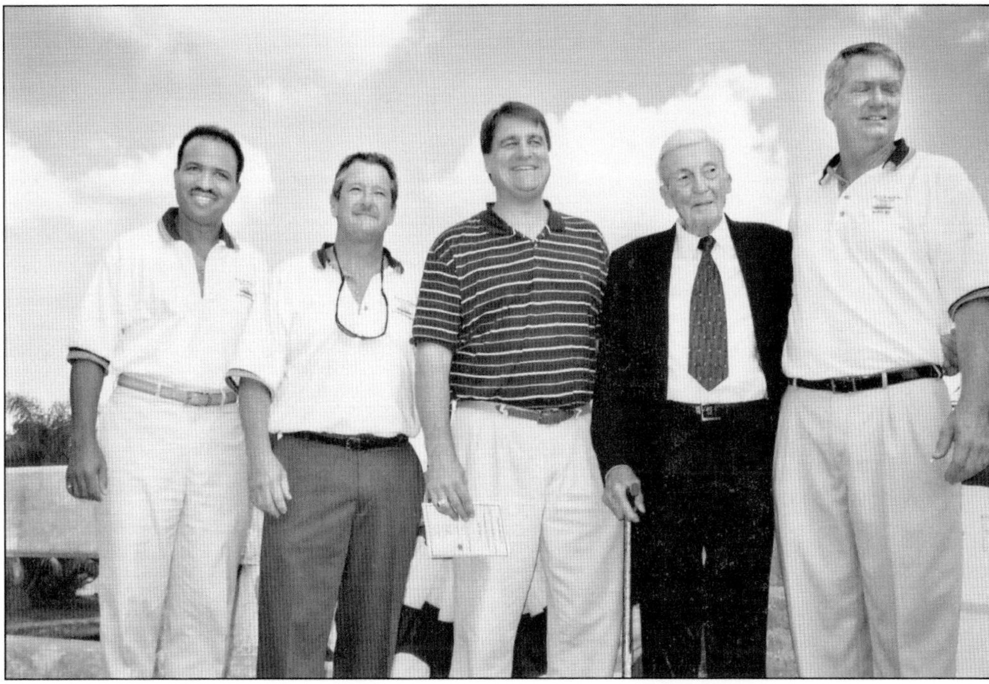

The dedication ceremonies for the James C. Dean Memorial Bridge did not draw 2,000 spectators as the original event did, but it was well-attended nonetheless. From left, commissioner Joe Angelos, commissioner Ted Galatis, state representative and former mayor Jack Seiler, James Dean, and Mayor Scott Newton are all smiles at the event. (Hope Gallegos.)

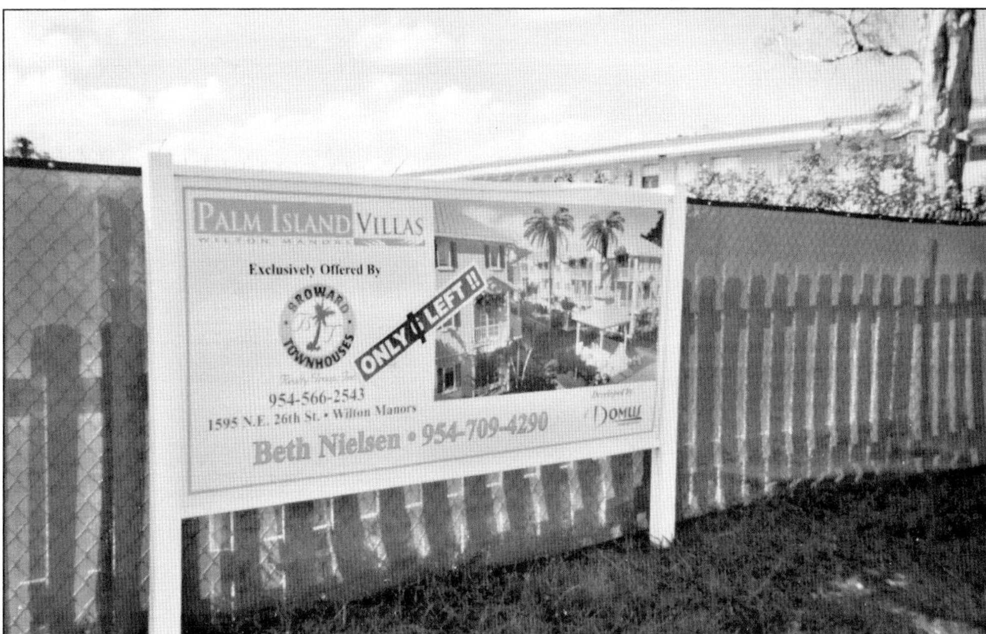


By 2004, the signs of the times in the Island City were not stop signs, but rather construction signs. By 1997, the city's 50th birthday, the city was 99 percent built out, requiring builders to "bash and build."

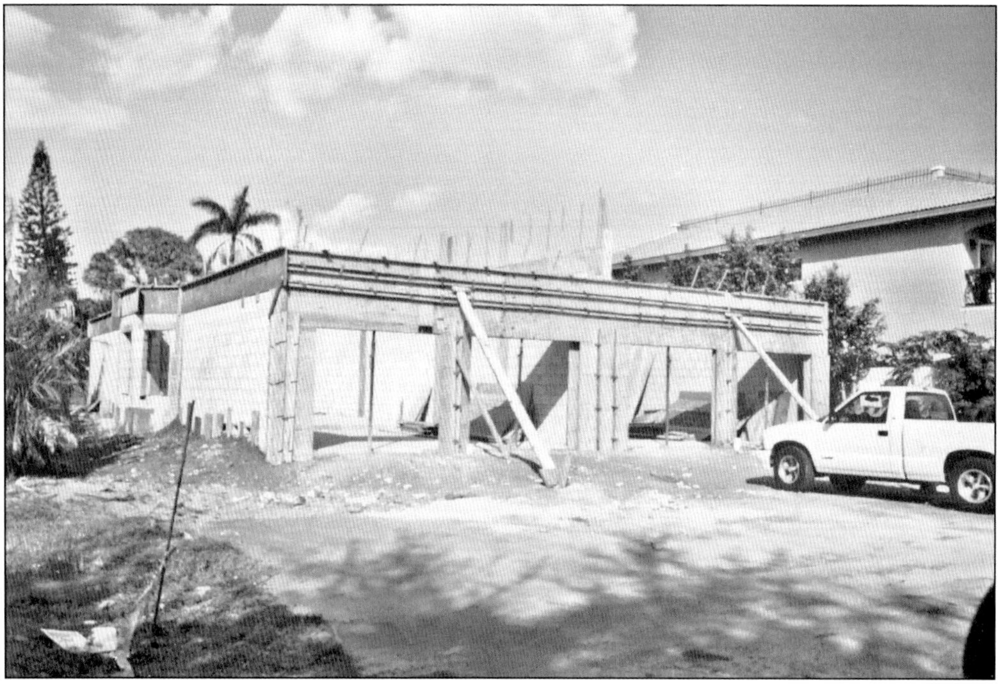

This townhouse is being constructed on property formerly occupied by chicken coops. Early developer John P. Pedersen built them during World War II because he could obtain lumber for the coops, but not for building apartments. After the war, the chickens were evicted and the buildings were refurbished for apartments.

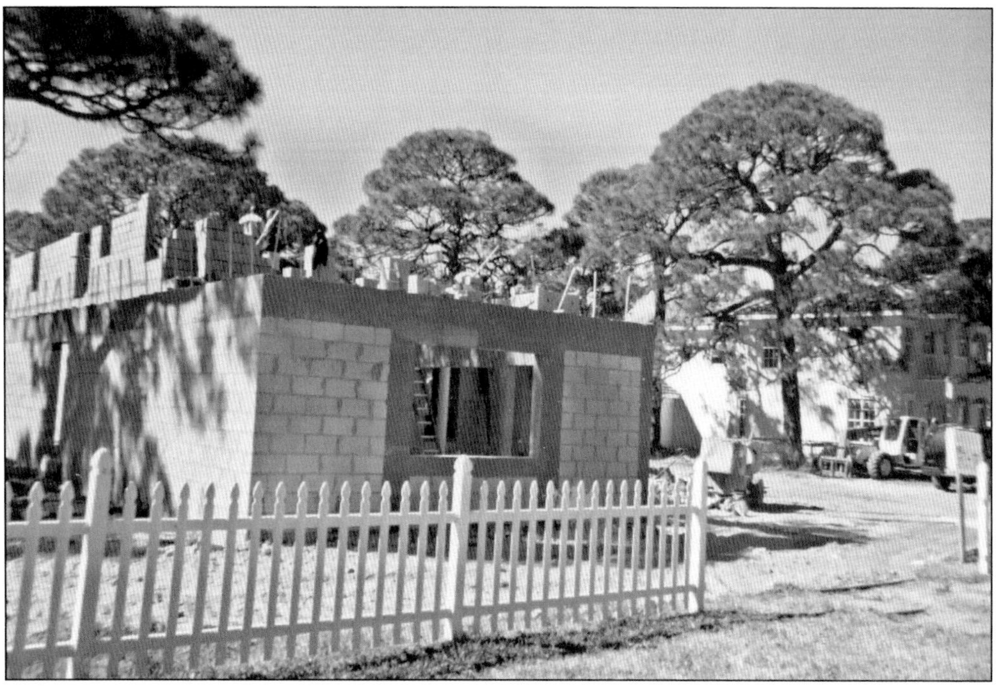

Wilton Cove rises on one of the few remaining undeveloped land parcels, on property formerly owned by the McJunkin family. Wilton Cove will feature 18 four-bedroom luxury homes.

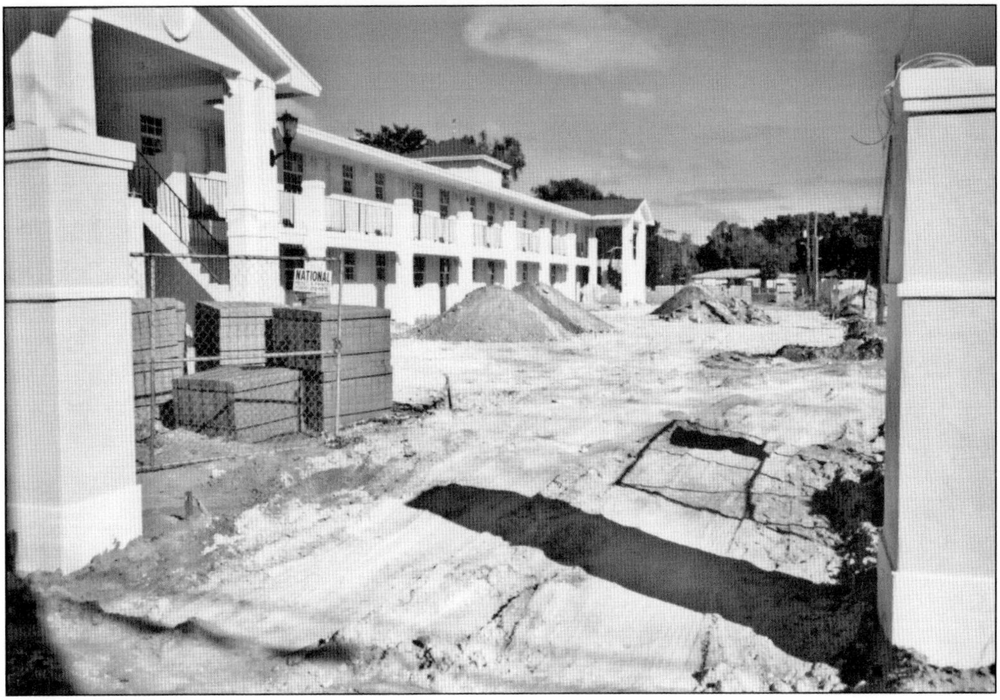

The Grove at Wilton Manors rises on Northeast Eighth Avenue in the city's Highland Estates section.

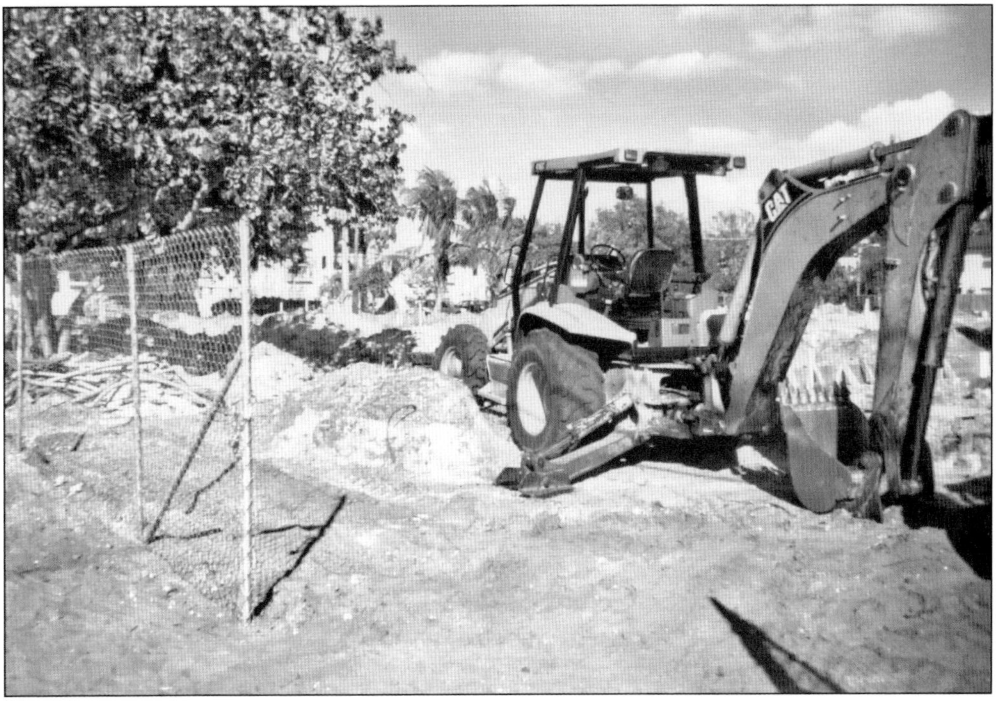

Highland Estates was annexed into Wilton Manors in 1951; before annexation, it had less stringent zoning requirements, so the flurry of development has served to help weed out some older buildings.

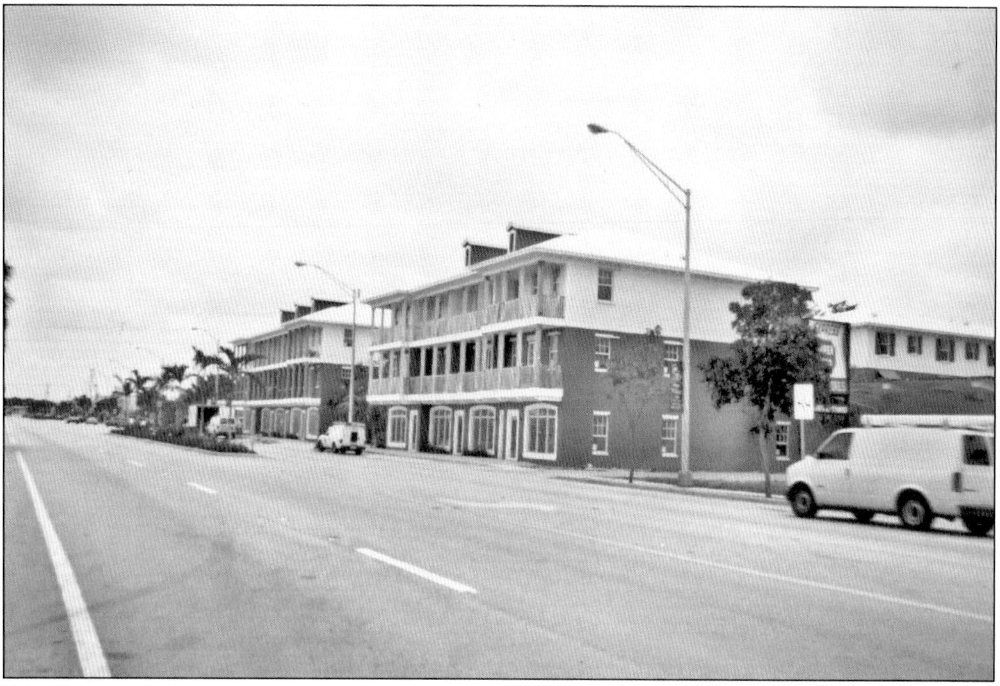

In 2004, work began on a mixed-use development on the former Trailer Haven site. The project, Belle Isle, slated to open in 2005, will feature 51 townhomes and 9 live-work units with apartments above commercial storefronts.

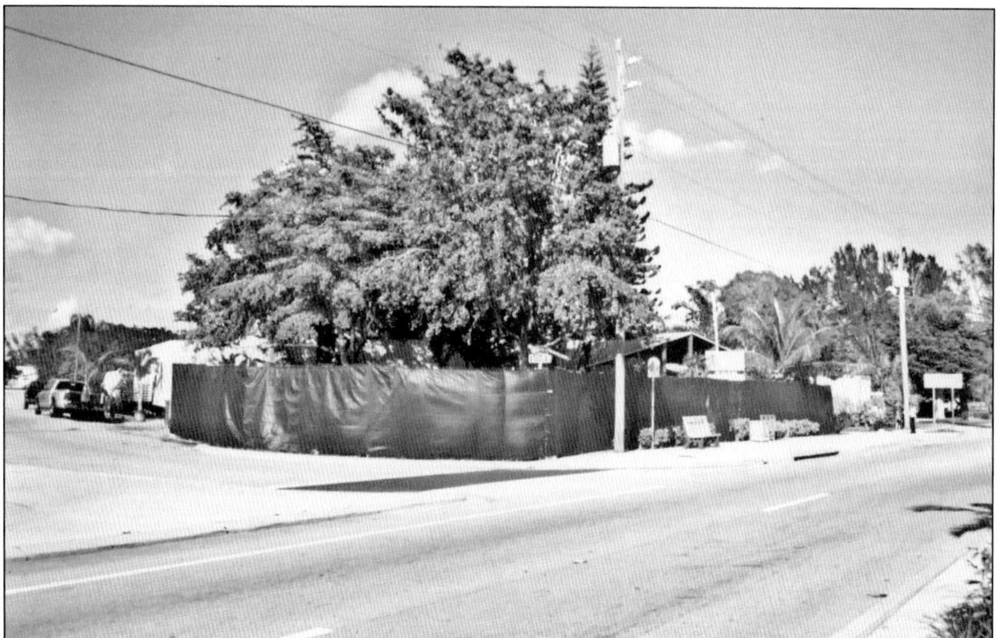

Behind the construction screen, awaiting demolition, is the building that formerly housed Secord Funeral Home at Wilton Drive and Northeast Seventh Avenue. It also was used by a church for youth activities and long served as Spectrum House, a drug-treatment facility. It will be razed in 2005 for residential development.

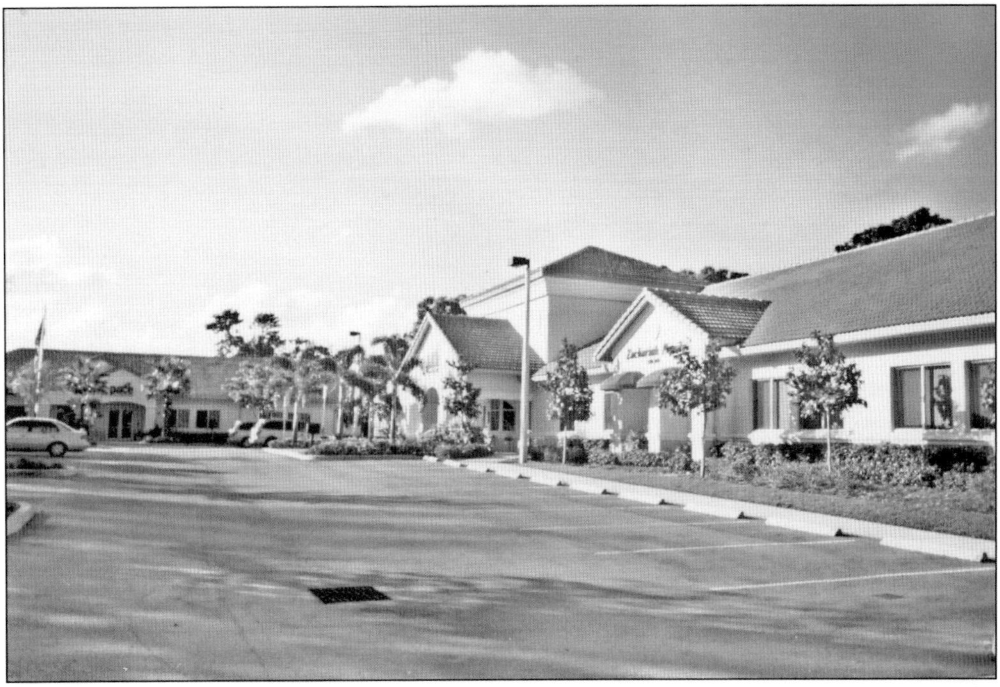

The PACE Center for Girls on Andrews Avenue in Wilton Manors is one of 18 statewide, providing education, counseling, and social services for at-risk teenagers and "tweens." The PACE program was established in 1985, and the Broward unit was established in 1992.

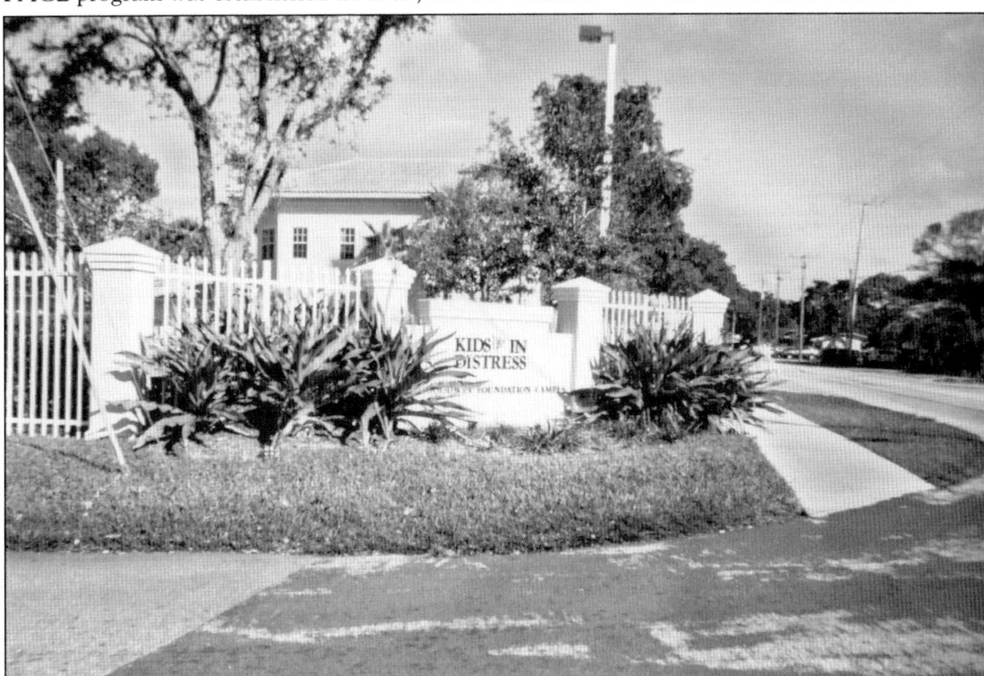


Kids in Distress, on Northeast Twenty-sixth Street, was incorporated in 1979, but the group's campus has been in a three-stage growth mode recently, adding 48,000 square feet of space, and planning to add more. Older homes were razed to provide space.

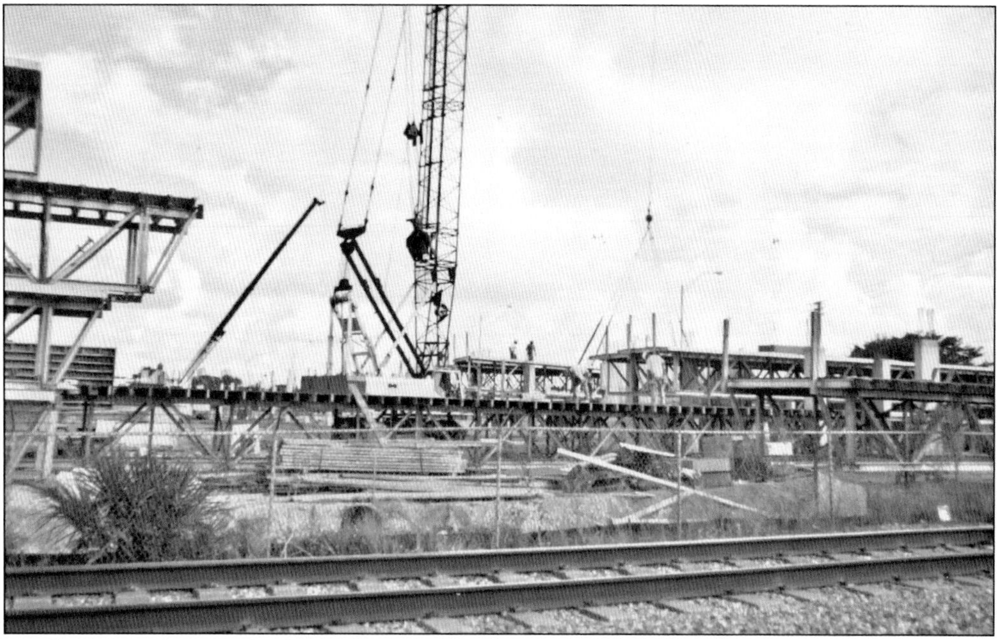

At the start of 2005, the biggest construction underway was Wilton Station, which broke ground in 2004 for 272 housing units and a selection of boutique retailers. The community will provide private garages/storage units and will offer amenities such as a clubhouse, pool, pet park, and docks.

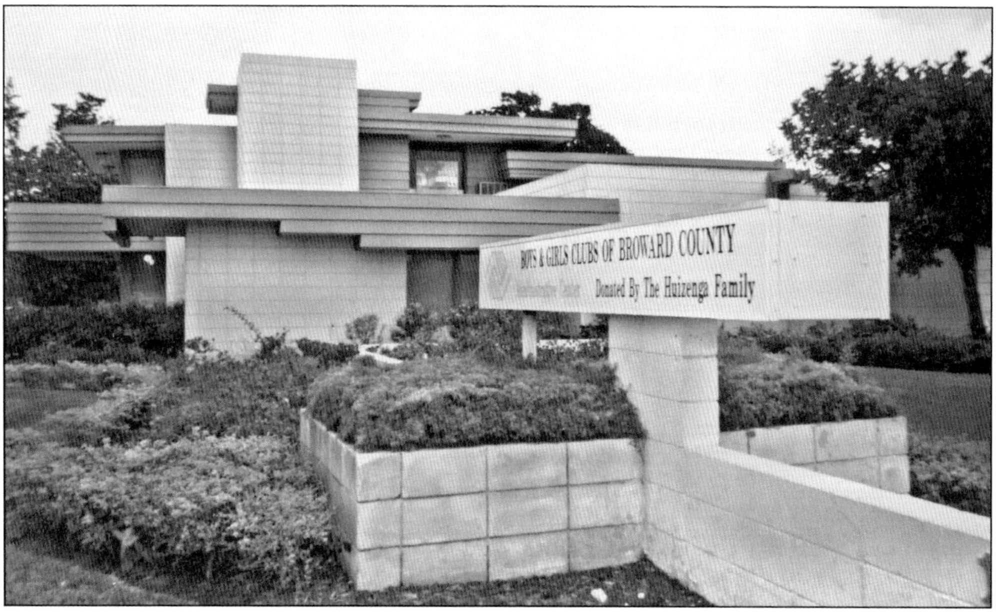


Many individuals and groups have been content to adapt older buildings to their needs rather than raze and rebuild. Doing so has helped preserve some of the community's historic places. One such example is the administrative center for the Boys and Girls Clubs of Broward County, which was originally built in 1964 as Robinson's Beauty School. Fort Lauderdale architect Dan C. Duckham's organic design remains as strong and contemporary today as when it was first built. Duckham has designed residences and commercial buildings around the world.

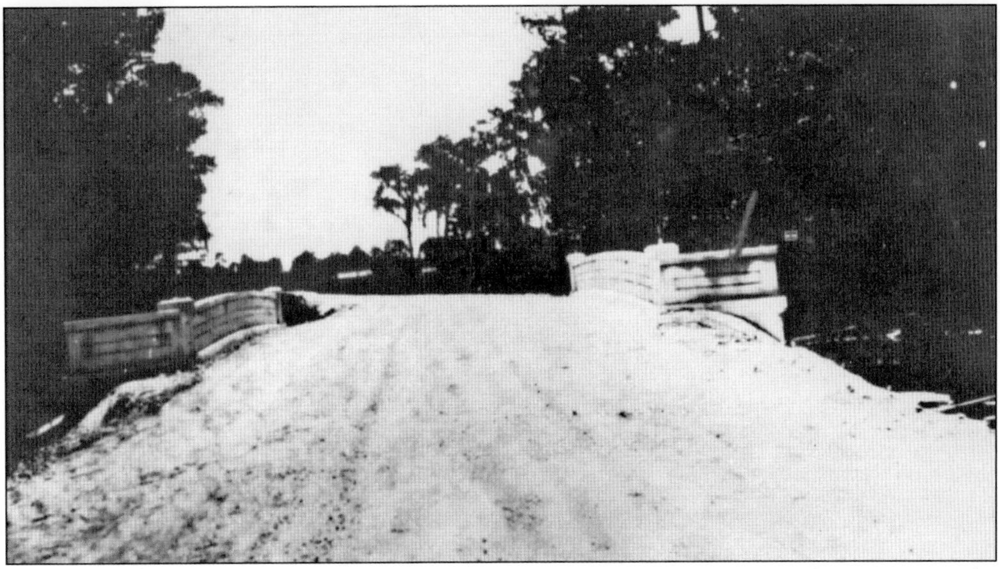

One of Broward County's oldest bridges is one of the 11 that lead into Wilton Manors. The southern Dixie Highway Bridge was built in 1923 by the Luten Bridge Company of York, Pennsylvania. (Broward County Historical Commission.)

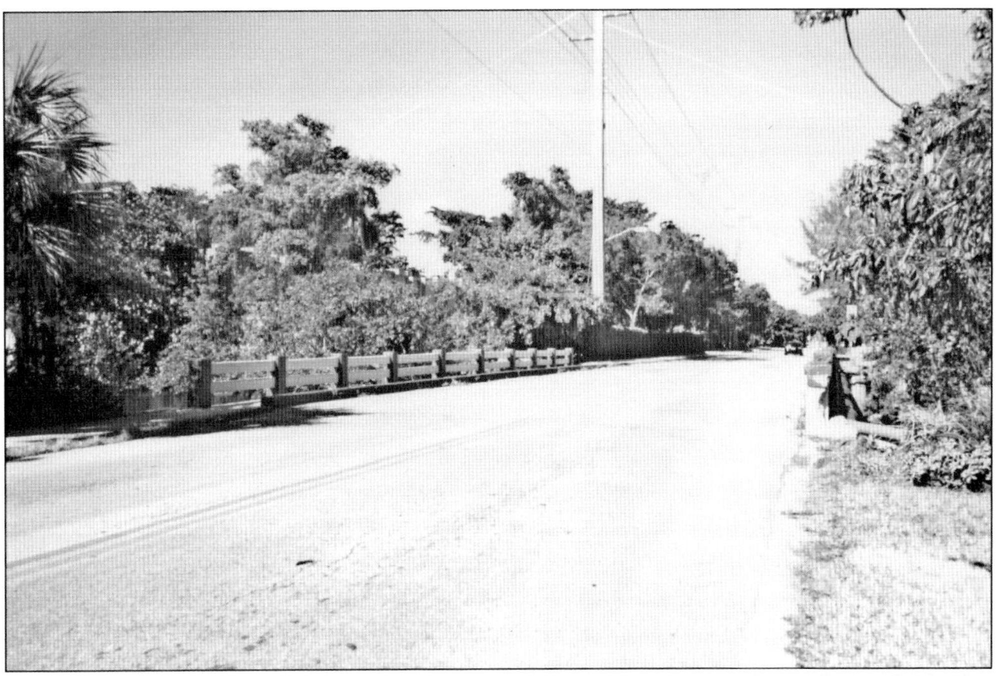

Given a fresh coat of paint every few years and checked for structural soundness, the bridge remains in service today. The bridge, like many aspects of Wilton Manors, demonstrates that residents and business owners alike usually prefer to renovate rather than rebuild to help preserve Wilton Manors's small-town feel.

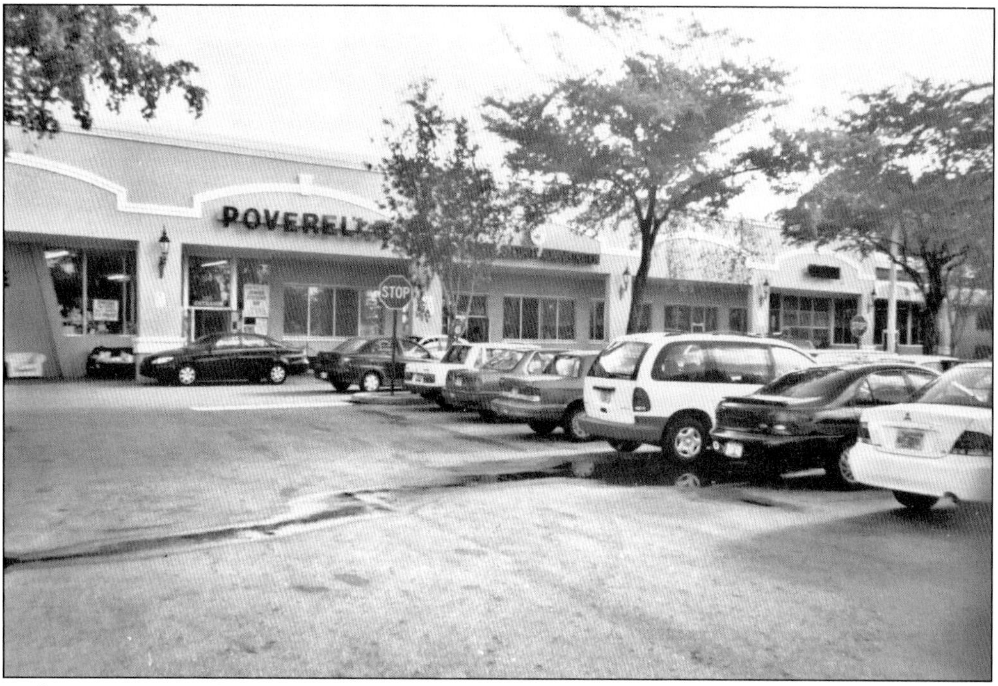


Built as Stevens Market and long open as Grand Union supermarket, this structure was divided into the eastern portion of the Shoppes of Wilton Manors. Among the tenants are the Poverello Food Bank and Thrift Shop and the Social Security Administration office.

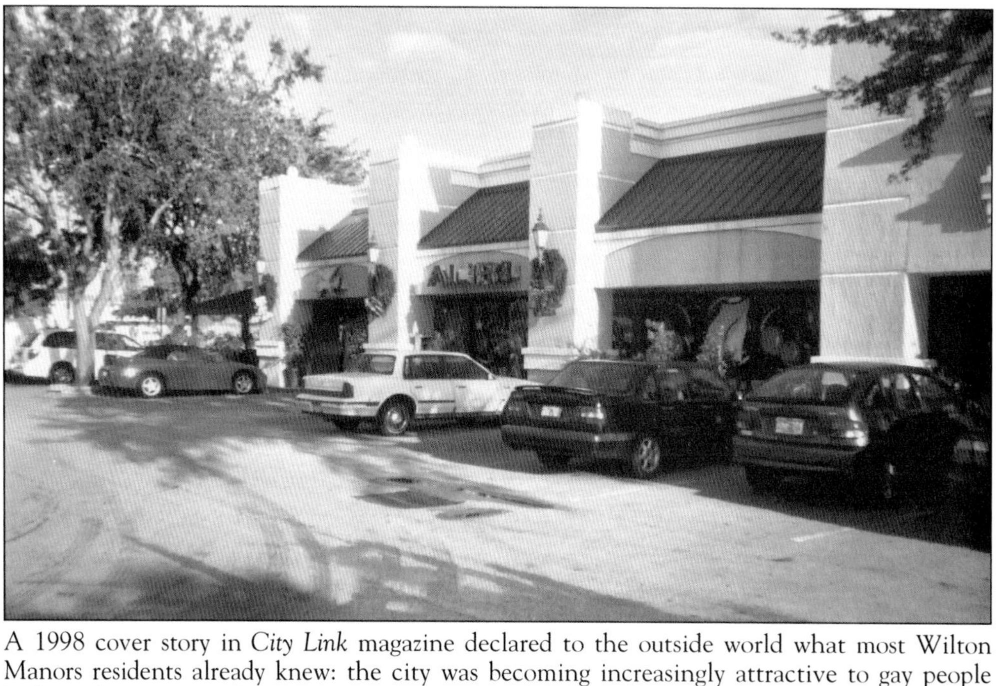

A 1998 cover story in *City Link* magazine declared to the outside world what most Wilton Manors residents already knew: the city was becoming increasingly attractive to gay people looking for a quiet, tolerant community to settle in. One of the pioneers at the front of the influx was George Kessinger, who, in April 1997, opened Georgie's Alibi, a restaurant, sports bar, and meeting spot for the gay community.

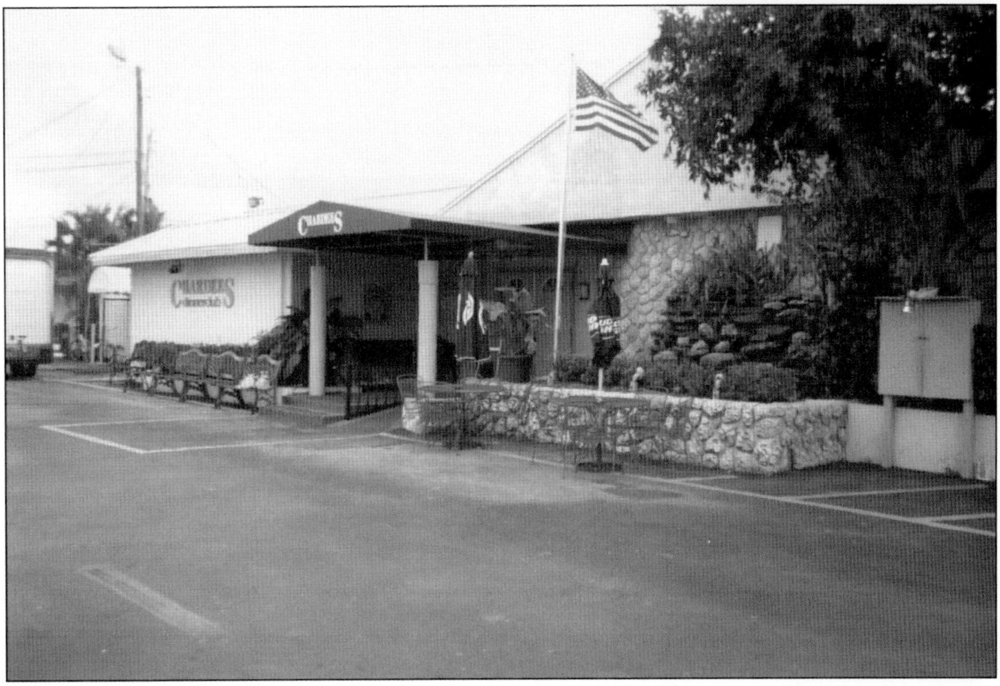

Across the street from the Shoppes of Wilton Manors are the Shoppes of Plaza Dee North and Chardee's Dinner Club, occupying the space where Manor Market stood. After Manor Market closed following the drowning death of Lamar Braddy, the building was used for Manor Flame restaurant, where former major leaguer Max Carey addressed the 1960 state champion baseball squad at their end-of-the-season banquet. After Manor Flame and several other incarnations, the restaurant became Chardee's, and attracted a gay clientele. Entrepreneur Tony Dee bought Chardee's in 1990, refurbished it, and brought in live entertainment nightly.

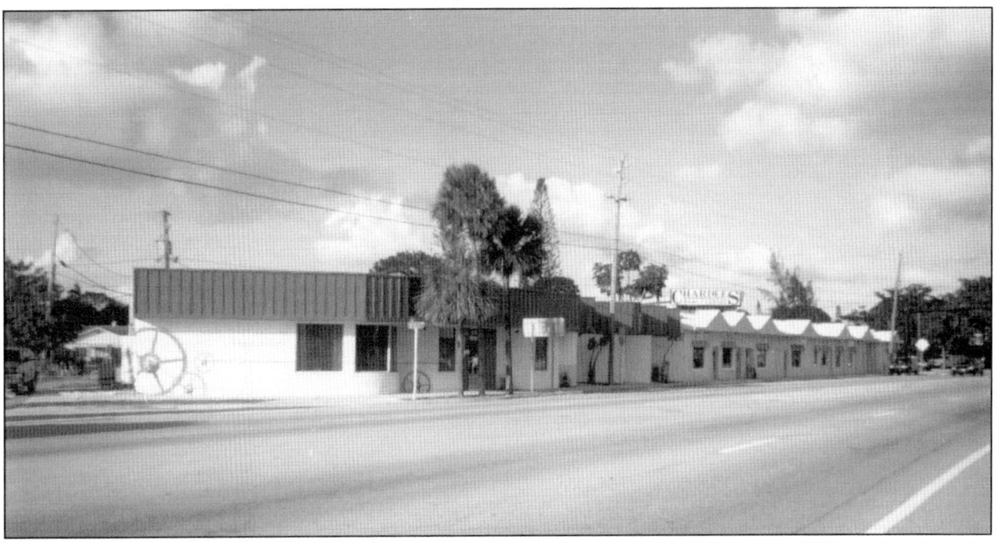

Dee bought the remainder of the plaza in 1992 and named it the Shoppes of Plaza Dee North. Once home to a dentist, a shoe repair store, a women's wrestling organization, a photography studio, and a public relations firm, it is now home to a variety of businesses largely catering to the needs of the gay community.

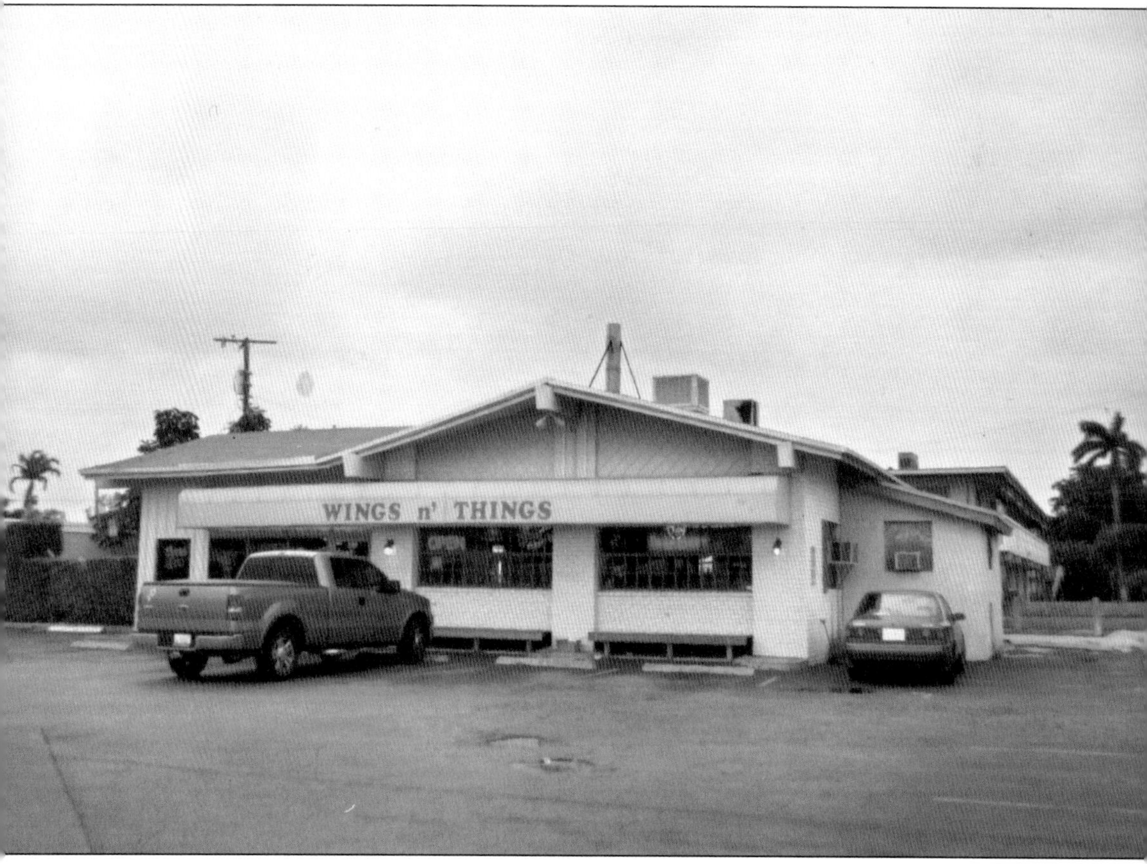


Across Northeast Twenty-second Street from the Shops of Plaza Dee North is a longtime favorite location for Buffalo-style chicken wing devotees, Wings 'n Things. Constructed and operated as a full-service gas station, the Manor Service Station was owned by Pat Dickson, who sold Standard Oil products there. Dickson sold it to Harold Price in 1954. Price's Pure station was a hub of community activity; Price, a native of Lykens, Pennsylvania, quickly became active in a variety of city activities as well, including the volunteer fire department. In 1956, he was elected to the city council, and he started a 10-year stint as mayor in 1960. He also served as president of the Broward County League of Municipalities and the Wilton Manors Chamber of Commerce. In the mid-1970s, Price sold to Ed Hauck Sr., a harness horse owner, driver, and trainer from Buffalo, New York. Hauck converted the gas station to a restaurant serving Buffalo-style chicken wings. Thirty years later, the wings are still in demand.

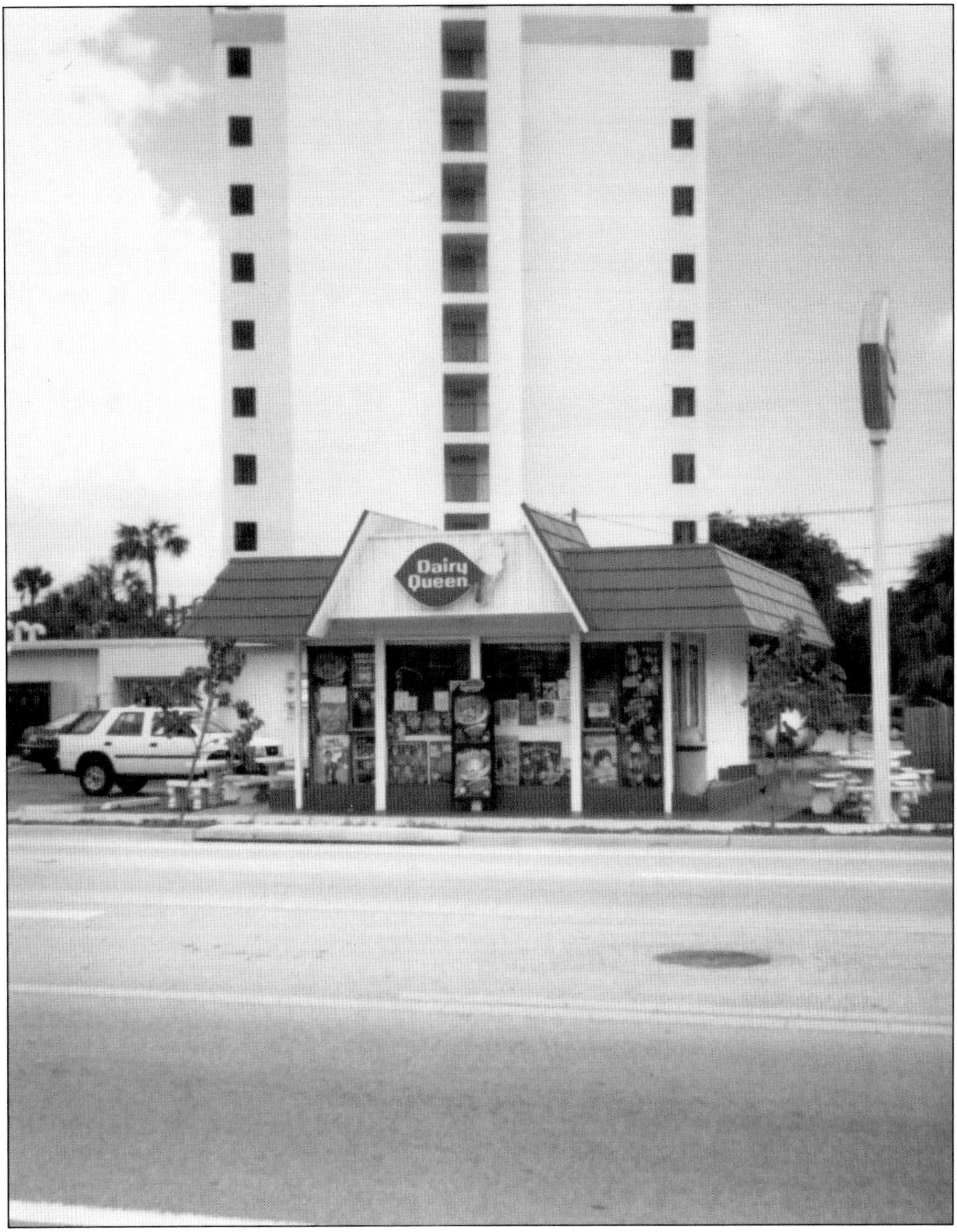


Originally opened in 1953, the Dairy Queen near the Northeast Fourth Avenue gateway to the city has filled the sweet tooth for many people in north-central Broward County. In the late 1990s, when Lynn Lawrence bought the popular soft-serve ice cream stand from Mariam Khandwalla, she updated the building and added a greater variety of items for sale, making it more appealing to ice-cream lovers. The low building behind the Dairy Queen is a coin laundry that also has served city residents since the 1950s. The building looming in the background is Wilton Towers apartments, the city's tallest building.

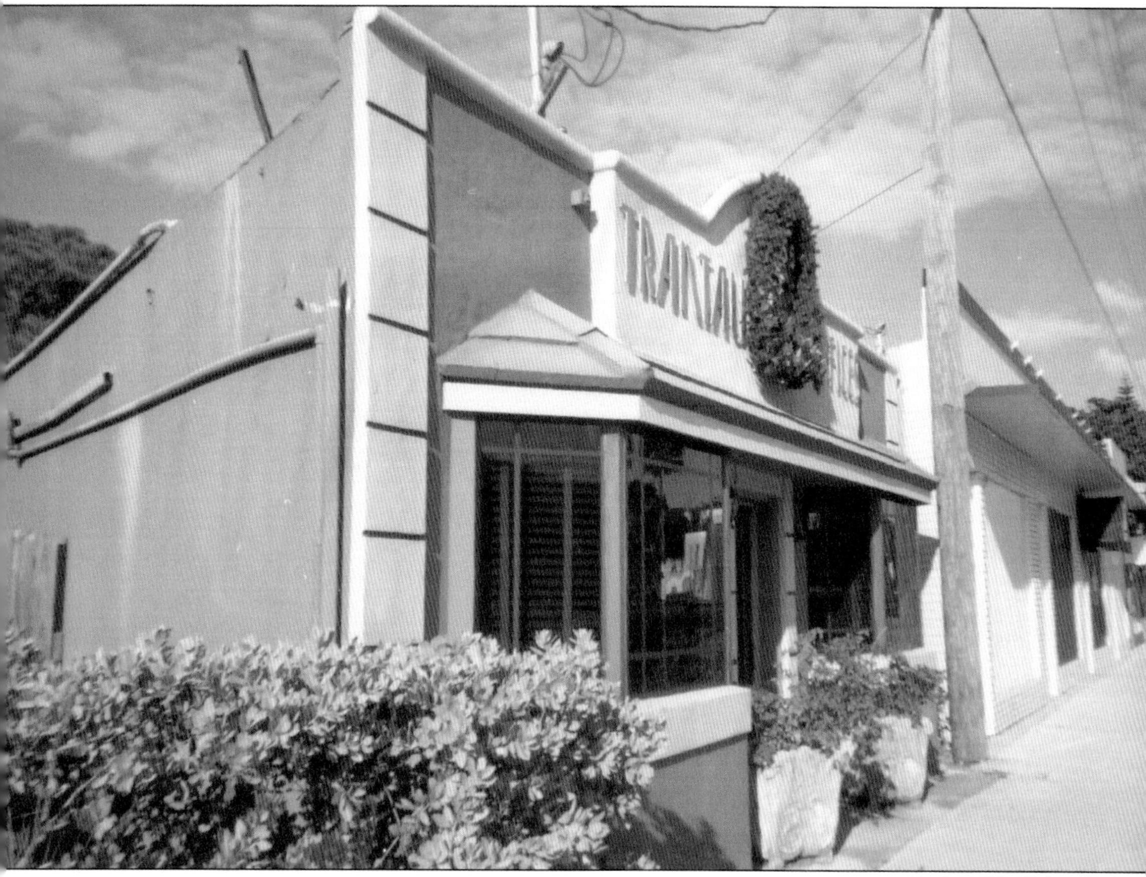

Fort Lauderdale city commissioner Dean Trantalis established his law office at 2255 Wilton Drive, in a building long used by insurance companies, including the A. Mann Insurance Agency in the late 1950s and, later, Mann and Turgeon. Next to Trantalis's office is the Big Dog Saloon.

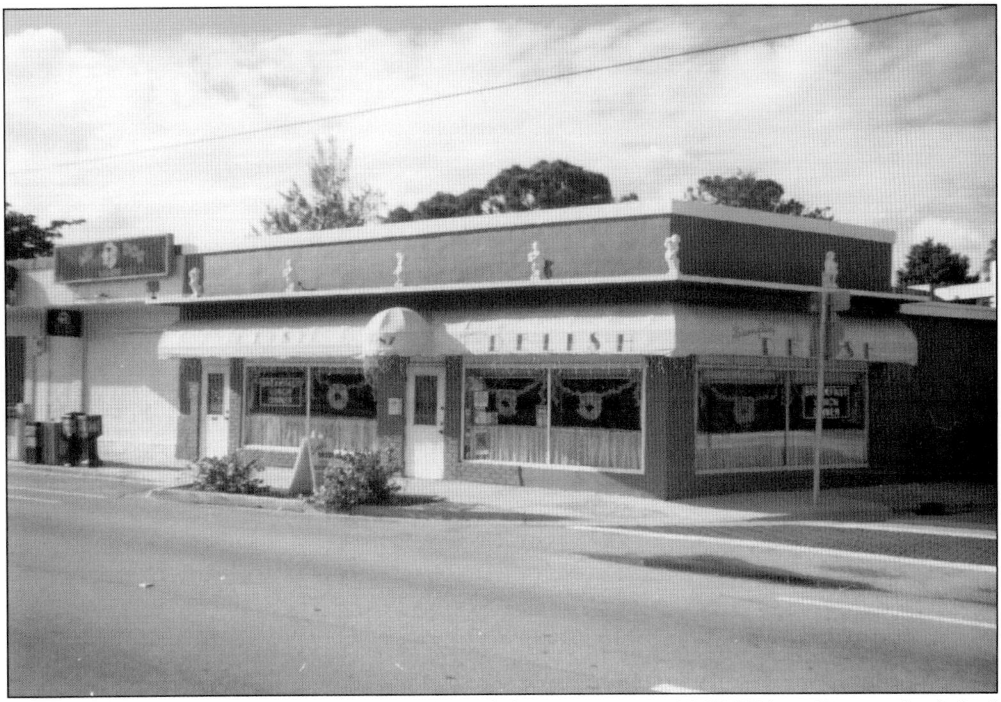

Next to the Big Dog Saloon is the Simply Delish restaurant at 2287 Wilton Drive, which had earlier served as an appliance store.

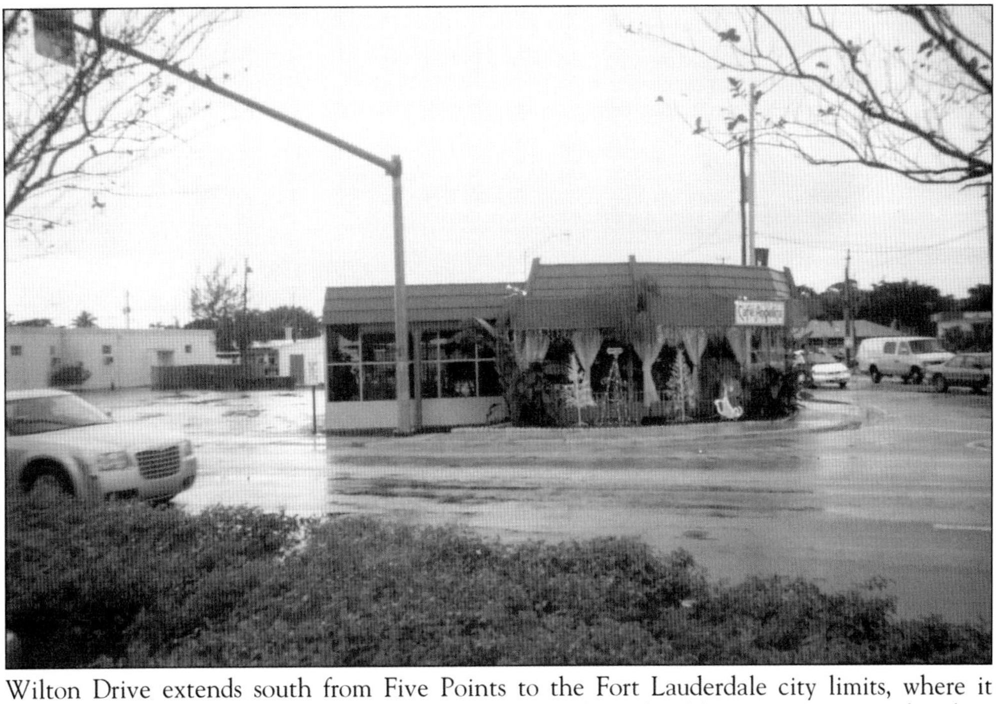

Wilton Drive extends south from Five Points to the Fort Lauderdale city limits, where it becomes Northeast Fourth Avenue. At Five Points, where the Abreu entryway stood earlier, Café Angelica is one of several restaurants that have occupied the corner since the A&W Root Beer stand closed.

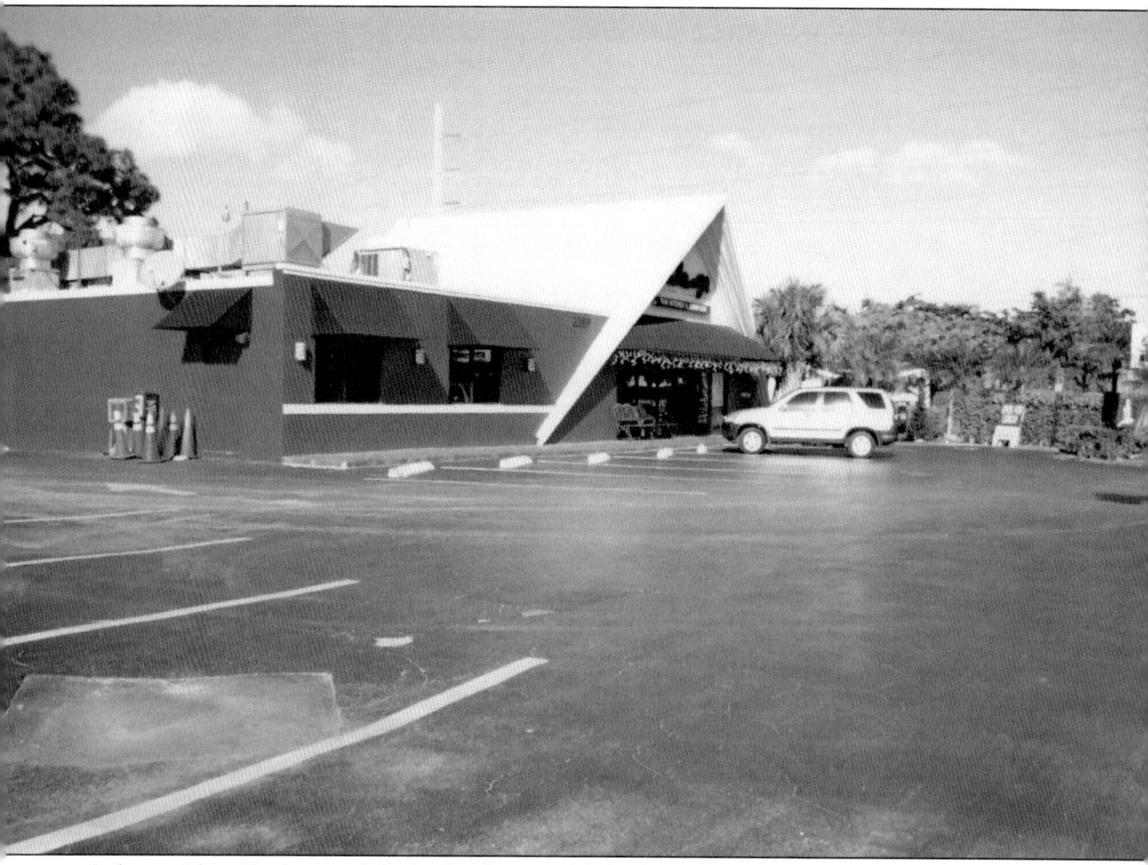

Galanga Thai Kitchen and Sushi Bar has established itself in a building long used as a photo shop at 2389 Wilton Drive. Its name comes from *Kaempferia galanga*, the aromatic spice from the ginger family widely used in Southeast Asian cuisine. Nearby are other restaurants in refurbished buildings, such as Hamburger Mary's, in what was formerly a Burger King, and Dorothy's Deli, in a former Pizza Hut that also served incarnations as a British pub and a health foods café.

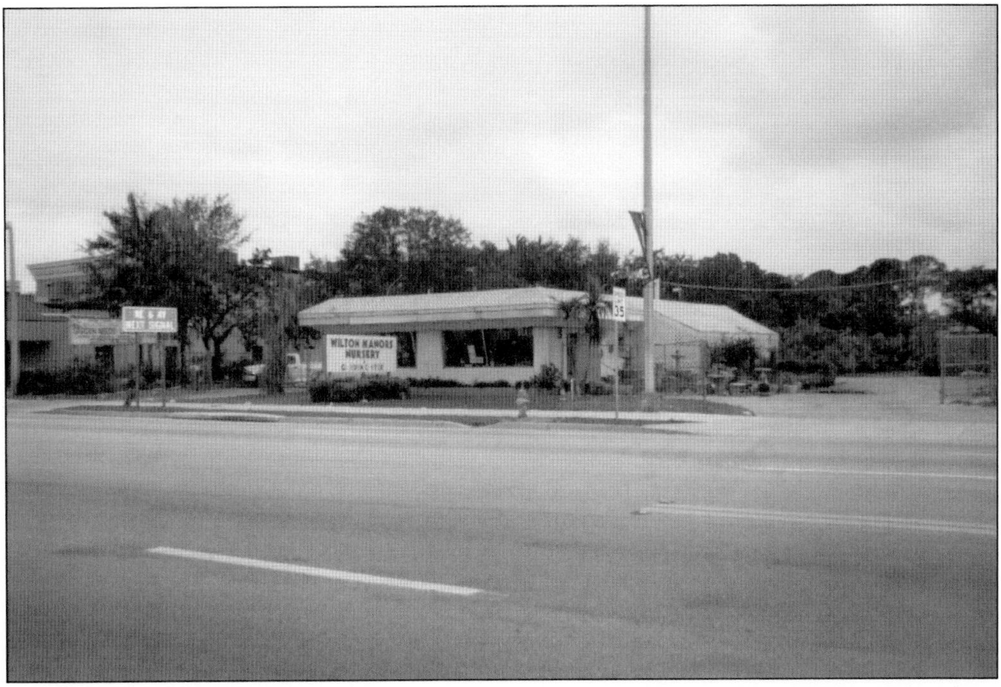

Constructed and first used as a drive-in restaurant, the building at 2194 Wilton Drive long served as Hull TV. It is now Wilton Manors Nursery and Garden Center.

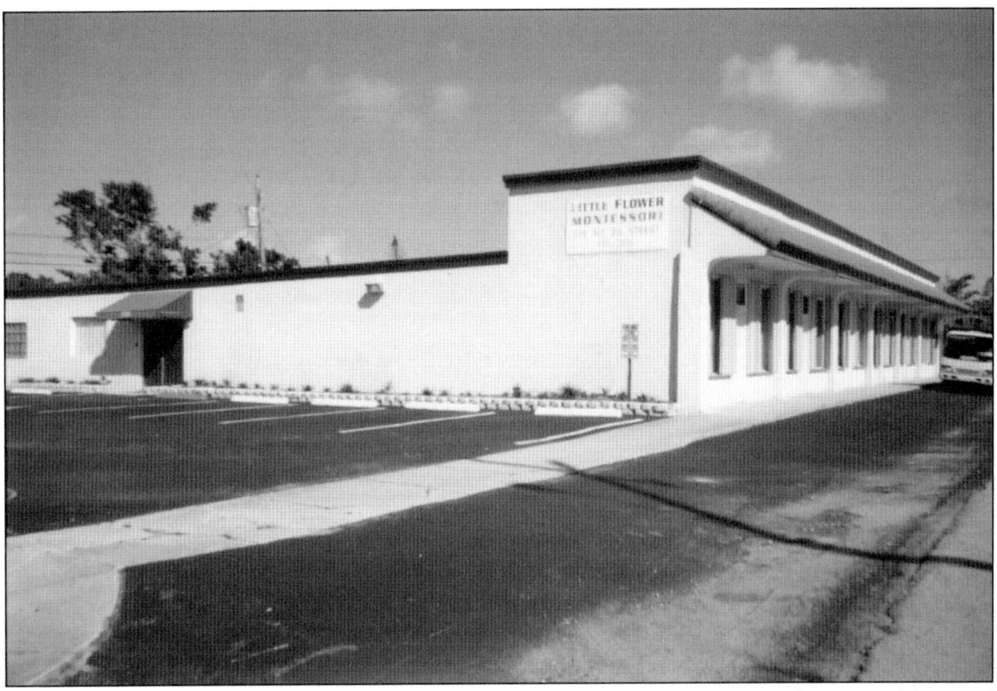

The Little Flower Montessori School on Northeast Twenty-sixth Street was the original home of Miss Jordan's School, which opened in 1950. It was later used as a drapery and home furnishings store before becoming a Montessori school.

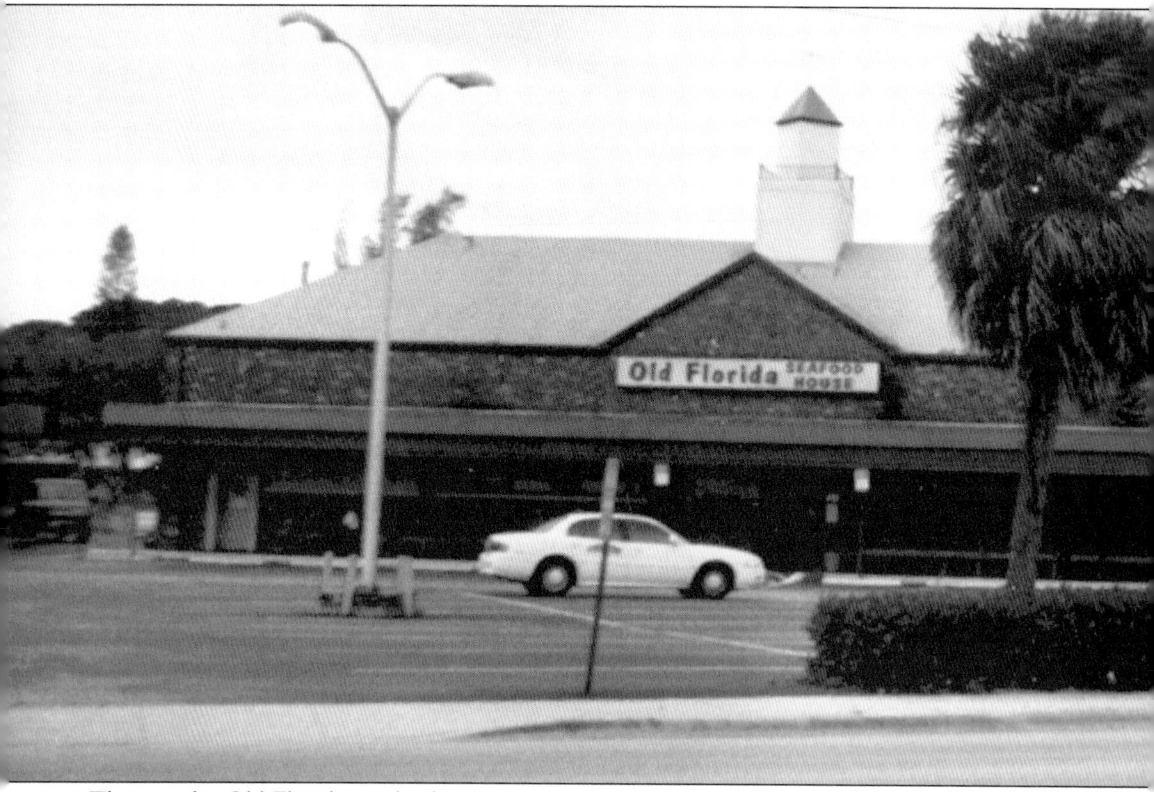


The popular Old Florida Seafood House first served as an A&P supermarket. The Holy Cross physicians' offices were originally used as Williams City Drug Store. A United States Postal

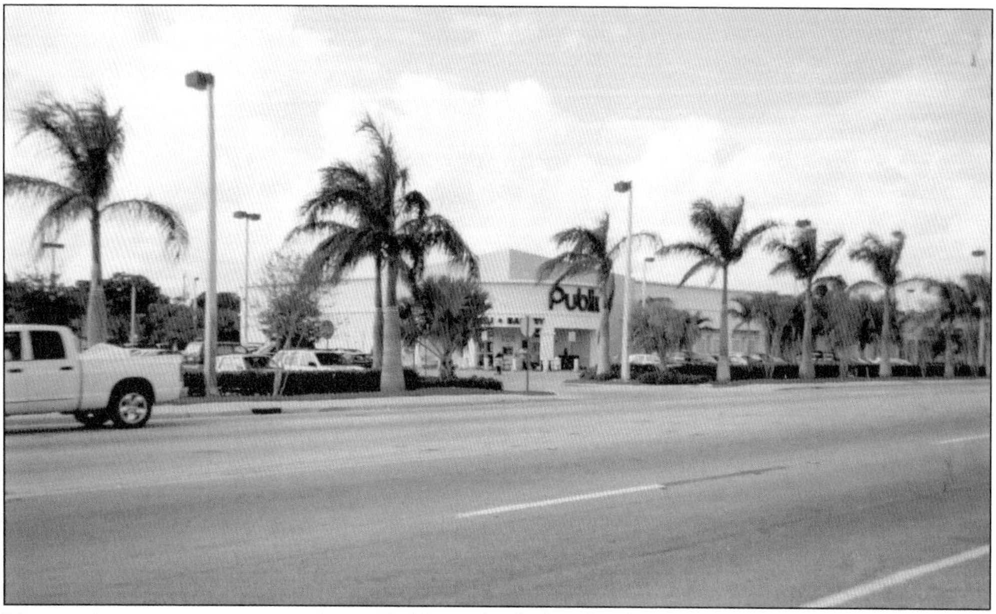

The city's remaining supermarket is Publix, which faced a design dilemma when it decided to update its store at Five Points. The result is a store that offers a greater selection and better uses the space it has available.

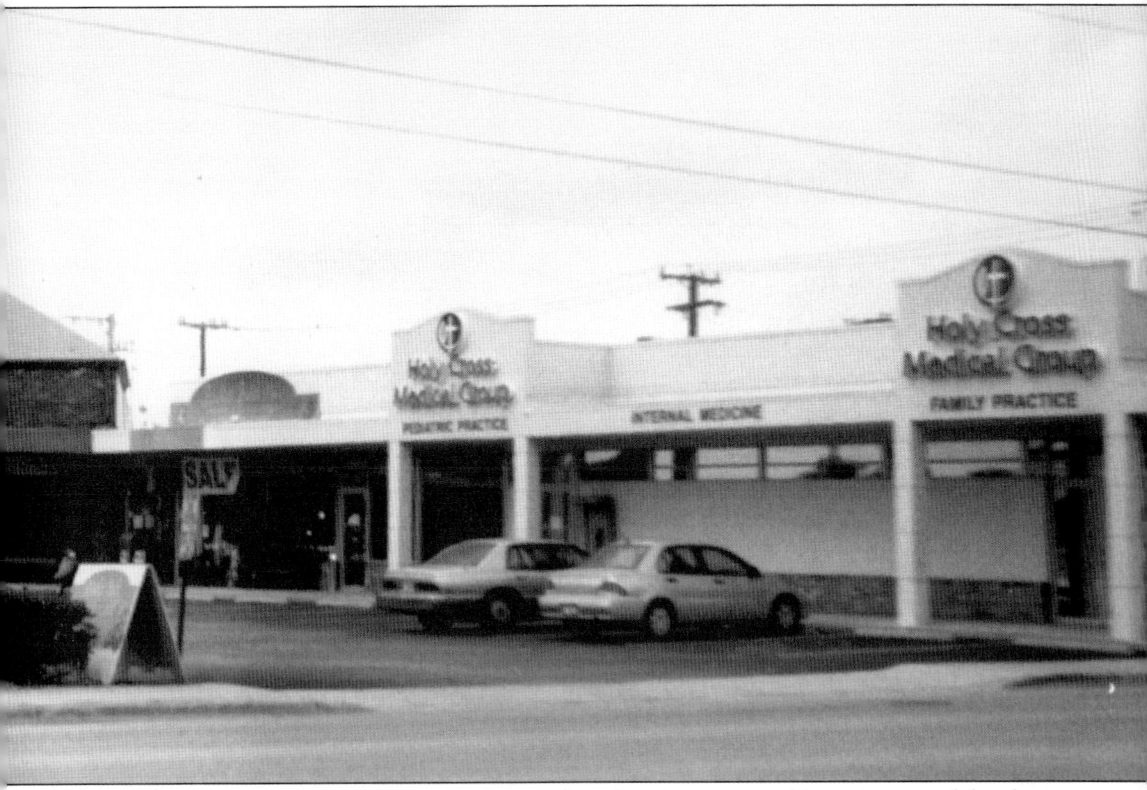


Service branch once operated a small office within the pharmacy and later, in one of the shops between the pharmacy and where the seafood restaurant now stands.

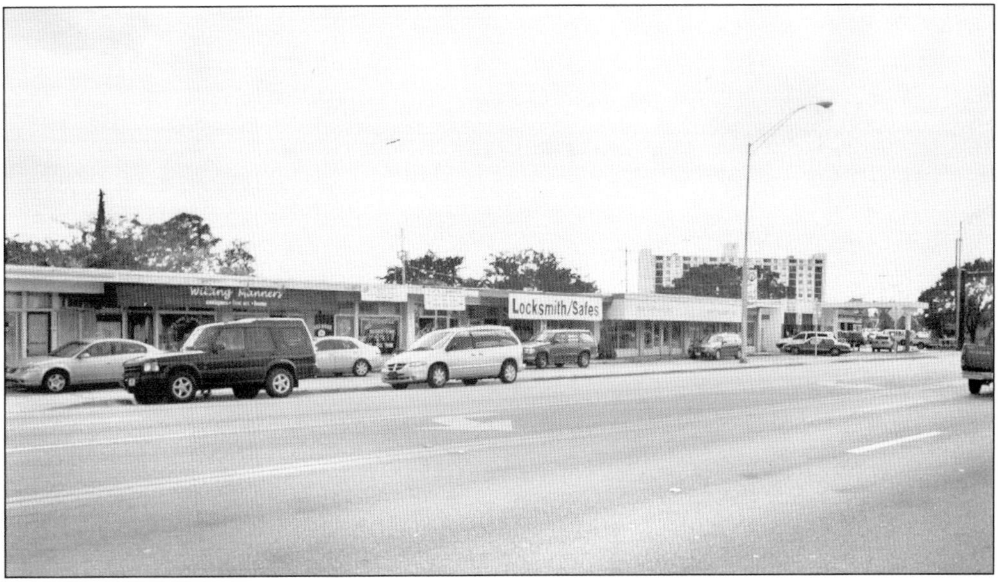


The strip of shops along the eastern side of Wilton Drive has long served the community. The building that now serves as the home of Marsupium Inc., to the right of the locksmith/safes sign, was formerly the home of Broward 5 & 10. Later, Bob and Mary Pearce moved from Indianapolis and bought the shop, operating it for years as Pearce's 5 & 10.

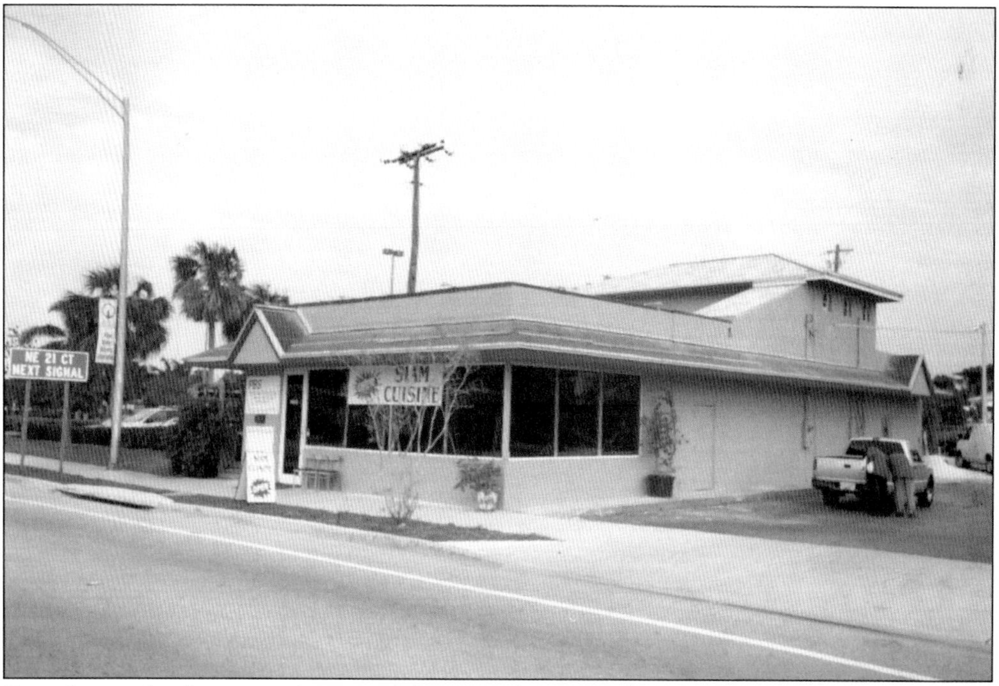


Siam Cuisine has long served up spicy Thai specialties to Wilton Manors residents, and in 2004, it underwent a face lift and expansion. The restaurant originally operated as Royal Castle, a Miami-based hamburger chain that specialized in small, steamed hamburgers and birch beer.

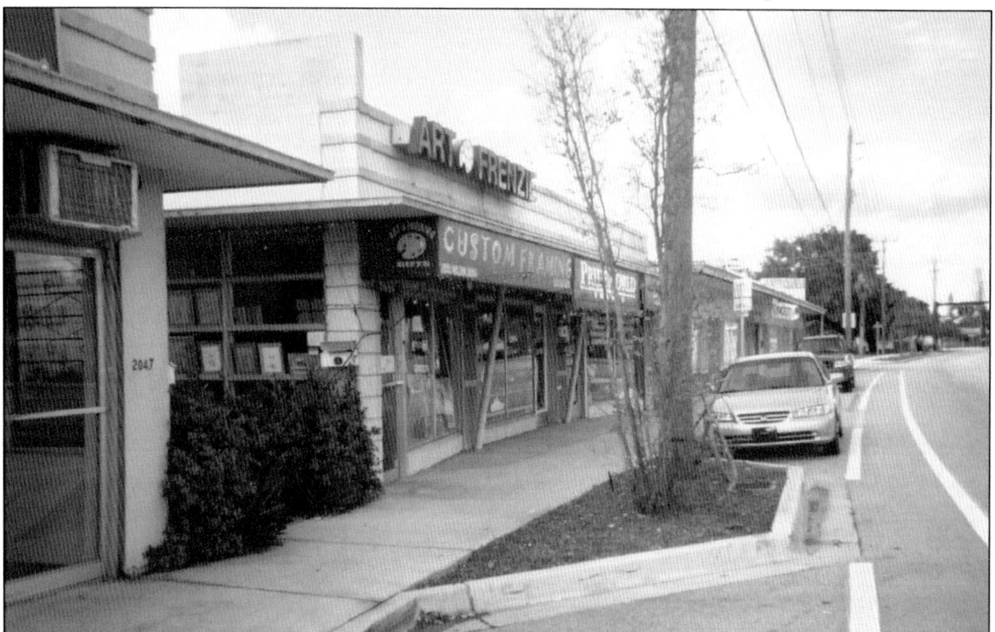


This strip mall on Wilton Drive has several of its tenant stores undergoing transformation. The mall's anchor had formerly been a furniture store. When the furniture store closed, it was operated for a while as an antique mall. It is now the Main Street Gym. Other stores in the mall include Pride World Travel, Art Frenzie, New Creations Interiors, and Hair BrainZ Salon.

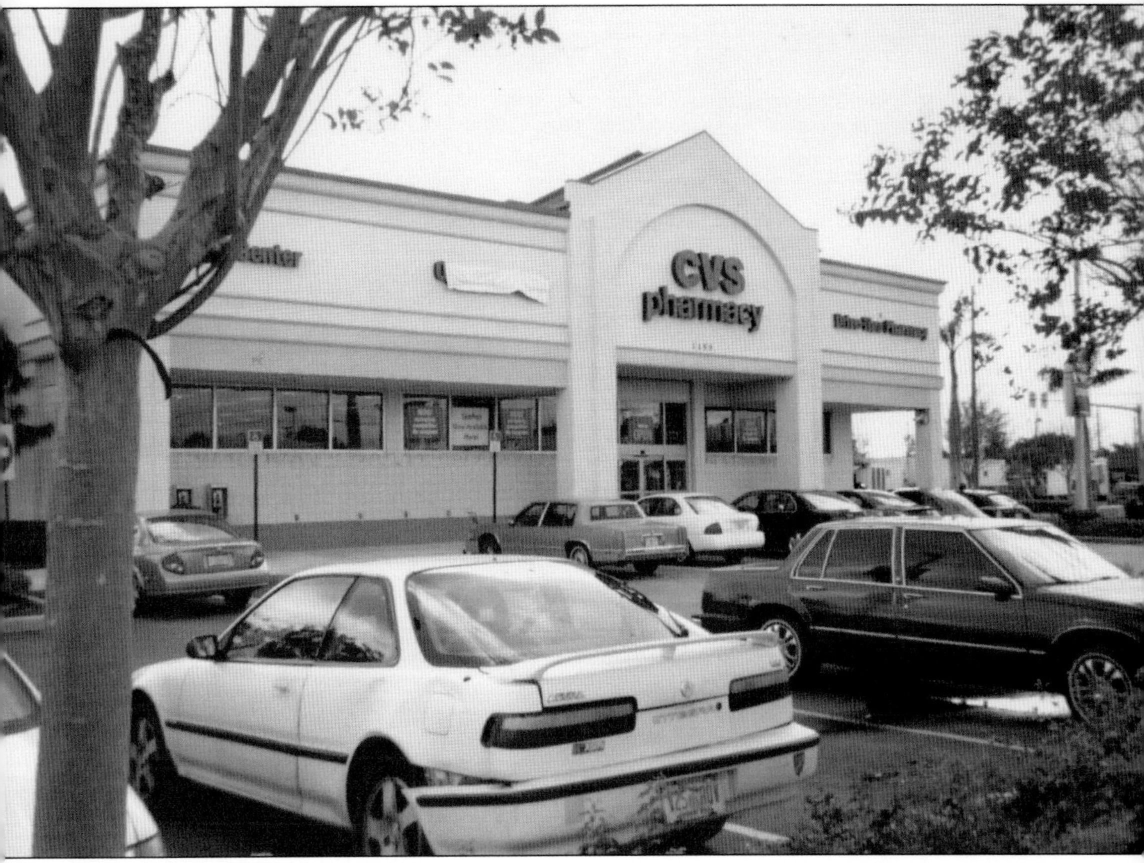


Ground was broken for the Eckerd's Drugs at Five Points on May 1, 1998. The pharmacy replaced the Five Points Home and Garden Center and Taylor & Turner Pest Control. In 2004, CVS Pharmacy bought out Eckerd's.

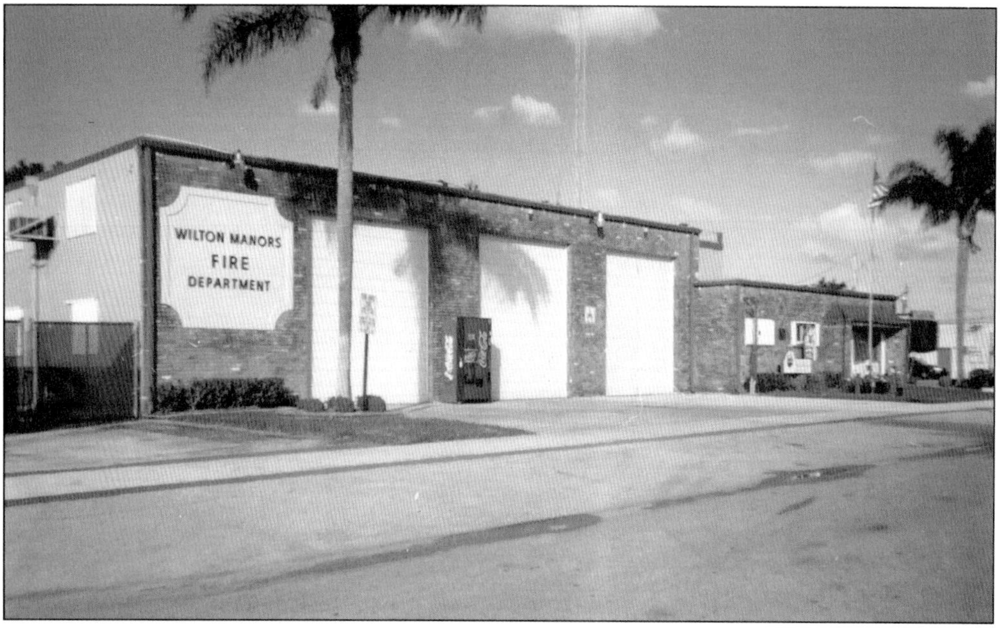


Some parts of the city are gone forever, but will never be forgotten. The fire station on Northeast Twenty-second Street still exists, with brass plaque affixed to the front of the building dedicating it to John Miller, but the Wilton Manors Volunteer Fire Department and Auxiliary are gone, replaced by the Fort Lauderdale Fire Department, which the city contracted for fire services starting in 2000. The Wilton Manors station is now Station 16.

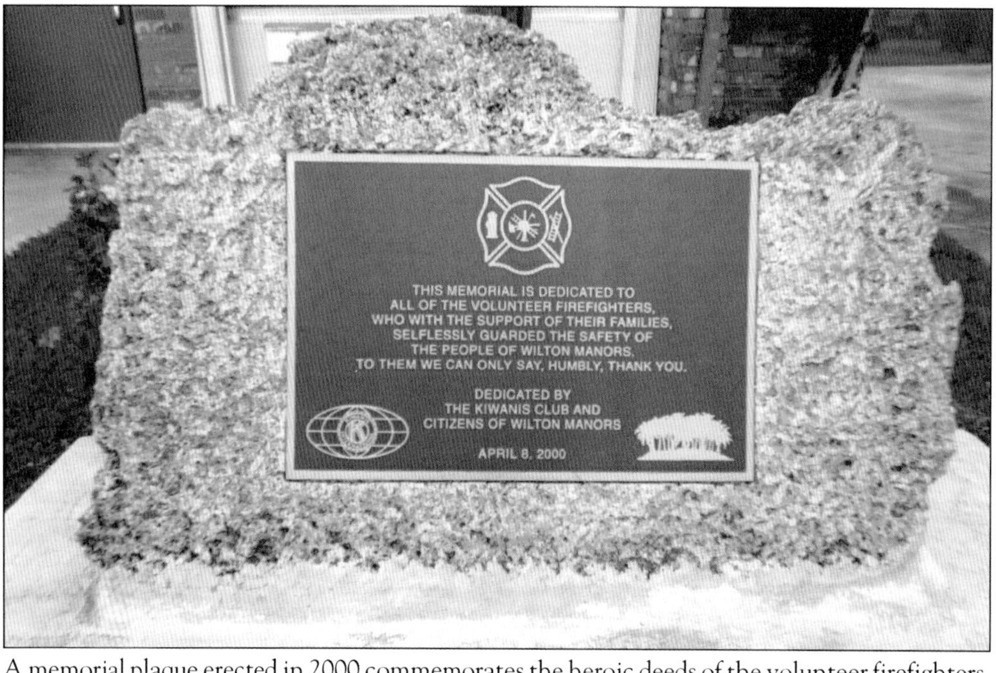


A memorial plaque erected in 2000 commemorates the heroic deeds of the volunteer firefighters. It reads: "This memorial is dedicated to all of the volunteer firefighters, who with the support of their families, selflessly guarded the safety of the people of Wilton Manors. To them we can only say, humbly, thank you."